The Software Project Manager's Bridge to Agility

The Agile Software Development Series

Alistair Cockburn and Jim Highsmith, Series Editors

Agile software development centers on four values identified in the Agile Alliance's Manifesto:

- Individuals and interactions over processes and tools
- Working software over comprehensive documentation
- Customer collaboration over contract negotiation
- Responding to change over following a plan

The development of Agile software requires innovation and responsiveness, based on generating and sharing knowledge within a development team and with the customer. Agile software developers draw on the strengths of customers, users, and developers, finding just enough process to balance quality and agility.

The books in The Agile Software Development Series focus on sharing the experiences of such Agile developers. Individual books address individual techniques (such as Use Cases), group techniques (such as collaborative decision making), and proven solutions to different problems from a variety of organizational cultures. The result is a core of Agile best practices that will enrich your experience and improve your work.

Titles in the Series:

Steve Adolph, Paul Bramble, Alistair Cockburn, and Andy Pols; *Patterns for Effective Use Cases;* 0201721848

Alistair Cockburn; *Agile Software Development, Second Edition;* 0321482751

Alistair Cockburn; *Crystal Clear;* 0201699478

Alistair Cockburn; *Surviving Object-Oriented Projects;* 0201498340

Alistair Cockburn; *Writing Effective Use Cases;* 0201702258

Anne Mette Jonassen Hass; *Configuration Management Principles and Practice;* 0321117662

Jim Highsmith; *Agile Software Development Ecosystems;* 0201760436

Jim Highsmith; *Agile Project Management;* 0321219775

Craig Larman; *Agile and Iterative Development;* 0131111558

Dean Leffingwell; *Scaling Software Agility;* 0321458192

Mary Poppendieck and Tom Poppendieck; *Lean Software Development;* 0321150783

Jean Tabaka; *Collaboration Explained;* 0321268776

Kevin Tate; *Sustainable Software Development;* 0321286081

The Software Project Manager's Bridge to Agility

Michele Sliger
Stacia Broderick

✦ Addison-Wesley

Upper Saddle River, NJ • Boston • Indianapolis • San Francisco
New York • Toronto • Montreal • London • Munich • Paris • Madrid
Cape Town • Sydney • Tokyo • Singapore • Mexico City

The publisher offers excellent discounts on this book when ordered in quantity for bulk purchases or special sales, which may include electronic versions and/or custom covers and content particular to your business, training goals, marketing focus, and branding interests. For more information, please contact:

U.S. Corporate and Government Sales
(800) 382-3419
corpsales@pearsontechgroup.com

For sales outside the United States please contact:

International Sales
international@pearsoned.com

Library of Congress Cataloging-in-Publication Data

Sliger, Michele, 1964-
  The software project manager's bridge to agility / Michele Sliger, Stacia Broderick.
    p. cm.
  Includes bibliographical references and index.
  ISBN 0-321-50275-2 (pbk. : alk. paper) 1. Computer software—Development—Management.
2. Agile software development . I. Broderick, Stacia, 1974- II. Title.

  QA76.76.D47S563 2008
  005.1068—dc22

                              2008008524

ISBN-13: 978-0-321-50275-9
ISBN-10: 0-321-50275-2

Text printed in the United States on recycled paper at RR Donnelley in Crawfordsville, Indiana.
First printing May 2008

This Book Is Safari Enabled

The Safari® Enabled icon on the cover of your favorite technology book means the book is available through Safari Bookshelf. When you buy this book, you get free access to the online edition for 45 days.

Safari Bookshelf is an electronic reference library that lets you easily search thousands of technical books, find code samples, download chapters, and access technical information whenever and wherever you need it.

To gain 45-day Safari Enabled access to this book:

- Go to http://www.informit.com/onlineedition
- Complete the brief registration form
- Enter the coupon code I1GL-5UBF-62GU-7QF5-HBBE

If you have difficulty registering on Safari Bookshelf or accessing the online edition, please e-mail customer-service@safaribooksonline.com.

Editor-in-Chief
Karen Gettman

Executive Editor
Chris Guzikowski

Senior Development Editor
Chris Zahn

Managing Editor
Kristy Hart

Project Editor
Betsy Harris

Copy Editor
Bart Reed

Indexer
Erika Millen

Proofreader
Paula Lowell

Publishing Coordinator
Raina Chrobak

Cover Designer
Alan Clements

Compositor
Nonie Ratcliff

For Jesse, who would have been proud.
—Michele

To Mike, for his patience and support.
—Stacia

Contents

Preface

We are dedicated to the use of agile practices in software development (a.k.a. agilists), but we didn't start out that way. We began as Project Management Professionals (PMP®)[1] who used more traditional methods in the development of software.

Why We Wrote This Book

We followed the approaches outlined in the Project Management Institute's *A Guide to the Project Management Body of Knowledge—Third Edition* (*PMBOK® Guide*) for much of our careers, and in moving to agile approaches we became more aware of the misconceptions out there surrounding the subject matter of this book—incorrect ideas that we once believed as well. Now as agile consultants, we continue to hear our clients say that they believe (incorrectly) that if they are to keep their PMP certification and follow the practices outlined in the *PMBOK® Guide* that they must use a waterfall-like methodology. We also hear the mistaken belief that agile approaches lack discipline and rigor. And we see the fear and dismay of those who believe that their investment in the Project Management Institute (PMI) may be for naught if they follow the path to agility.

It is our goal to dispel these myths in our book and show that the Third Edition of the *PMBOK® Guide* does in fact support agile software development methods and that the investment that project managers have made in the PMI and in the practices outlined in the *PMBOK® Guide* are still solid and appropriate to pursue. It is clear to us that the *PMBOK® Guide* is methodology-neutral and supports good project management practices regardless of the approach chosen. Although many are already aware of this fact, we find that there are still many who are not. As PMPs who are now agile enthusiasts, we feel it is important to also dispel the mistaken notion in the agile community that PMPs cannot be good agile project managers. We would like to build a bridge between the two—thus the need for this book.

Structure and Content of the Book

Accordingly, we've put much of the detail concerning this bridging in Part II, where we map the *PMBOK® Guide's* practices to agile practices. It is our intent to show project managers that in moving to an agile methodology, they do not move away from implementing PMI-recommended practices—they simply implement the practices in a different way, making sure that the intent behind these practices remains true. In some chapters you'll find a clear mapping, whereas in others the mapping is more imprecise. This book is intended to be a guide, a way to take the lexicon you are already familiar with and relate it to a new way of developing software. This book will not replace any of the more specific agile practice books in the market today, and we encourage you to supplement this reading with other books on particular agile methods (Scrum, XP, Lean, Crystal, and so on).

The next several sections provide a quick preview of the book.

Part I: An Agile Overview

Part I introduces you to the basic terms and concepts of agile software development. We begin in the first chapter ("What Is Agile?") with a look back at the emergence of agile ideas in the history of software development. You may be surprised to learn that even Winston Royce's paper on the waterfall approach recommended an iterative cycle and the involvement of the end user in the whole of the project! From this history we move forward and review the concepts behind the Agile Manifesto and its associated principles, which are the basis of all agile software development frameworks.

In Chapter 2, "Mapping from the *PMBOK® Guide* to Agile," we look at the history of the PMI and its most famous contribution to the practice of project management, the *PMBOK® Guide*. We'll examine how the *PMBOK® Guide* project lifecycle phases and project management process groups can be related to the Agile Fractal. And we'll reiterate again that you can be agile and be in keeping with the recommendations outlined in the *PMBOK® Guide*.

Chapter 3, "The Agile Project Lifecycle in Detail," describes the agile project lifecycle—from release planning to iteration planning to daily planning—and how demos, reviews, and retrospectives at the end of each iteration allow the team to continually improve. This chapter begins the use of terminology and concepts that we expand on throughout the rest of the book.

Part II: The Bridge: Relating *PMBOK® Guide* Practices to Agile Practices

This is the part of the book where we review each of the *PMBOK® Guide* knowledge areas and discuss what you used to do as a traditional project manager, and what you should consider doing instead as an agile project manager. As the title implies, we are trying to build an explicit bridge between the traditional and the agile, and provide you with guidance on what tasks and activities you should substitute—or keep.

As it is in the *PMBOK® Guide,* the knowledge areas are not in any type of chronological order. In both traditional and agile project management settings, you will find yourself doing most of these activities in parallel.

Because there is some overlap in the knowledge areas, you may find some ideas and concepts repeated. We did this intentionally, because we expect many of you to use this part of the book as a reference guide, and may therefore start with any of these chapters in any order. However, to keep the repetition to a minimum, we do use references to other chapters rather than rewrite large sections.

The chapters in Part II include the following:

- Chapter 4: "Integration Management"
- Chapter 5: "Scope Management"
- Chapter 6: "Time Management"
- Chapter 7: "Cost Management"
- Chapter 8: "Quality Management"
- Chapter 9: "Human Resources Management"
- Chapter 10: "Communications Management"
- Chapter 11: "Risk Management"
- Chapter 12: "Procurement Management"

Part III: Crossing the Bridge to Agile

Whereas Part II covers the specific practical activity changes, Part III covers the softer skills of being an agent of change and what this change means for you personally and professionally. Having answered much of the "what" you need to do in Part II, we turn our focus to "how" to make these changes in Part III. From how your role changes, to how you'll work with others who aren't agile, to what to watch out for, we respond to the commonly asked questions of those who are about to cross the bridge. The chapters in Part III complete the main body of the book:

- Chapter 13: "How Will My Responsibilities Change?"
- Chapter 14: "How Will I Work with Other Teams Who Aren't Agile?"
- Chapter 15: "How Can a Project Management Office Support Agile?"
- Chapter 16: "Selling the Benefits of Agile"
- Chapter 17: "Common Mistakes"

Appendixes

We've included two appendixes we hope you will find useful. Appendix A, "Agile Methodologies," runs down a number of the software development methodologies that fall under the agile umbrella. Appendix B, "Agile Artifacts," includes a look at the typical agile project "artifacts."

Who This Book Is For

Although this book is targeted at software project managers who are members of the PMI, anyone who is doing traditional software project management will benefit from seeing agility presented in terminology to which they are accustomed. We will refer to these long-established methodologies as "waterfall," "plan-driven," or "traditional," all of which refer to sequential, phased, noniterative approaches to software development.

Final Thoughts

We should also make it clear that we are not sanctioned by PMI or any of its representatives. This book is the result of our research, interpretation, and experience. Although we used the Third Edition of the *PMBOK® Guide* in our studies, we expect that as the *PMBOK® Guide* goes through further revisions, you will still find the concepts presented here to be relevant.

Endnote

1. "PMP," "PMI," and "PMBOK Guide" are registered marks of Project Management Institute, Inc.

Acknowledgments

The authors would like to jointly express their appreciation to the following individuals who helped to make this book a reality:

- The editors at *Better Software* magazine and StickyMinds.com, particularly Lee Copeland and Francesca Matteu. This book originally started out as a whitepaper that won an award at the 2005 Better Software conference in San Francisco, and led to a series of supporting articles on StickyMinds.com. Lee, Francesca, and all the editors at their organization have helped us to become better writers.
- Mike Cohn, who encouraged us throughout the process and provided us with early feedback on our chapters.
- Dennis Bolles, Ted Boccuzzi, Greg Githens, Kent McDonald, and Bob Tarne, our reviewers who spent a great deal of time and effort in helping us to figure out how to better communicate our thoughts and ideas.
- The agile coaches and trainers who began to reference our book even before it was published.
- The numerous teams who have provided us with so many learning experiences and who have allowed us to share our experiences with them.

Michele Sliger would like to thank:

- Jean Tabaka, who taught me the importance of collaboration and facilitation.
- The folks at Rally Software, who pushed me to grow, excel, inspect, and adapt.
- My agile mentor Mike Cohn and my Scrum buddy Alicia Yanik. No matter how crazy my question, they are always kind enough to respond.

- Shelly Wilbanks, my dearest friend, for her unending encouragement and support—and free legal advice for life (there, it's in writing!).
- The kids at Judi's House—they remind me of what's really important and fill me with endless wonder at the power of self-organizing teams and the agility of the human soul.
- Stacia, for writing the hard chapters!

Stacia Broderick would like to thank:

- Mike Broderick, my husband and rock, and Bodie Broderick, who always wore a smile and a wagging tail.
- Ken Schwaber, who mentored me through the valley of despair.
- Bob Schatz, who taught me how to become a leader.
- My family, who put up with my absence at family events and gatherings. It will be nice to get back to those things.
- My Nikes, for helping me sort my thoughts and clear my head.
- Michele, for writing the hard chapters!

About the Authors

Michele Sliger has extensive experience in agile software development, having transitioned to Scrum and XP practices in 2000 after starting her career following the traditional waterfall approach. A self-described "bridge builder," her passion lies in helping those in traditional software development environments cross the bridge to agility. Michele is the owner of Sliger Consulting Inc., where she consults with businesses ranging from small startups to Fortune 500 companies, helping teams with their agile adoption, and helping organizations prepare for the changes that agile adoption brings. A frequent conference speaker and regular contributor to software industry publications, Michele is a strong advocate of agile principles and value-driven development practices. She is a certified Project Management Professional (PMP®) and a Certified Scrum Trainer (CST). She has an undergraduate MIS degree and an MBA. When not working, Michele volunteers as a grief facilitator for teens at Judi's House, a nonprofit dedicated to helping children learn how to cope with the loss of a loved one.

Stacia Broderick has worked as a project manager for fifteen years, the last eight in software development. She was fortunate to be helped across the bridge under the mentorship of Ken Schwaber while working for Primavera Systems in 2003 and ever since has helped hundreds of teams the world over embrace the principles of and transition to an agile way of creating products. Stacia founded her company, AgileEvolution, Inc., in 2006 based on the belief that agile practices present a humane, logical way for teams and companies to deliver products. Stacia is a Certified Scrum Trainer as well as a PMP®, a mix that proves valuable when assisting organizations' transition from traditional to modern practices. Stacia enjoys running, playing classical violin, and spending time with her family.

How One Project Manager Crossed the Bridge

I'm Stacia Broderick, and I want to convey a deeply personal story of change in hopes of helping you recognize the importance of listening to yourself and learning how to grow, even when it is quite uncomfortable and scary.

I have been a project manager since 1993, agile since 2003. I am also a PMP, formally trained in the lexicon of the thousands of certified Project Management Professionals who went before me. When I started managing projects, I took certain pride in my abilities to plan a project, learned how to enter data into a project management tool, held status meetings, negotiated with contractors and third-party sourcing for resources and materials, mitigated risks in the project and, of course, controlled scope. I could perform forward- and backward-pass calculations in my sleep.

Project management was a perfect fit for me, who, as a third-grader, resource-loaded my two sisters and I into weekly rotating chore schedules. I even designed a process for reducing the number of dishwashing loads by only emptying the dishwasher based on a pull-and-batch system (pull a dish only when needed, and no more frequently; gather all dirty dishes in the sink until time to reload dishwasher; reload all at once), but my father did not support this new approach. For me—a self-admitted control freak— project management was a perfect fit.

My conflict with Scrum, one of the agile approaches to software development, began in 2003. I was vehemently opposed to this new, lightweight, not-sponsored-by-any-formal-governing-body methodology (or so I had thought). My life was turned upside down when Ken Schwaber came to train and mentor our team of managers and software developers. As a devout PMP, or perhaps as a result of still being relatively new to software development, I was a bit leery of Ken's initial teachings about self-managed teams and iterative development. As I drifted in and out of the two days of ScrumMaster training, the line that caught most of my attention was, "You have no power." Ken meant it in the sense that the product owner and delivery team roles would be collaborative in nature, and that a project manager wasn't the decision-maker in Scrum. Like a mantra, I repeated this line to see if I could get used to it. I kept thinking, "How could you possibly manage a project or people without power? Wasn't it a prerequisite that you had to muscle your way through a project and demand that people work overtime and weekends (but promise to feed them free pizza)? As the project team grew fatter and physically slower, didn't this mean you could more easily beat them into submission?" (I kid, I kid.)

When my boss failed to show up to ScrumMaster training, I was automatically thrown to the lions as my (now ex)-boss's replacement. Congratulations to me: I was the newly minted ScrumMaster of three project teams.

Wow. So now I had to lead people. I had never *lead* people before. I had certainly managed them, and collected the status of their tasks, and quizzed them on how much time was remaining on those tasks. And, of course, I questioned their estimates. (Everyone knows that developers are horrible estimators!) I sometimes even gave my helpful opinion on whether certain technical tasks were easy or difficult, much to the developers' delight, I am sure.

Of course, what I didn't realize at the time was that I really had no power to begin with. You see, I had always managed a group of knowledge workers—folks who grew up crunching numbers, writing complex code, creatively banging out products that at their roots consisted of only 1s and 0s. I truly believe that up until learning to lead, these knowledge workers merely tolerated me. I had never really managed them. They managed me by deciding to make me happy by filling out their timesheets. They humored me when I asked to be walked through the testing phase of the project plan, *again.* They certainly knew way more about how stuff really worked than I did. My life was ruled by impossible project plans (see Figure I-1). For a few months straight I made great overtime by staying late at the office to perfect the Gantt chart, knowing in my heart that it would be out of date the very next day, if not the very next minute. Often, I was asked to "create a dashboard" for the executives: a report that I knew reflected a false, positive reality. Now that I look back, I wonder how I survived the "manager" title.

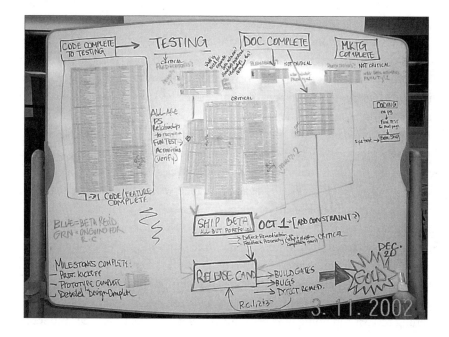

Figure I-1
Author's rendering of the "impossible project plan"

My first thoughts turned to tracking the status of projects. How will we know "where we are"? How will we know how much value we've earned? (My CEO at the time had written a book on earned value management.) How will we manage scope? (I had produced a scope change management process for the department and had spent weeks perfecting the diagram.) Most frightening of all, I wondered how insane our customers would think we are since we'd no longer be able to tell them when they could have everything they wanted. And what's with the paltry Scrum project tracking mechanisms? A burndown chart? What does that possibly tell us? That can't possibly tell us if we're on track! I want my percent-complete status reports! And let me say that the first few meetings with executives were disasters. I know that I left red-faced on many occasions.

All of these questions were fueled by the personal struggle I was going through: "Wow, if teams are self-managing, they'll no longer need me.

I don't have a place in this organization now that we're using Scrum." I had no idea how to act within this new realm. I had a very real struggle with getting past the "me" and focusing on the team. I was also troubled with ownership issues. I routinely struggled with not owning the administrative task of updating the product backlog; for me, this represented scope, and not having it within my charge was very frightening. I felt powerless and as if I had no role.

Somewhere around the third sprint, I started to get it. Once the teams started delivering real value that could be seen and touched, the light bulb went on. What were once yelling product owners were now engaged, energized product owners, who actually worked *with* the teams to talk about the user experience, helping developers deliver *valuable* product increments. Observing collocated team members who were often heard laughing, working closely together, and enjoying their personal lives again touched me in a way that no perfectly calculated project Gantt chart or nested work breakdown structure ever could. I began to realize what it meant for teams to work at a sustainable pace and to focus their energy on what really mattered: creating software for the company that they work for, while being able to enjoy their personal lives the rest of the time (after all, isn't this the foundation that keeps us all sane?). Coupled with a VP who "got it" and banned overtime for the department, the agile principle of sustainable pace really lifted morale and improved the quality of work life. I even had time one evening to visit the home of one of our developers, meet his wife, and learn more about real Indian food. It was a wonderful, personal experience (and I now love soan papdi, a wonderful Indian dessert).

After my personal light bulb went off about the value of agile development, I began to realize how I could provide value as an agile project manager. First of all, I let go of the backlog, and it relinquished its grip on me. By doing so, I gave control to someone else, namely the product owner, and let him prioritize the list. This gave me more time to focus on building teams. I moved into the collocated space with one of my teams, and I worked on justifying budget for other teams to collocate (and succeeded!). I created a newsletter for all of the project teams, called the *Daily Collaborator,* that included photos, stories, and interesting facts about the project. I learned how to report to executives, which was no small feat, by understanding their needs and by asking the team to help me determine how to show the project data. I made sure that stakeholders were involved in product reviews; sometimes it was difficult to get their time. I involved people from training and support in our iteration reviews and garnered their support in the testing lab when we were manually testing part of the system. I helped set up product backlog meetings that replaced our traditional change control meetings. I worked with customers as they implemented early releases of our products to gather feedback and understand how we could improve their experiences. And when I was in a period of quietness, I observed, observed, and observed some more—in the team rooms, daily standup meetings, reviews, and general team interactions. These observations helped me determine which obstacles to tackle next; I kept detailed notes and added tasks to my own impediment backlog when I saw a change or an organizational impediment that needed attention. I was a chameleon and a peacock at the same time, retaining the ability to blend in with the environment, while standing out and displaying my feathers when the environment needed to change.

We celebrated a very successful release nine months after instituting Scrum. It was a proud moment for us all; we had each traveled a personal journey and transformation unlike any other. Our release t-shirts said "Develop with Heart; Deliver with Pride." That department of 85 people always will remain my fondest memory of a truly performing Scrum development organization.

My first three Scrum teams—the ones that truly scared the bejeezus out of me—will forever remain in my heart as the kind people who taught me the tough lessons of letting go.

The best day of my professional life was the day that I walked into one of my Scrum team's daily meetings and the team looked at me, smiling, and said, "We don't need you here, Stacia. Maybe you can use this time to work on other things or to help another team. We've got it under control." And you know, they did have it under control. I walked away on the verge of tears, but the tears weren't for me and my "loss"; they were from the happiness I felt at being able to let go and know that all would be just fine, and from the satisfaction I felt from helping individuals become empowered.

For me to cross the agility bridge, I had to understand what it meant to put others before me. This wasn't something that came naturally to me; because of a tough upbringing and lack of sense of self, I created a strong identity in my project manager title. I had to learn how to facilitate and listen for problems underneath the surface. Most importantly, I had to learn that the people doing the work know the work the best and will figure out the best way to get from point A to Z. All they really needed me for was to clear the path. They knew this already; Scrum helped me see it.

Whereas Michele got it right away, it took me awhile. We each came from very different places when embarking on our own personal bridges to agility. Michele's bridge was short and level; mine was a swaying suspension bridge, on a 45-degree angle, fraught with high winds and torrential downpours. What we both agree on is that since we've been helping teams—hundreds of teams—move to agile methods, we have never been happier in our professional careers. In the following chapters, we are pleased to present some ideas for translating what you already know about managing projects into your own agile paradigm. We'll dig deeper into what you should expect, how to successfully make the transition, and what steps you'll need to take in order to cross the bridge to agility.

Part I

An Agile Overview

IN THIS PART

Chapter 1

What Is "Agile"?

In the struggle for survival, the fittest win out at the expense of their rivals because they succeed in adapting themselves best to their environment.

—*Charles Darwin*

Darwin's famous voyage on the HMS *Beagle* took four years, nine months, and five days, ending in 1836. We are all familiar with the story: Darwin set sail and discovered unique species of plants and animals in South America and other regions of the world, resulting in years of work that culminated in his Theory of Evolution.[1] Darwin began his adventure much to the disappointment of his family, who felt that it would delay his anticipated admission into the clergy. After his return from the voyage, and aware of the Victorians' strong belief in the divine, he kept his emerging theories quiet for twenty years while he studied barnacles to derive enough data to one day prove and thoroughly support his point. He knew the uproar that his thoughts and beliefs (or disbeliefs!) would create.

The rest is history, as the cliché goes. Darwin's theories were so profound, so prolific, that they still fuel debates in school systems and in medical research around the globe today. His discoveries threatened the religious norms of the time and prod at that belief system today, more than 125 years since his death.

Darwin's voyage is like the project manager's walk across the bridge to agility: the leap of faith, venturing out into the unknown, the process of discovery, and the sometimes unpredictable results. Both Darwin and the new agile project manager wonder about what to make of their newfound knowledge and how to blend that knowledge within the current context of society or the business organization.

Even though agile ways of doing development have been around since the 1960s, only recently has the agile movement gained so much momentum that one in seven companies is piloting or exploring the methods.[2] We are living in a time of a major movement within the software industry. This movement has caused many project managers to investigate what it means to be "agile." What they find is that, like Darwin's discoveries, agile methodologies are different from the traditional norms of software development, norms that often represent the societal structure for their business organizations. For some of you reading this book, agile methodologies will be a completely new island; yet, for others, the approaches might represent a way of working with which you're already familiar.

One trip to the Agile Manifesto web page yields thousands of names of supporters of the process. A random sampling of the comments on that web page produce quotes such as "The Agile Manifesto is an important first step in reforging the craft of software development."[3] And, as evidenced by the thousands of postings, the support is global: "Me siento feliz porque nuevamente me siento emocionado por los avances en mi profesion." (*I feel happy because again I feel touched by the advances in my profesion [sic].*)[4]

Although agile has a lot of support, it also has its fair share of critics who believe that it is a fad and does not work. There are websites and blogs from people who insist that a plan-driven, prescriptive approach is more appropriate for delivering software. Our experiences have shown that successful agile projects and agile teams exist all over the world. It is our opinion that when teams are supported by management, and can interact with the customer, they are much more successful than teams who create software using a sequential, prescriptive approach.

We realize that traditional project managers with no agile experience who visit an agile team's room for the first time must feel a bit like Darwin when he discovered the unique creatures and life on the Galapagos Islands, as the landscape is quite different: Teams deliver incremental product releases, which allow the organization to be responsive and proactive in resolving issues; teams are safe places for individuals whereby trust, collaboration, and hard work are the founding values; people talk to each other.

This chapter provides you with a solid understanding of the origins, values, and principles of agile methods so that you will understand what the other island looks like.

What Are the Origins of Agile?

Agile describes a set of principles and practices for delivering software. What we know as agile today has actually emerged over a long period of time.

A look at the origins of agile takes us back several decades in time. The United States Department of Defense (DoD) and NASA have used iterative and incremental development (IID) since the 1950s.[5] IID is an approach to building systems characterized by executing several iterations in sequence, each iteration containing a release of new features. IID enables flexibility because decisions can be made based on working software.

In the 1960s, Evolutionary project management, also called Evo, was conceptualized by Thomas Gilb, who formally introduced it in 1976. Evo recommends one- to two-week iterations, focusing on the delivery of product each iteration. Like IID, Evo "emphasizes delivering a partial solution into production early, in order to obtain early business value, and feedback to guide and evolve future deliverables."[6] Evo also substantiated the incremental, iterative, and feedback elements of agile software development.

Even Dr. Winston Royce's 1970 paper, "Managing the Development of Large Software Systems," which first introduced the concept of the "waterfall" approach, discussed the value of iterative software development. Indeed, Royce stated that the waterfall model "is risky and invites failure" because it leaves testing until the end, when major design flaws might then be found and require substantial rework: "In effect the development process has returned to the origin and one can expect up to a 100% overrun in schedule and/or costs."[7] Seven of the nine pages in his paper are then devoted to improvements to the basic waterfall model, including iterative development and involving the customer throughout the process. In reading the paper, it makes you wonder how we could have missed his final recommendations and instead implemented his base model. Ironically, it was the limited adoption of Royce's ideas by industry that created the waterfall approach to software development, not Royce's ideas themselves.

In 1986, "The New New Product Development Game," a whitepaper published by Takeuchi and Nonaka, suggests that "the rules of the game in product development are changing. Many companies have discovered that it takes more than the accepted basics of high quality, low cost, and differentiation to excel in today's competitive market. It also takes speed and flexibility."[8] Additionally, Takeuchi and Nonaka discuss the "rugby approach" of dedicated, self-organizing teams, the members of which, like actual rugby scrum teams who work together to gain control of a ball and move it up the field, all work together to deliver product. Takeuchi and Nonaka found that in a sequential, "relay-like" system, "crucial problems tend to occur at the points where one group passes the project to the next. The rugby approach smooths out this problem by maintaining continuity across phases." Takeuchi and Nonaka introduced another agile principle: dedicated, cross-functional, self-organizing teams that reduce the bottlenecks created by functional groups (silos) of people. This whitepaper is the foundation of the Scrum approach; you may read more about Scrum and other agile approaches in Appendix A, "Agile Methodologies."

Moreover, ideas from Lean Product Development, as propagated by the Toyota Production System (TPS), provide even more foundation for the agile family of software development approaches. Lean focuses on eliminating waste through continuous improvement, getting quality right the first time and producing only what was requested by the customer. Agile teams do something very similar in that they only create the features that are needed by the customer now, by focusing on the highest value items in a ranked product backlog. Mary and Tom Poppendieck immortalized these Lean concepts as applied to software product development in *Lean Software Development: An Agile Toolkit*.[9]

When we speak of the progression of agile throughout the years, some agilists say that it is a movement in the software industry against the management style carried over from the manufacturing business culture of the 1920s. Frederick Taylor, who was innovative in his time, introduced segregation of management (white collars) from ordinary workers (blue collars). Manufacturers who followed Taylor's "scientific management' approach broke down work into manageable chunks and assigned managers to the responsible workers. Managers would then time the best approach to get the work done, and hand out "instruction cards" to the workers based on these time and motion studies. Workers' incentive was simple: Do the work by way of the manager's card and get paid in return. The explicit message: Managers know the work better than the workers.

At the end of World War I, Taylor's management theories were supported and proven appropriate for the workforce at the time. In years since, however, workers have become more specialized and educated. The global reduction of manufacturing jobs in recent years—11 percent from 1995 to 2002[10]—has caused a shift in education and employment choices. In fact, a

2005 United States labor market report stated, "three out of ten occupations predicted to grow the fastest are computer related."[11] This growing crop of "knowledge workers," a term coined by Peter Drucker in the 1960s, refers to a new breed of employees who employ their knowledge and brainpower, instead of their hands, as a means to income.

It is in this new era of knowledge workers that the old organization paradigm no longer works, and the shift to agile principles and practices begins. Now workers must be treated as "volunteers," because like volunteers, these workers can leave and take with them their "means of production": their knowledge. Also like volunteers, knowledge workers do not want to be ordered around. Instead they want to be engaged, they want to participate, and they want to know where they're going and what impact their work will have on others. They want to be challenged, and feel as though their efforts are appreciated. This means that the old approach of commanding workers must be replaced with the newer approach of information sharing and persuasion. As Drucker states, "one does not begin with the question, What do we want? One begins with the questions, What does the other party want? What are its values? What are its goals? What does it consider results? … The starting point may have to be managing for performance…the starting point may be a definition of results."[12] And so in agile, we focus on providing value to the customer and constantly improving our productivity as we do so.

The 1990s saw a flurry of agile approaches that ran the gamut from Scrum at Easel Corporation to Extreme Programming at Chrysler Corporation to Crystal Methods and IBM's Rational Unified Process at various organizations. Additionally, the Dynamic Systems Development Method (DSDM) was added to the mix in Europe. It was evident that lighter-weight approaches were cropping up all over the global software development landscape. The mid- to late '90s showed a significant increase in the use of these agile methods to create product, culminating in 2001 with the writing of the Agile Manifesto.

What Is the Agile Manifesto?

In 2001, a group of 17 "lightweight" methodologists met in Snowbird, Utah, to discuss their approaches to delivering software. This group of people consisted of representatives from eXtreme Programming (XP), Scrum,

DSDM, Adaptive Software Development, and others "sympathetic to the need for an alternative to documentation driven, heavyweight software development process."[13] Jim Highsmith says that most of the agile principles boil down to "mushy stuff" and that "the meteoric rise of interest in and sometimes tremendous criticism of Agile Methodologies is about the mushy stuff of values and culture."[14] After much discussion about said mushy stuff and the ways in which they were creating software, the Agile Manifesto was written: [15]

We are uncovering better ways of developing software by doing it and helping others do it. Through this work we have come to value:

- Individuals and Interactions over Processes and Tools
- Working Software over Comprehensive Documentation
- Customer Collaboration over Contract Negotiation
- Responding to Change over Following a Plan

That is, while there is value in the items on the right, we value the items on the left more.

Kent Beck	James Grenning	Robert C. Martin
Mike Beedle	Jim Highsmith	Steve Mellor
Arie van Bennekum	Andrew Hunt	Ken Schwaber
Alistair Cockburn	Ron Jeffries	Jeff Sutherland
Ward Cunningham	Jon Kern	Dave Thomas
Martin Fowler	Brian Marick	

Although the four value statements are discussed in the following sections, we feel that it is important to emphasize the last statement of the Manifesto. The writers were not claiming that agile teams do not write documentation, for example, although this myth surrounds agile teams. Rather, agile teams question the value of the documentation that they have traditionally produced, and whittle that away to only write documentation that is useful and valuable, such as tests or high-level designs, or end-user documentation deliverables such as online help or manuals. When thinking about the last statement of the Manifesto, it is important to remember to stress the items on the left as value statements and employ the items on the right as needed and when they add value. Now let's explore the Agile Manifesto in more depth.

Individuals and Interactions over Processes and Tools

This first value of the manifesto underscores the importance of individuals and interactions when building software systems. All agile approaches focus on empowered, self-managing teams; autonomous teams do not need the day-to-day intervention of management. Instead, if management protects a team from outside interference, and focuses on removing obstacles in the way of creating product, teams become highly effective and productive.[16] Additionally, it is widely accepted that complex systems cannot be predicted[17] and that they're best managed using empirical process controls;[18] therefore, management allows self-managing agile teams to build systems in an empirical manner.

Agile teams are empowered to make the necessary decisions in order to get the work done. Takeuchi and Nonaka referred to this as "self-transcendent," meaning that the team should be in a "never-ending quest to find the limit."[19] Empowered teams take the guidelines that management gives them and create their own goals from those directives; they find a way around a problem through devising unique solutions as a team.

Agile teams are composed of a mix of skills—everyone necessary to create the product increment is on the team. This means that an agile team is composed of developers, testers, database experts, writers, business analysts, user interface experts, and other skilled professionals. Through working together daily to meet the goals of the iteration, the individuals on the team start to create a shared direction for the product. Ideas overlap. Leadership emerges. Agile team members are able to step in for each other as necessary; they create the system as a team and not as a series of handoffs that we normally associate with a serial process. They apply what they've learned, and the collective knowledge grows; design, quality and productivity is improved as a result.

Humans have tried to create tools to replace face-to-face communication. From collaboration portals, to online communities, to virtual whiteboards, the tech space abounds with products to help us get better at communicating. Unfortunately, for many, these tools have been touted as the penultimate communication vehicle. What many teams have learned, however, is that practicing ventriloquism through tool and process marionettes has created phenomenal waste in our product development processes. The Agile Manifesto, by focusing on individuals and interactions, forces teams to rethink the best approaches to communication, realizing the power of team members collaborating in person to solve a mutual problem. And when the team members aren't face to face (this is indeed a global market), tools can help support—not replace—those conversations. Never underestimate the value of a simple phone call.

Working Software over Comprehensive Documentation

Agile projects value working software, which is a profoundly different emphasis from traditional, phased projects. Traditionally, one would measure a project's progress by the percent complete of the functional milestones (that is, analysis complete, documentation complete, code complete, and so on). In agile projects, however, working software is the ultimate quantification of project status. Instead of status meetings where everyone reports, "I'm 90 percent complete," agile teams provide actual working product as a status report, called a "product review," at the end of each iteration. Inspecting software that works enables us to respond appropriately to the true state of the project. Everything is visible; decisions can be made based on product that exists, not documented representations thereof.

This value statement of the Agile Manifesto is two-fold; the second idea behind this statement is that many teams consider some documentation wasteful. In fact, we've been told very directly by some developers that they don't need "no stinkin' specs." In business terms, spending lots of time up front to capture every design detail in a specification can be a waste of time. Most agile teams say that design changes as the system is built, which results in outdated documentation; therefore, why waste time documenting ideas that will most likely change as implementation begins, and as customer feedback is received? The famous Standish Group finding that more than "60% of software functionality is rarely or never used"[20] speaks to the waste introduced by comprehensive documentation. How is this so? Well, in traditional projects when the scope is defined up front, the scope is protected in order to keep the project "on schedule and within budget," even when the features defined up front need to change or even be dropped based on changes in the customer's environment. Therefore, why should we develop something that will not be used by our customers? In fact, why even write about it?

One developer stated it very succinctly:

> If someone hands me a 40-page document and tells me to go code, I won't know what to work on first. In fact, I would probably tackle the architecture stuff first, or maybe I'd work on something that was interesting and exciting to me. It probably won't be the most valuable feature for the customer. So now the waste of writing the document is compounded by the waste of me coding whatever it is that I think I should start with—and it probably won't be the right thing.

Besides the waste factor, agile teams prefer face-to-face communication over documentation because it is simpler, faster, and more reliable.

With that said, there are various forms of documentation that teams consider valuable within the context of their organization. For example, one organization could not live without end-user documentation; in fact, it was so important that it became a criterion that each feature had to pass in order to be accepted at the end of each iteration. Another team decided to document its decisions every iteration because it had just previously lost five valuable team members to a hostile team takeover. And yet another organization had to pass government regulatory compliance, so it had to work with its auditors to find the "right" level of documentation that could pass audits. Even though the stress is on working software, all documentation is not bad. If in doubt, ask the team: Is it valuable? Are we better off for writing it? Are we obligated by law, and, if so, how can we find out what is the minimum we can do?

Customer Collaboration over Contract Negotiation

Contract negotiation in the traditional sense means that we identify and define everything the customer wants and then draw up the contract that spells out the payment and date specifications. This has resulted in many fixed-price/fixed-scope situations. What we have learned is that this isn't always the best approach for software development projects. Too many teams have found themselves in death-march[21] situations, working 80 hours a week to meet the deadline set forth in the contract—a contract that was estimated and agreed to by somebody other than the team in the first place. Just as bad, customers have found themselves committed to work that no longer makes sense, all in the name of a contract.

Agile "customer collaboration," on the other hand, implies that customers become a part of the development process. To develop the right system, customer feedback is essential. Agile teams value the contributions made by the customer—or the customer representative—and learn to let the customer make the business decision. In turn, customers rely on important technical information that the team can provide in order to make appropriate decisions. Sometimes customers don't know what they want until they can see it.

We see a tremendous focus on contracts these days that are better suited for agile projects. Mary Poppendieck talks about building in cost responsibility for both parties, based on Toyota's contracting examples with its die makers. Their contracts are written based on a target cost principle—that once the target cost of the contract has been met, Toyota and the customer share the excessive cost of change. This is an incentive for both parties to minimize the cost of change, yet recognizes and allows it to happen. Another type of contract—the "staged contract"—allows for built-in checkpoints in the contract to provide the customer visibility and go/no-go decision points along the way. These contract types are not new, but they are gaining more visibility as more viable alternatives for software development teams.

Teams can build a system that meets the customer's needs if the customer provides feedback and guides them along the way. Writing specs down and throwing them over the fence is simply not effective, and has landed many a team in the position of working overtime to fix the system to meet the needs of the customer. Perhaps, if the customer had been involved along the way, the team wouldn't be in such a predicament. We've coached many teams who have ended up in this situation and are using agile methods as a way of changing this.

Responding to Change over Following a Plan

It's much easier to respond to change when the organization and the customer share a clear understanding of the project's status. Focusing on increments of working software and collaborating with the customer allow development teams to more readily respond to change.

In plan-driven environments, all requirements are specified up front, broken down to the task level and estimated. Costs and dates are calculated bottom-up from these very granular tasks. The resulting schedule becomes a baseline for the project and is utilized to measure the project's performance. Therefore, it is very important to stay on task and control scope creep in a plan-driven project setting to limit or eliminate cost overruns or schedule slippage.

The Agile Manifesto does not say that plans are not important. In fact, agile teams are very disciplined and dedicated to planning and to revisiting those plans; because they are involved in the creation of the plans, they are deeply committed. Agile plans follow more of a rolling wave approach using top-down planning, into which we'll take a deeper look later in this book.

What Are the Agile Principles That Guide Teams?

The Agile Manifesto was written along with a set of 12 principles to guide teams. We have listed each principle, along with a brief description of each:

- *Our highest priority is to satisfy the customer through early and continuous delivery of valuable software.*
  This principle underscores the focus of delivering value to the customer. At the end of the day, it is this philosophy of customer satisfaction that drives agile teams.

- *Welcome changing requirements, even late in development. Agile processes harness change for the customer's competitive advantage.*
  In a plan-based project, staying on scope means that scope changes are often discouraged. By allowing for change, we can be certain that we're building products that help bring value to our customers. By delivering early and continuously, while also allowing for change, we can stay flexible and thus "agile" in our ability to meet changing conditions.

- *Deliver working software frequently, from a couple of weeks to a couple of months, with a preference to the shorter timescale.*

  This principle specifies the timebox as a way of delivering continuously to the customer. A shorter timescale means that the team doesn't create product for too long a time without getting feedback. This is a way to mitigate the risk posed by building in long development cycles in which the customer is surprised at the end. In agile, by delivering very frequently, there are seldom surprises. Some say that agile removes the "Tada!" moment.[22]

- *Business people and developers must work together daily throughout the project.*

  Business people, or stakeholders, represent the business needs for a product. Just like customers, they have certain ideas and beliefs about how the system should work. Also, just like customers, they don't necessarily know what those needs are until they see the system. Therefore, when business people collaborate with developers, they ensure that their business interests will be better met by sharing contexts, ideas, and answers.

- *Build projects around motivated individuals. Give them the environment and support they need, and trust them to get the job done.*

  In agile projects, teams are said to be self-managing within the timebox; that is, while building product during the iteration, they should be able to have all the necessary resources at their fingertips and the trust of management to get the job done.

- *The most efficient and effective method of conveying information to and within a development team is face-to-face conversation.*

  Although seemingly common sense, this statement refers to replacing some documentation with words. Instead of writing detailed design specifications, for example, the team members will work together to discuss and explore ideas about how the software should be built. This is not to say that agile teams do not document—they do. Instead, it's to say that documentation is not the primary vehicle of communication. We are aware that many teams are distributed across thousands of miles, and sometimes it may seem that the only way to communicate is through extensive documents; however, many teams have successfully implemented instant messenger, video conferencing, wikis, updated engineering environments, and other uses of technology to support effective collaboration.

- *Working software is the primary measure of progress.*
  There is no better way to understand the status of our project than by inspecting the current state of our system. What has been delivered? How does it work? How can we be sure that it works the way we need it to? By having a look at the product as it's being built, business people and customers can ask these questions—and get answers by looking at the emerging product!

- *Agile processes promote sustainable development. The sponsors, developers, and users should be able to maintain a constant pace indefinitely.*
  Working at a sustainable pace is important to the quality of life for everyone involved in the project. Not only the quality of life, but the quality of the product can suffer if overworked engineers are struggling to focus and finish.

- *Continuous attention to technical excellence and good design enhances agility.*
  Professionalism in anyone's craft is paramount. Technical professionals who write software based on good, simple design are able to respond to change quickly and effectively. This flexibility allows for organizations to be agile.

- *Simplicity—the art of maximizing the amount of work not done—is essential.*
  Simplicity is the anti-gold-plating mechanism of agile. Agile teams only build what the customer wants, and no more. This very simple principle ensures that teams are not building functionality that a customer does not want or will not use. Once a feature is built, it must be maintained for the life of the system, or the investment must be made to back it out. Either way, this is waste that should be avoided.

- *The best architectures, requirements, and designs emerge from self-organizing teams.*
  The collective wisdom of a team magnificently outweighs the wisdom of one individual. When team members get their heads together, they collaborate to build the best system possible. This agile principle echoes Drucker's teachings about the knowledge worker.

- *At regular intervals, the team reflects on how to become more effective, then tunes and adjusts its behavior accordingly.*

  Although product can be inspected and adapted at the end of each iteration, this principle discusses the need for process tuning. Agile teams retrospect in order to determine which processes are working well and which are not. Team members work together to collectively solve any challenges with their processes and focus on improvement over time.

To some, agile represents a people approach to project management; to others, it describes lean development and removing waste from a process. And yet to others, it describes a way to work in a fast-paced world full of churn and change. What will it mean to you on your island?

Summary

Here are the takeaways from this chapter:

- Agile project management is purposely different from traditional project development.
- Agile development has been with us since the 1960s. The Agile Manifesto was a formal reconciliation of the guiding principles of the existing "lightweight" methodologies in existence in 2001.
- Agile proposes a new emphasis:
  - Individuals and interactions over processes and tools
  - Working software over comprehensive documentation
  - Customer collaboration over contract negotiation
  - Responding to change over following a plan

"That is, while there is value in the items on the right, we value the items on the left more."

Endnotes

1. Charles R. Darwin. *On the Origin of Species by Means of Natural Selection, or the Preservation of Favoured Races in the Struggle for Life.* (London: John Murray, 1859) 1–6.

2. Carey Schwaber. "Corporate IT Leads the Second Wave of Agile Adoption." Trends, a Forrester Research Inc. report. November 30, 2005, 2.

3. Kent Beck, et al. "Independent Signatories of the Manifesto for Agile Software Development." http://www.agilemanifesto.org/sign/display.cgi.

4. Kent Beck, et al. Translation: "I feel happy because again I feel touched by the advances in my profesion [sic]."

5. Craig Larman and Victor R. Basili. "Iterative & Incremental Development: A Brief History." Computer, June 2003.

6. Craig Larman. *Agile and Iterative Development: A Manager's Guide.* (Boston: Addison-Wesley, 2004), 225.

7. Winston W. Royce. "Managing the Development of Large Software Systems: Concepts and Techniques." (paper presented at the Western Electronic Show and Convention [WesCon]), Los Angeles, CA, August 25–28, 1970), 329.

8. Hirotaka Takeuchi and Ikujiro Nonaka. "The New New Product Development Game." *Harvard Business Review*, January–February 1986 (reprint 86116), page 1.

9. Mary Poppendieck and Tom Poppendieck. *Lean Software Development: An Agile Toolkit.* (Upper Saddle River, NJ: Addison-Wesley, 2003), xxiv–xxv.

10. Tim Kane, et al. "Ten Myths About Jobs and Outsourcing." The Heritage Foundation, http://www.heritage.org/Research/TradeandForeignAid/wm467.cfm.

11. Bureau of Labor Statistics. "Charting the US Labor Market in 2005." U.S. Department of Labor, http://www.bls.gov/cps/labor2005/home.htm.

12. Peter F. Drucker. *Age of Discontinuity: Guidelines to Our Changing Society.* (New York: Harper & Row, 1968), 264.

13. Kent Beck, et al. http://www.agilemanifesto.org/.

14. Ibid.

15. Ibid.

16. Takeuchi. "New New Product Development Game."

17. Ralph D. Stacey. *Strategic Management and Organisational Dynamics, Fifth Edition.* (New York: Prentice Hall/Financial Times, 2007).

18. Babatunde A. Ogunnaike and W. Harmon Ray. *Process Dynamics, Modeling and Control.* (New York: Oxford University Press, 1994).

19. Takeuchi and Nonaka, 4.

20. Jim Johnson, "The Cost of Big Requirements Up Front (BRUF)." Keynote presentation at the annual XP (eXtreme Programming) Conference. Alghero, Sardinia, May 2002.

21. Ed Yourdon. *Death March.* (Upper Saddle River, NJ: Prentice Hall, 2003), xv–xviii.

22. Michele Sliger refers to this instead as the "Oh, crap!" moment.

Chapter 2

Mapping from the *PMBOK® Guide* to Agile

A new doctrine goes through three stages. It is attacked and declared absurd; then it is admitted as true and obvious but insignificant. Finally, its true importance is recognized and its adversaries claim the honor of having discovered it.

—*William James*

When you change the way you look at things, the things you look at change.

—*Max Planck*

Now that you have a clear understanding of what agile is and what might be waiting for you on that island, let's begin our journey by building the first few steps of our bridge to agility. First we must examine the origins of the *PMBOK® Guide,* the book most often used as a reference by project managers. Then we'll see how its project management lifecycle and processes correlate to those of agile.

The Project Management Institute and the *PMBOK® Guide*

The Project Management Institute was founded in 1969 at the Georgia Institute of Technology by five volunteers: James Snyder, Gordon Davis, Eric Jenett, A.E. Engman, and Susan C. Gallagher.[1] Its original purpose was to form an organization where members could share their experiences in project management and discuss issues. The purpose has expanded today to advancing practice knowledge and application in the profession of project management.

To this end, in 1983 the PMI created a publication titled "PMI Special Report on Ethics, Standards, and Accreditation." The "Standards" portion of this document was the "Project Management Body of Knowledge." In 1996 the first edition of *A Guide to the Project Management Body of Knowledge (PMBOK® Guide),* a book that outlined project management knowledge areas, processes, and practices, was published. The *PMBOK® Guide* became a standard for generally recognized good practices in project management. Now in its third edition, the *PMBOK® Guide* has sold more than a million copies worldwide. For years this has been the de facto archetype that *all* project managers follow—not just software project managers.

Although the *PMBOK® Guide* does not dictate methodology, many software project managers nevertheless began to associate the waterfall model with the processes outlined in the *PMBOK® Guide.* Perhaps it was because the waterfall model was the prevalent methodology at the time, or perhaps it was because the waterfall model provided a framework that supported all the *PMBOK® Guide* practices. Whatever the reason, it has been a hard misconception to shake, even though the third edition of the *PMBOK® Guide* makes it very clear that it is up to the reader to determine what processes are most appropriate to use in his or her situation.

Indeed, the *PMBOK® Guide* has paradoxically become broader in its context, even as it becomes more detailed in its processes and practices. As an important and noted change from the 2000 edition, the third edition states clearly that "there is no single best way to define an ideal project life cycle."[2] It further goes on to say that "the project manager, in collaboration with the project team, is always responsible for determining what processes are appropriate, and the appropriate degree of rigor for each process, for any given project."[3] Whereas the 2000 edition might have made it difficult to make a case that agile practices are in keeping with best practices as outlined in the *PMBOK® Guide*, the third edition makes it easy.

It is not only the *PMBOK® Guide* that is clear in its support for the validity of the newer agile methodologies. PMI's magazine *PM Network*[®4] started talking specifically about agile practices in April 2005, when Peter Fretty's feature article "Reconciling Differences" shined a spotlight on how agile practices had improved productivity, quality, and customer satisfaction at Shine Technologies.[5] That was the first of several articles that have since appeared in the magazine touting agility. Although that article was clear that the changes were the result of adopting agile practices, most of the subsequent magazine articles seem to shy away from the term "agile." Instead, these features discuss how collaboration, team empowerment, the use of team norms, and the project manager's shift away from a command-and-control management style to one of leadership in service to the team are improving the project and the product.

PMI is also supporting the training of its project managers in Agile Project Management courses and presentations in PMI-sponsored programs such as PMI Seminars World®, PMI Global Congresses®, and chapter symposiums and conferences.

Individual members of the Project Management Institute are also embracing agile methodologies; the authors of this book are an obvious case in point. We are still a minority, but feel strongly that this is starting to change. We are seeing more and more certified Project Management Professional (PMP®) attendees in our agile courses, hoping to expand their knowledge of software development approaches and project management. PMI volunteers at all levels of the organization are taking part in bringing agile to its constituents, including the volunteers who organized and authored the third edition of the *PMBOK® Guide*—many of whom graciously volunteered their time yet again, this time to review this book.

The PMI does not advocate any particular methodology. It only supplies a standard of good project management practices, and whether individuals choose to follow a waterfall or an agile approach, the *PMBOK® Guide* will support them both. You don't have to cast aside your PMP designation to be agile. (We certainly didn't!) All you need to do is change how you implement the practices. Well, there is a little more to it, so please keep reading—this is what we will focus on in Part II of the book.

But before diving into the *PMBOK® Guide* knowledge areas and mapping its practices to agile practices, let's first look at how the *PMBOK® Guide* version of the project lifecycle corresponds to a generic agile version.

Project Lifecycle

The project lifecycle is defined as "a collection of generally sequential project phases whose name and number are determined by the control needs of the organization or organizations involved in the project."[6] These phases are a collection of logical groupings of related activities that usually culminate in a deliverable. The *PMBOK® Guide* describes their sequence as beginning with an initial phase, followed by a series of intermediate phases, and ending in a final phase (see Figure 2-1).[7] Processes that aid in the completion of the deliverable are performed in each phase.

Figure 2-1
Project lifecycle
phases

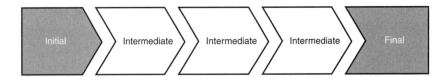

Project Management Institute, *A Guide to the Project Management Body of Knowledge (PMBOK® Guide), Third Edition*, Project Management Institute, Inc., 2004. Copyright and all rights reserved. Material from this publication has been reproduced with the permission of PMI.

In traditional approaches to software development, these phases have typically followed the waterfall methodology (see Figure 2-2). For example, one phase might be Design, and the deliverable for this phase would be some type of a system design document. Many times sign-offs are required before proceeding to the next phase, but this is the result of the methodology and not a mandate by the *PMBOK® Guide.*

Let's look at how this translates to an agile project lifecycle. In the definition "a collection of generally sequential project phases," the word "sequential" is often the biggest stumbling block. This is due to the popular misconception that "sequential" equals "waterfall." Agile has sequential project phases that we call "iterations," with the deliverable in each iteration being working code. However, all of the processes typically done sequentially—analysis, design, code, test—are done within a single phase in agile to produce an increment of code.

Waterfall Model

Figure 2-2
Waterfall approach to software development

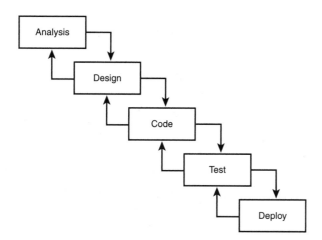

You may even want to consider these iterations as subphases of a larger phase, known as the release, where the major deliverable is a set of those increments of code such that they can be put into production and/or delivered to the customer.

The second part of the project lifecycle definition points out that the number (and in our agile interpretation, the duration) of the phases is "determined by the control needs of the organization." In agile, the number of iterations is decided on by the customer, based on what they define as the minimum amount of functionality deemed acceptable for a release. The length of the iterations—generally between one and six weeks—is determined by the "control needs" of the customer (or customer representative), that is, how often the customer will want to change what the delivery team is working on. The volatility of the industry, the amount of risk, and the clarity of the vision are all factors that affect the length of the iteration and define the organization's need for flexibility.

In the initial phase of agile projects, a planning process is part of the first iteration, and the deliverable is the high-level plan for the project (and in most cases, the first increment of working code is delivered as well).

Intermediate phases in agile are the releases and/or iterations where additional features are delivered in the form of working code. The final phase in an agile project is the hardening or production-readiness phase (*not* a test-fix phase), where process activities that prepare the system for delivery are conducted, along with the final project retrospective and other closing processes.

The *PMBOK® Guide* states that the transition from one phase to another usually involves some type of technical transfer or handoff.[8] This is the type of phrasing that might lead readers to believe that only a waterfall methodology is appropriate when following *PMBOK® Guide* practices. However, if we interpret "handoff" to mean that there is a handoff of an increment of code to the customer to use as they see fit, then agile is still in keeping with the basic tenets of the *PMBOK® Guide*. At the end of each iteration an increment of code is completed by the team and reviewed by the customer. Regardless of the outcome, the next iteration begins as planned (unless the project is cancelled); only the content of the work for that iteration is subject to change.

Because of this regular rhythm of incremental delivery, many have proffered that each iteration of an agile project is itself a project, having a start and stop date, and delivering a product as a result. We disagree with this assessment, however, believing it to be colored by years of waterfall practice. The waterfall methodology outlines the processes of analysis, design, coding, testing, and deployment, which were all done as part of a project. Because these are things that are all done within an iteration in agile, the logical assumption for many was that an iteration equaled a project. But an iteration is more properly referred to as a phase or subphase of the project, if you are using *PMBOK® Guide* terminology. Projects are "undertaken to create a lasting outcome,"[9] with the project team generally remaining the same until the project ends. In agile, the delivery team is kept together from iteration to iteration, with each delivered increment an enhancement and/or evolution of the previous increment. The *PMBOK® Guide* refers to this as "progressive elaboration,"[10] and includes this as being a characteristic of some projects. It defines agile projects perfectly.

The *PMBOK® Guide* notes that each phase (iteration) should have a formal initiation outlining what deliverables are expected in that phase and a formal review at the end to conclude the phase with permissions obtained to continue or a decision made to stop the project. Agile iterations work on this premise as well. The initiation is done by the customer, whether informally with a verbal committal that work should begin or approval that work should continue or formally through the use of contracts (or internal budget cycles). Agile iterations begin with a planning meeting to define what will be completed in the iteration and end with a review to learn from the events and obtain customer acceptance of the features delivered. During the review, the project can be cancelled, approved to continue, or a release can be requested and implemented immediately or implemented in the next iteration.

Figure 2-3 shows how the project lifecycle, as depicted in the *PMBOK® Guide,* can be mapped to the agile project lifecycle. In fact, the agile project lifecycle is simply a fractal, as illustrated by the expanded phases in the figure. An agile project can be made up of multiple releases or periods of calendar time (quarters are commonly used), which in turn are made up of iterations in which teams create the increment of working code. Each has an initial phase (where planning is a key process), intermediate phases, and a final phase (where reviews and retrospectives are key processes).

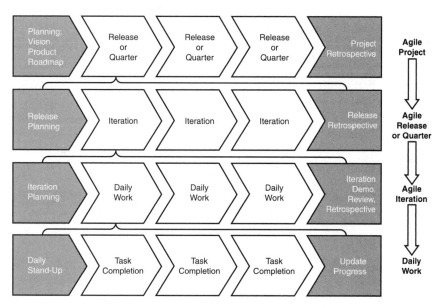

Figure 2-3
Phases and sub-phases in an agile project lifecycle (agile fractal)

One area where agile and the *PMBOK® Guide* disagree is in the involvement of the stakeholders. In agile, there is an expectation of the active involvement of a customer or customer representative throughout the duration of the project. This individual sets the direction for the product at the outset of the project and refines that vision at the beginning of each iteration, with the same high level of influence over the characteristics of the product at each iteration until the product is released. The *PMBOK® Guide* takes the view that stakeholder influence occurs up front and then declines throughout the rest of the project.[11] In agile, however, the stakeholders' influence remains strong and does not decrease until the product is released and the project is over. Agile welcomes change and provides a framework that manages that change through the use of iterative and incremental development with regular customer feedback, reviews, and retrospective analysis.

Project Management Processes

W. Edwards Deming's modified model of Walter A. Shewhart's Plan-Do-Study-Act is also referred to as the Plan-Do-Check-Act cycle. The *PMBOK® Guide* acknowledges this iterative method of continuous improvement, and maps its project management process groups to the PDCA cycle (see Figure 2-4). These project management process groups defined by the *PMBOK® Guide* are Initiating, Planning, Executing, Monitoring and Controlling, and Closing. The graphic on the right in Figure 2-4 is from the *PMBOK® Guide*.[12]

Figure 2-4
Plan-Do-Check-Act
and the *PMBOK® Guide* process groups

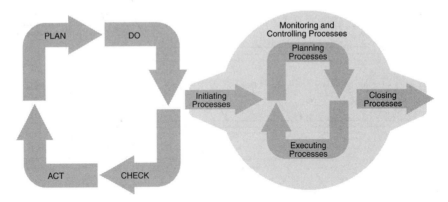

Project Management Institute, *A Guide to the Project Management Body of Knowledge (PMBOK® Guide), Third Edition,* Project Management Institute, Inc., 2004. Copyright and all rights reserved. Material from this publication has been reproduced with the permission of PMI.

The process groups are not phases, but rather they are an integrated set of processes applied iteratively throughout the project and revised as needed. As with the project lifecycle, we can map the process groups to the agile fractal—at the overall project level, at the release level, at the iteration level, and even at the daily level of activities done by an agile team (see Table 2-1). This is what we will discuss in more detail in Part II—how to map the traditional practices that support these processes to those typically done in agile projects. And we'll follow the same format that the *PMBOK® Guide* uses, and provide this information organized by the nine key knowledge areas: Integration, Scope, Time, Cost, Quality, Human Resources, Communications, Risk, and Procurement.

Table 2-1
Process Groups and the Agile Fractal

Agile Fractal	Project Management Process Groups				
	Initiation	**Planning**	**Executing**	**Monitoring & Controlling**	**Closing**
Project	Business case or feasibility study or contract	Project kickoff and visioning meeting Release roadmap planning	Iterative and incremental delivery of working software	Regular reviews of deliverables, progress, and process	Project retrospective
Release	Roadmap and release definition	Release planning meeting	Iterative and incremental delivery of working software	Regular reviews of deliverables, progress, and process	Release retrospective
Iteration	Iteration planning meeting	Iteration planning meeting	Work features through to completion	Task boards, burndown charts, daily stand-ups, acceptance of completed features	Iteration demo, review, and retrospective
Daily work	Morning coffee or tea	Daily stand-up meeting	Work tasks through to completion	Attention to obstacles identified by the team	Record progress on task board and burndown chart

Summary

Here are the takeaways from this chapter:

- The *PMBOK® Guide* is a standard for generally recognized good practices in project management. Misconceptions still exist regarding the type of methodologies that can be used to implement the practices outlined in the *PMBOK® Guide*. It is perfectly fine to use agile—you can still be in keeping with the recommendations in the *PMBOK® Guide.*
- The *PMBOK® Guide* outlines project lifecycle phases that correspond to agile releases and/or iterations. An agile project can be made up of multiple releases or quarters, which in turn are made up of iterations. An iteration's work, in turn, is represented by a set of daily tasks.
- The initial phase in an agile project includes planning processes and usually a delivery of an increment of code; the final phase includes hardening and production readiness processes as well as a final project retrospective. All intermediate phases focus on the delivery of increments of working code.
- Agile projects use Deming's Plan-Do-Check-Act cycle as part of the integrated processes in each agile fractal.

Endnotes

1. Project Management Institute. "The Institute," from a datasheet included in their media kit. http://www.pmi.org/Pages/default.aspx (accessed September 2006).

2. Project Management Institute. *A Guide to the Project Management Body of Knowledge (PMBOK® Guide), Third Edition.* (Newtown Square, PA: Project Management Institute, Inc., 2004), 20.

3. Ibid., 37.

4. "PM Network," "PMI Seminars World," "PMI Global Congress," and "PMP" are registered marks of Project Management Institute, Inc.

5. Peter Fretty. "Reconciling Differences." *PM Network,* April 2005, 40.

6. *PMBOK® Guide,* 368.

7. Ibid., 23.

8. Ibid., 20.

9. Ibid., 5.

10. Ibid., 6, 8.

11. Ibid., 21.

12. Ibid., 40.

Chapter 3

The Agile Project Lifecycle in Detail

It is not the ship so much as the skillful sailing that assures the prosperous voyage.

—George William Curtis

The emphasis is on steering the project—which is quite straightforward—rather than an exact prediction of what will be needed and how long it will take—which is quite difficult.

—Ron Jeffries

In this chapter, we expand the general agile project lifecycle that was introduced to you in the previous chapter. As we explained, the agile project lifecycle is composed of a series of phases, called "releases," and the iterations that fit within releases. This chapter will help you understand what happens at the project, release, iteration, and daily levels within the agile project lifecycle. Although any lifecycle is impossible to ideally define, this chapter draws on principles from some of the more popular agile methods to give you some ideas about an agile project lifecycle. Focusing on iterative and incremental development, embracing changing requirements, and maintaining a strong relationship with the customer are among the ideas we want to impart as we explain the approach, and this will also form the foundation of the rest of the book as we map the *PMBOK*® *Guide* processes to agile processes in Part II, "The Bridge: Relating *PMBOK*® *Guide* Practices to Agile Practices."

What Does an Agile Project Lifecycle Look Like?

Besides a set of values that have supported the rapid and robust translation of ideas into innovations, agile can also be expressed as a general approach to delivering software incrementally and iteratively. So, the term "agile" not only describes what teams are trying to be but also how they try to get there. Agile is often referred to as a value-driven approach, as opposed to the more traditional plan-driven approach, often called the "waterfall." In agile, the value of the features to the customer drives the order of the work, and the values outlined in the manifesto drive the way the work itself is done.

Each agile methodology has its particular focus—Scrum, for example, is a project management framework. XP, on the other hand, turns "the dials" on good technical development practices "up to ten."[1] As was demonstrated in the previous chapter, we can extract from these various methods a general agile approach. We refer to this agile project lifecycle, shown in Figure 3-1, throughout the remainder of the book.

Figure 3-1
The agile project life-cycle (agile fractal)

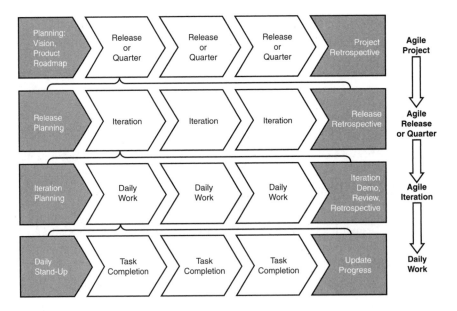

Let's take a deeper look at what happens within each layer of the agile fractal.

Agile Project

An agile project is a project that is planned and executed based on the tenets of the Agile Manifesto. It is a generally accepted best practice that long-term agile projects are executed using sequential releases, or collections of iterations, in order to break up the work of the overall project into manageable chunks. The *PMBOK® Guide* calls releases "phases."

The agile project is kicked off by at least three processes: visioning, product roadmap planning, and product backlog definition. These processes loosely correlate to the *PMBOK® Guide* processes of Develop Project Charter and Develop Preliminary Project Scope Statement; however, the product roadmap depicts the evolution of the product over time, defining what each release "chunk" will look like as well as a providing a timeframe for each delivery. More details about product roadmap planning are provided in Chapter 5, "Scope Management."

Other types of processes you may see in an initial agile project phase are environment setup, architectural documentation, release planning, team coding standards development, and actual delivery of a working product increment. Additionally, some organizations conduct other initiation processes, such as feasibility studies, research and development, and business case identification, during this initial phase of the project, whereas other organizations consider these activities to be business-facing and outside the project's boundaries. You will have to analyze your organization and projects and make this determination for yourself.

The interim phases in the agile project are the project releases. An agile project release is like a milestone, except that in an agile project, the release milestone deliverable is a working set of features. The release may be internal or external. A release is made up of several iterations, as we will discuss in the next section.

The final process in the agile project is the project retrospective. Similar to project postmortems, the project retrospective involves the entire project management team, stakeholders, and sometimes customers, in an effort to reflect on the project in its entirety and make overall management improvements for the next project. This is a project closing process. Other typical project closing processes you are probably already familiar with are activities such as contract closure and administration of the project schedule; these types of processes will still occur as necessary in the final phase of the agile project.

Figure 3-2 represents the agile project with release phases and planning and retrospective process bookends.

Agile Release

An agile release is a phase made up of several iterations, which are similar to what the *PMBOK® Guide* calls subphases. A common timeframe for a release is on a quarterly basis, and this would entail several iterations' worth of work. A release may be internal or external, depending on the needs of the organization at the time.

The process that kicks off an agile release is called "release planning," which is a one- or two-day event involving the entire team. Release planning is very useful in painting the big picture; the output of release planning—the release plan—is a set of goals, assumptions, and decisions that guide the team in delivering value to the customer. The release plan loosely correlates to the project schedule, except that a release plan is generally only created for the release at hand, and not for the overall agile project, especially in the case of long-term projects. When a project is shorter in duration, the agile project plan is equivalent to the release plan.

Interim phases in a release are the iterations themselves, with a release retrospective as the final closing process for the release. Figure 3-3 represents the phases of an agile release; planning and retrospection serve as bookends for the release iterations.

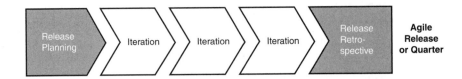

The inputs to release planning are a prioritized, estimated product backlog and a velocity measurement (or estimate) as determined by the team. A product backlog is a list of items to be implemented in the product, whereas velocity is the measured rate at which teams turn product backlog items into running tested features (if no velocity exists, the team will estimate its velocity based on its capacity for work). A product vision and roadmap are helpful information to have on hand. The team and the customer[2] attend this meeting and come up with a high-level plan for a collection of iterations. The inputs, attendees, and outputs are listed for you in Figure 3-4.

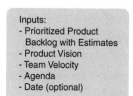

Inputs:
- Prioritized Product Backlog with Estimates
- Product Vision
- Team Velocity
- Agenda
- Date (optional)

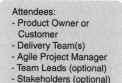

Attendees:
- Product Owner or Customer
- Delivery Team(s)
- Agile Project Manager
- Team Leads (optional)
- Stakeholders (optional)

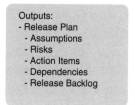

Outputs:
- Release Plan
  - Assumptions
  - Risks
  - Action Items
  - Dependencies
  - Release Backlog

Figure 3-4
Inputs, attendees, and outputs of a release planning session

In Figure 3-5, we have illustrated how a release plan guides delivery over the course of, in this case, three iterations. We have also designated the planning and review processes, along with the outputs of each iteration.

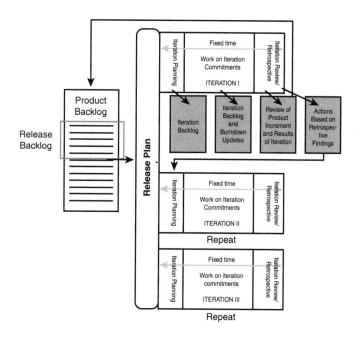

Figure 3-5
A visual representation of the iteration phases and how they relate to the product backlog and release planning processes.

Agile Iteration

An agile iteration is one timebox of work. A timebox is a length of time with a fixed start date and a fixed end date in which agile teams complete their work. Iterations are generally one week to six weeks in duration and are the level at which a team self-manages its day-to-day tasks.

Once an iteration has been given the green light by the customer, the team will meet to plan the iteration. In this meeting, the team works with the customer to determine what features can be delivered in the iteration; additionally, the team breaks down the features into tasks with hourly estimates and then signs up for the tasks.[3] This is the only time in an agile project in which tasks (or activities) appear. The deliverables and expectations of the iteration are clearly defined and committed to by the team; the output of the iteration planning process is the iteration backlog that captures all the team members' tasks and estimates.

Iteration Planning

As you can see in Figure 3-6, the inputs and attendees of iteration planning are almost identical to those of release planning. Iteration planning and release planning follow a similar agenda, but the outputs of each are different. Whereas a release plan is a high-level strategic plan for a collection of iterations, an iteration plan is a detailed task list that serves as a tactical guide to help accomplish an iteration's goal. Both release and iteration plans are created by the team as a response to negotiating and collaborating with the customer in the respective planning meetings.

Figure 3-6
Inputs, attendees, and outputs of iteration planning

Inputs:	Attendees:	Outputs:
- Prioritized Product Backlog with Estimates	- Product Owner or Customer	- Iteration Plan
- Product Vision	- Delivery Team(s)	- Iteration Backlog
- Team Velocity	- Agile Project Manager	- Assumptions
- Iteration Start/End Dates	- Team Leads	- Risks
- Optional: Release Plan	- Stakeholders (optional)	- Actions
		- Communications
		- Dependencies

The team is responsible for managing its work within the confines of the iteration. The iteration plan that the team creates in iteration planning is critical to good iteration execution; however, as with any plan, the team updates the iteration plan to reflect reality.

Several processes must be conducted when an iteration is formally closed in our general agile approach: the iteration review, when the product is reviewed for feedback purposes; updates to the product backlog based on the results of the iteration; and, finally, an iteration retrospective, at which point the team inspects and adapts its process. Your organization may utilize additional processes as necessary.

Iteration Review

The iteration review provides a designated time and space for collaborative decision-making about the product, as well as an opportunity to review the metrics and overall progress of the iteration. As Ken Schwaber, the co-creator of Scrum, states, "Collaboration, further exposure of salient information, and brainstorming should occur so that decisions are made with the best information possible."[4]

Think of the iteration review as a magnifying glass into the current state of the product. The team works for an iteration and at this review pulls out the magnifying glass to bring others clarity as to what they've built. The review meeting is typically low-ceremony with minimal preparation. The product should be tested and meet the criteria set forth to meet the agile value of "working software."

As shown in Figure 3-7, the team provides a walkthrough of the work it completed for the iteration, as well as a review of the work it did not complete during the iteration. Additionally, many teams will review their iteration metrics, such as test coverage, burndown charts, and velocity. This very clearly paints the picture of project status for all the stakeholders and attendees of the review meeting.

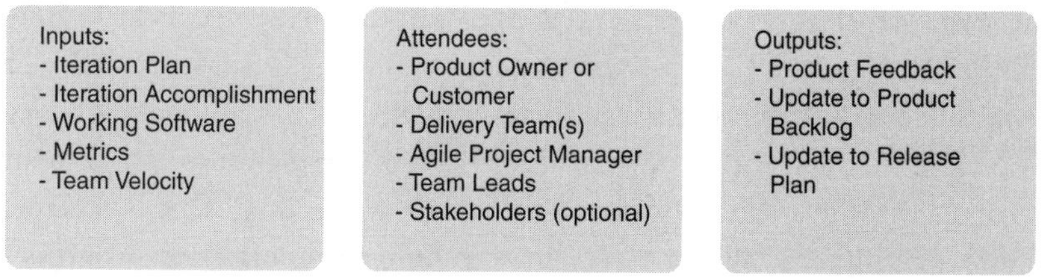

Inputs:
- Iteration Plan
- Iteration Accomplishment
- Working Software
- Metrics
- Team Velocity

Attendees:
- Product Owner or Customer
- Delivery Team(s)
- Agile Project Manager
- Team Leads
- Stakeholders (optional)

Outputs:
- Product Feedback
- Update to Product Backlog
- Update to Release Plan

Figure 3-7
Iteration review inputs, attendees, and resulting outputs

Iteration Retrospective

The iteration retrospective follows the review and is the final closing process for an iteration. In this meeting, the team identifies what worked well in the previous iteration, what did not work well, which items it can control, and what actions it would like to take to improve the process. Unlike a project postmortem, or lessons learned, which is held once at the end of the entire project, iteration retrospectives are conducted at the end of every iteration, with the idea that stopping for a process check during the project lifecycle will ultimately lead to overall improved project execution.

The resulting decisions and adaptive actions flow into the next iteration. The actions that the team can directly control go on its next iteration backlog; anything else goes onto the agile project manager's "impediment backlog." Figure 3-8 represents this flow.

Figure 3-8
Iteration retrospective
results flow

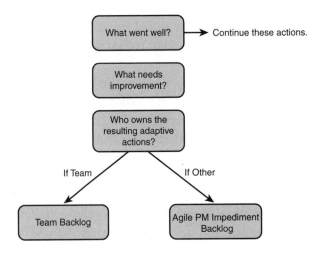

Daily Work

The lowest level of the agile fractal is daily work, represented as tasks in the iteration plan that are completed by team members (see Figure 3-9). The project manager does not manage this work; therefore, team members need to check in with each other daily to stay in synch. A common way agile teams do this is through the use of the daily stand-up meeting. This is a fifteen-minute meeting that allows the team members to report their progress to each other and adapt their iteration plan as needed.

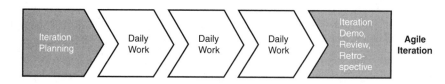

Figure 3-9
The daily work level
of the agile fractal

If you do your agile homework, the daily work level is the point at which you will read and hear about many different and interesting approaches. For example, XP teams have figured out that to get from "idea" to "running tested feature" within two weeks usually means that automated tests need to be implemented to run against continuous builds. Because the team is moving so fast, it needs mechanisms in place to quickly know the status of the system. Scrum, however, doesn't suggest any methods to utilize to get to "potentially shippable product increment," and DSDM is quite prescriptive about what to do within the iteration. If you'd like more information about these different approaches, refer to Appendix A, "Agile Methodologies."

We are not going to prescribe a set of practices in this section, but we highly recommend that you read more about XP development practices as a means to delivering high-quality, complete product increments each iteration. The final word about the work in an iteration is that the team is empowered to make whatever decisions necessary to complete its work, in keeping with the tenet of "working software," and the team manages and directs its own work, adjusting as necessary.

Rinse, Repeat

It is important to remember that the project lifecycle starts with a planning process and ends with closing processes such as the iteration review and retrospective. Some teams we've coached had never previously learned about visioning, roadmap, or release planning in an agile context. Our experience with this process is that it is light enough so as to remain flexible, and valuable so as to provide some predictive ability when it comes to contracts and procurement or resource planning at a high level. It is important to remember that each step in this lifecycle involves the team, and daily work is owned and managed by the team.

You will notice that our set of processes is quite a bit lighter than that of the *PMBOK® Guide*. We feel as though the identified processes in this chapter are sufficient to run an agile project. However, we provide even more detail as we dive deeper into the mapping of traditional and agile approaches in Part II of this book.

How Is Agile Different from a Plan-Driven Approach?

As you can see, we still plan and create plans in agile, we still create documentation in agile, and we still test in agile. In fact, many teams who begin their adoption of agile do so by conducting "mini-waterfalls" each iteration, with a code freeze about two-thirds of the way through in order to leave time for testing and integration. Although this isn't ideal, it is a way to start learning about the urgency of timeboxing and how to break down large chunks of functionality into smaller pieces.

The differences between agile approaches and traditional approaches are in two areas: the timing and depth of the practices, and the mindset of those involved. The focus on iterative and incremental development means that agile teams plan enough to get started and focus on simplicity, or maximizing the amount of work not done. The mindset differences are made clear by how we refer to these methods: value-driven (agile) versus plan-driven (traditional). Agile approaches are value-driven in two ways. One is in the focus on features that provide the highest value to the customer and the importance of working on those features first. The other is in the values that drive how teams choose to work together. These are the values outlined in the manifesto's principles, and values that are often distinctly cited in each of the agile methods. Values such as courage, respect, and communication are all drivers of behavior, and are key to the proper implementation of any agile method. This is not to say that plan-driven approaches have no values; it is to say that in agile, we make them explicit and discuss them often.

Agile practices and processes are iterative and incremental in keeping with agile frameworks. In our next part of this book, we dive into the agile processes as they relate to the processes outlined by the *PMBOK® Guide*.

Summary

The takeaways from this chapter include the following:

- Agile projects are made up of agile releases. Agile releases are synonymous with the *PMBOK® Guide*'s project phases.
- An agile release consists of multiple iterations and provides agile teams with a way to plan over an extended period of time.
- A release can be internal, external, or simply a forecast for the project. It is a collection of iterations.
- Release planning is optional but highly encouraged; iteration planning is required.
- Iterations loosely correlate to *PMBOK® Guide* subphases. Iterations are initiated by the customer, planned, executed, and closed, just like phases of a project.
- Iteration planning is the meeting in which the team selects a subset of the product backlog and plans all of the tasks necessary to complete the selected product backlog items.
- The iteration review meeting is held so that the team can receive feedback from customers and stakeholders about the emerging product. Additionally, agile teams provide information regarding iteration metrics and measurements, making progress visible and transparent to all.
- Daily work is planned and completed by the team members and is not managed by the agile project manager.
- A product backlog is a list of items to be implemented in the product. The product backlog is estimated by the team and is ranked in order of priority by the customer.
- Retrospectives at the end of each iteration, release, and project are a critical and required part of the agile project lifecycle. Retrospectives provide the team members an opportunity to reflect on previous events and refine the ways in which they work together.

Endnotes

1. Kent Beck. *Extreme Programming Explained.* (Boston: Addison-Wesley, 2000), xvi.

2. We've used the word "customer" to represent the person who can make decisions about what is desired in the product. Depending on your organization, the voice of the customer may be represented by an internal person. We've seen titles such as business analyst, product manager, end user, product owner, marketing manager, and even salesperson as stand-ins for the customer.

3. We've found that new agile teams will go through the process of assigning owners to tasks. As teams mature and as team members begin to feel comfortable switching contexts, they stop assigning owners during iteration planning. Although they continue to task out the work in iteration planning, they leave the tasks without owners, allowing anyone who's available to pick the next task on the list during the execution of the iteration.

4. Ken Schwaber. "No Applause, Please." Scrum Alliance, http://www.scrumalliance.org/articles/31.

Part II

The Bridge

Relating *PMBOK*® *Guide* Practices to Agile Practices

IN THIS PART

Chapter 4

Integration Management

Integration, in the context of managing a project, is making choices about where to concentrate resources and effort on any given day, anticipating potential issues, dealing with these issues before they become critical, and coordinating work for the overall project good.

—*PMBOK® Guide*

I love it when a plan comes together!

—*Colonel John "Hannibal" Smith on the popular 1980s television show* The A-Team

We have a "strategic" plan. It's called doing things.

—*Herb Kelleher, chairman and founder of Southwest Airlines, the only U.S. carrier to be profitable every year since 1972*

Integration management is about pulling all of the project management processes together into one unified whole—a juggling act of trade-offs and coordination as part of balancing the project execution and the expectations of the stakeholders. Agile project managers are like the directors of a play, making sure the actors understand the playwright's vision, giving them goals to accomplish and motivation to guide them, and then standing in the wings while the performers do their jobs and improvise when they need to. From the beginning of the project where the vision is communicated, to the end of the project where the group reflects on their accomplishments and failures, the project manager is there to guide everyone through the process.

Rob Austin and Lee Devin describe the process of preparing a theatrical production appears in their book *Artful Making*.[1]

> Through repeated iteration, actors transform conflicting actions into a coherent and unified form. Such a process—uncoordinated, simultaneous, individual acts of creation punctuated by arduous episodes of bringing everything together—can seem disorganized. It can appear "poorly managed" when it is, in fact, expertly managed. Although rigorously structured by its iterative shape, rehearsal doesn't manifest an orderly appearance the way planning-based methods can.

Iteration Planning Meetings

Iteration planning meetings can look a bit like cocktail parties without the cocktails. It's a bit disconcerting to those who haven't seen meetings run in this fashion before, as I discovered when helping a client with his first planning meeting. I was delighted with how well it was going and said so to the project manager, who took a long look at the chaos in the room and asked, "Are you sure?" I explained that there is both good and bad chaos, and that what he was witnessing was the good kind that rejuvenates the team and prepares them to meet the challenges ahead. Agile provides a framework to contain, focus, and direct this chaos, and lively discussions are part and parcel of the whole.

This is a perfect description of how it looks in agile teams as well! The agile type of chaos is carefully controlled by the practices and disciplines of the framework, yet still enables energy, enthusiasm, and excitement in meeting and conquering challenges.

In the following sections, we'll look at how the *PMBOK® Guide* description of integration management relates to the practices typically performed in an agile project.

Develop the Project Charter and Preliminary Scope Statement

The project charter is a formal document used to justify, explain, define, and ultimately authorize a project. Although the *PMBOK® Guide* states that the project charter is prepared by a sponsor or other party external to the organization, it has been our experience that a project manager within the organization often drives this effort in conjunction with the business sponsor. In this section, we'll look at developing the charter from the latter viewpoint.

There are two ways to develop a project charter in an agile environment. One is to continue along the traditional route of preparing the paperwork needed in order to obtain approval (sometimes called the "project initiation process"), as this then translates into funding and charge codes and the formation of the team. The other way presumes that either provisional funding has been awarded or that tacit approval has already occurred without the need for internal paperwork. For example, those accepting contracts from outside sources, working on special projects, or working in smaller organizations may find themselves in this category. For these teams, conducting a four-to-eight-hour vision meeting will result in the deliverables associated with the preparation of a project charter.

Barely Sufficient Is Just Good Enough

I counseled one team to use Alistair Cockburn's "barely sufficient" philosophy in order to prevent doing more than was absolutely necessary when having to prepare its project charter.[2] The team had been newly christened as an agile pilot team when it found that it still had to go through the traditional project approval process. Using this "barely sufficient" guideline, the team asked, "Is this something that we really must do, and if it is, then what is the simplest thing we can do to satisfy this requirement?" The team, working with the financial controllers, determined that project approval was an organizational requirement for the team. Without the approval, the project team would be disbanded, and the monies and staff would go to other already approved projects. But the controllers conceded that the documentation required for the approval process could be streamlined and simplified, saving the team from doing the big upfront design that goes against agile philosophy. Based on the discussions the team had with the financial controllers, it went ahead and did the barely sufficient analysis and design work required to produce a technical specification document, which along with its business case, was submitted for approval. The design spec was a high-level overview of the system, and included high-level functional specifications—but avoided the detailed requirements writing that would have taken the team weeks to complete. The team's documents were considered just good enough for the review process, and the project was approved.[3]

Vision Meeting

The goal of the vision meeting is to define the boundaries and intent of the project by sharing the vision and needs of the business. See Figure 4-1 for an example of a typical vision meeting agenda for an agile project. Note that the agenda items also help the team to define a preliminary scope statement as part of the project data sheet.

Vision Meeting Agenda

- Executive welcome! (Project champion or sponsor)
- Introductions, ground rules, review of agenda (Project manager)
- What is our goal in this meeting? What is our scope of authority? And What's in It for Me (WIIFM)? (Project manager and customer/product owner)
- What is this project expected to accomplish? Do we have an architectural plan to get us there? Share the vision! (Customer/product owner and architect)
- Who's going to help us? (Project manager)
- What questions/suggestions/concerns do we have? (Team)
- Can we create the elevator statement? (Team)
- Can we design the box? (Team)
- Given our work so far, do we have enough information to fill out a project datasheet? (Team)
- Do we know what our high-level project schedule looks like? (Customer/product owner and team)
- What issues/risks might impact the vision/project? (Team)
- What does our final elevator statement, box, and datasheet look like now? (Team)
- What are our team working agreements? (Team)
- Close: communications plan, empty parking lot, action items, next steps

Figure 4-1
Vision meeting agenda

Elevator Statement

Included in this agenda example are two vision exercises recommended by Jim Highsmith in his book *Agile Project Management*. The first is the elevator statement, which is a brief statement designed to impart the intent of the project within two minutes.[4] The idea sprang from the notion that should you ever find yourself on the elevator with the CEO, you'd have about two minutes on the ride to the top floor to explain what it was you were working on and why it was important—thus ensuring your continued employment and maybe even recognition come bonus time. This is the format to follow when preparing the statement:[5]

- For (target customer)
- Who (statement of need or opportunity)
- The (product name) is a (product category)
- That (key benefit, compelling reason to buy)
- Unlike (primary competitive alternative)
- Our product (statement of primary differentiation)

The final result should flow smoothly as if there were no bullet points separating the ideas. Here's an example you might see from one of the many online retailers: For men and women who care about their skin, and who prefer the convenience of shopping online, SuperSoft Skin is a product line of skin protection and repair products that make your skin feel like a newborn baby's. Unlike brands available in brick-and-mortar shops, our product is exclusive in its one-of-a-kind patented herbal mixture that is guaranteed to show results within 24 hours.

Once the architect and customer have explained the intent and use of the product, the team should split into groups of three or four and each create an elevator statement. This exercise should only take 30–60 minutes: 15 minutes for the teams to create the statements on flipcharts, and 15–45 minutes

Are Your Team Members All on the Same Elevator?

While conducting this exercise during a training class with a large traditional team, I had them split into teams along skill lines: developers, testers, technical writers, business sponsors and analysts, and managers. I tasked them with preparing the elevator statement for their current project, which they'd been working on for several weeks. The results were the classic example of the blind men and the elephant, as each group only could see a small piece of the overall vision. Even the managers conceded that their elevator statement failed to accurately depict the vision, after seeing what the others had produced. This exercise made the team members realize that they needed to revisit the objectives of their project.

to review each and combine the best pieces into one. If the elevator statements created by the groups are all vastly different, then more discussion is required to clarify the vision. The key benefit of this exercise is getting all the team members on the same page with a clear understanding of precisely what it is they are trying to accomplish and why.

Design the Box

The other exercise has the team, again in smaller groups, designing the box that would carry the product.[6] The front of the box will have the product name and logo, and a key statement about what it is that the product does. The back of the box will have some of the key features that, during the exercise debrief, can be transferred to sticky notes as the high-level features marking the beginning of the product backlog. You should do this exercise even if the real product won't be shipped in a box—it's this tangible representation of the vision that's important. Figure 4-2 shows an example with both the key statement and high-level features on the front of the box.

Figure 4-2
Design-the-box
example

Although these and other exercises will address the basic information needed to charter a project, there is still a need to make sure the project meets the overall corporate strategic objectives. The project as defined in the visioning meeting may meet a business need and be financially justifiable, and yet not be in keeping with the current company direction and goals. This is an issue that should be addressed either prior to the visioning meeting or as part of the meeting.

Summary Comparison

Table 4-1 presents a summary comparison of the traditional and agile approaches to developing the project charter and scope statement. In an agile project, this process would be referred to as "defining the vision."

Table 4-1
Develop Project Charter and Preliminary Scope Statement

Traditional	Agile
Obtain input and feedback from appropriate parties on project objectives and justifications.	Obtain input and feedback from the team and other appropriate parties on project objectives and justifications as part of a vision meeting.
Prepare a business case and associated documentation required by the company and/or project approval board in order to obtain project approval.	If needed, prepare a business case and associated documentation required by the company and/or project approval board in order to obtain project approval.
Use the company-sanctioned software development methodology and prepare accordingly.	Use an agile software development methodology and prepare accordingly.

Develop Project Management Plan

A key deliverable in the *PMBOK® Guide*'s integration management process is the project management plan document, which is prepared and owned by the project manager. This document contains details concerning how the project will be executed, monitored, and controlled. The agile framework you select will have guidelines that describe much of this information. Simply follow the approach as outlined by the author of the methodology, and inspect and adapt at regular intervals as you go.

The project management plan described in the *PMBOK® Guide* is not to be confused with the project schedule. A schedule baseline can be included as a part of the overall project management plan, however. Because this tends to be the item of most interest to stakeholders, it is often the portion of the plan that gets the most attention. Therefore, further discussion of how this might look in agile is warranted.

In agile software development, with its emphasis on just-in-time design and participatory decision-making, the project management planning activities translate into several different envisioning and planning exercises done on an iterative basis, referred to as "rolling wave planning"[7] or "multilevel planning." Rather than defining all the elements of a project plan at the beginning of the project (scope, work breakdown structure, schedule, assumptions, risks, and so on), the agile project manager will instead focus on planning for the visible horizon while staying within the boundaries agreed to in the vision meeting. And rather than requiring formal documentation, the agile team can use informal documentation consisting of whiteboards, flipcharts, sticky notes, photos, and so on. The decision on the level of documentation required depends on organizational requirements, team needs, and the value the documentation adds to the customer.

Let's recall our agile fractal diagram from Chapter 2. Release plans indicating the expected release date and the features to be worked in the iterations, and iteration plans indicating the level of effort in implementing a set of features within the defined timebox, are defined in planning meetings that involve the entire team. These plans also include items such as assumptions, risks, dependencies, a definition of what "done" means, resource availability, and so on. The team members must create, own, and commit to both the release plan and the iteration plan; they do not simply provide input. In other words, instead of the project manager creating the plan with the team's assistance, the team creates the plan while the agile project manager facilitates the process.

Release plans, iteration plans, and other planning outputs are then shared with all stakeholders in the most highly visible fashion possible. For co-located teams, this may mean something as simple as posting the plan on the wall; for geographically dispersed teams, technical solutions for communication are required, and SharePoint, wikis, or other third-party tools are well-equipped to provide this. Both wall and tool displays of project plans and progress are referred to in agile as "highly visible information radiators." Project managers go from writing a large detailed document defining the plan for the entire project to facilitating the team in its ongoing iterative planning efforts and sharing that information in the most available and visible way possible.

Team Working Agreements

One of the planning agenda items that an agile project manager must facilitate is the creation of team working agreements. Try to keep these between five and ten items—too few and you haven't covered enough, too many and the team won't be able to remember them all. Agreements can be, "If the build is broken then the whole team stops and works to fix it," and "We're not done until we meet our definition of 'done.'" One team I worked with decided that its number-one team working agreement would be, "We will be on time for meetings." The team's corporate culture had made showing up 10–15 minutes late a normal occurrence.

As with all things agile, remember that you can revisit the working agreements at the end of each iteration as part of the team retrospective discussion and make changes as needed.

Table 4-2 provides a summary comparison of traditional and agile approaches to developing the project management plan. In an agile project, developing the project management plan would be referred to as "developing the project plan and following the agile framework."

Table 4-2
Develop Project Management Plan

Traditional	Agile
Formally document the project management processes to be used by the team (quality management, communications, management, risk management, etc.), their level of implementation, and how they will be implemented.	Start with the agile framework as defined for the agile methodology the team has chosen and follow those guidelines, stopping at the end of each iteration to inspect and adapt.
Formally document the methods to be used for communication with stakeholders.	Follow the agile principle of having all project information highly visible and available to all interested parties at all times, and make arrangements accordingly to bring this about.

(continued)

Table 4-2
Develop Project Management Plan *(continued)*

Traditional	Agile
Define the timing for key management reviews.	Managers and other key stakeholders are welcome to review progress at any time by viewing the highly visible information radiators, with regular reviews occurring at the end of each iteration.
Determine and formally document how changes will be monitored and controlled.	Product changes are identified and addressed during demo and planning meetings and documented in the product backlog; process changes are identified and addressed during review and retrospective meetings and informally documented.
Determine and formally document how configuration management will be performed.	Determine how configuration management will be performed as part of deciding on team working agreements and document informally.

Direct and Manage Project Execution and Monitor and Control Project Work

Executing, monitoring, and controlling disciplines move from more directive, command-and-control tactics in the traditional environment to agile's facilitative, collaborative servant leadership. If you give the team members the tools they need, help them to understand the business problems they'll be solving, and give them the space and time to complete the job, they can self-organize and become a fully engaged and motivated team that produces high-quality products at a faster clip. Clearly, for many organizations, this change in tactics also leads to a shift in the culture and in the ways success is measured.

Project managers will find themselves learning how to guide their team in responding reliably to change instead of conforming to a plan, and learning how to do this in a completely new environment where the team makes decisions instead of being told what to do. It means more individual responsibility for team members and more facilitation skills required for the agile project manager. Most agile teams are uncomfortable with their new roles at first, and it is the project manager's responsibility to build team cohesion and foster good communication. Not everyone is willing to make this paradigm shift—project managers included. But for those who are willing, they'll find both the process and the new skills they've learned to be richly rewarding and well worth the effort involved. Read more about how your role as a project manager will change in Part III, "Crossing the Bridge to Agile."

Table 4-3 provides a summary comparison of traditional and agile approaches to directing and managing project execution and monitoring and controlling project work. In an agile project, this is referred to as "facilitating, serving, leading, and collaborating."

Table 4-3
Direct and Manage Project Execution and Monitor and Control Project Work

Traditional	Agile
Direct execution.	Provide leadership and foster a collaborative participatory decision-making environment.
Ensure conformance to plan.	Ensure the ability to respond to change by following the selected agile method.
Compare actual performance to what was planned.	Facilitate iteration review meetings.
Apply corrective action.	Facilitate retrospective meetings where the team defines what adaptive actions it will take.
Collect project data and report status.	Ensure the team has the space and materials needed to create highly visible information radiators; facilitate demo and review meetings; prepare an executive summary if appropriate.

Integrated Change Control

Integrated change control changes dramatically in agile methodologies. In keeping with the idea of minimum process to achieve maximum value, the change control process is streamlined and integrated into the daily routine of agile teams. Process changes are owned by the team, whereas product changes are owned by the customer.

Changes to the product scope are managed via the ranked backlog of features. This product backlog is managed by the customer (or whoever has the authority to make decisions about the product; often internally this is the "product owner" who is representing the customer). This individual is responsible for maintaining the list of items to be worked on, with the features that provide the most business value to the customer ranked highest. This backlog can contain items beyond functionality requests: technical support work and defects can also be placed in the backlog and ranked. During release and iteration planning, the highest-ranked items move from the backlog into the iterations, to be coded, tested, and finally accepted by the customer. At the end of each iteration, the working code that was developed is demonstrated, and feedback is gathered from stakeholders that may affect the ranking of and future decisions about the items in the backlog.

Process changes are also made at the end of the iterations, enabling the team to make course adjustments not only in the product, but also in the way they work. The team—customer, developer, tester, analyst, technical writer, project manager—can become the equivalent of a change control board, streamlining the process so that decisions are made quickly, collaboratively, and with little-to-no ceremony.

Notice how the agile project manager sits between the customer and the team. In traditional environments, the project manager is responsible for changes that occur in the plan. In an agile environment, the project manager facilitates the collaborative discussions of the customer and team to reach a decision regarding the proposed changes. Using the backlog as a change response tool, teams can educate the customer about the impact a request will have to the iteration and the overall release. The "something must drop if something is added" mentality is much easier to embrace when we speak in the terms of a flexible backlog versus a rigid change control list.[8]

Table 4-4 provides a summary comparison of integrated change control from the point of view of traditional and agile approaches. In agile projects, integrated change control is referred to as "continuous backlog management."

Table 4-4
Integrated Change Control

Traditional	Agile
Establish a change control board.	The team can be thought of as the change control board, with the customer being the final arbiter of product change decisions and the team being the final arbiter of process change decisions.
Determine and document change requests.	Change requests emerge from discussions around the product demo.
Determine and document resolution of change requests.	Product changes to be performed are documented as new items in the product backlog; process changes are documented as recommendations, team working agreements, and/or action items during the retrospective meeting.
Validate change request resolution.	The customer is responsible for approving the completed backlog items; the project manager is responsible for reminding the team of its process change agreements.
Determine and document how the change affects other project areas, such as scope, schedule, risks, etc.	Revisit plans at the end of each iteration and modify as needed.

Close Project

Project closure activities are quite similar in traditional or agile environments. Many agile teams will set aside an iteration at the end of the project to use for "hardening" (preparation for final rollout of the product). Note that this is *not* a bug-fixing iteration! For an internal release, this hardening iteration may consist of a variety of production-readiness activities, whereas for an external release, additional tasks such as capturing final screenshots for promotional materials and lining up production facilities might be items to consider.

Handoff Iteration

One agile team I was coaching discovered that having to deal with the hand-off to the production department meant allocating an extra iteration in order to prepare the formal documentation and other deliverables that production required. Passing through this required phase-gate of the production department meant that documentation, meetings, compatibility testing, and sign-offs had to be planned. The team decided to enter items in the backlog to represent each of the items on the production-ready checklist, and allocated an entire iteration to project closure or "production-readiness." Team members did not implement any new features during this iteration; instead, they attended hand-off and final approval meetings, and produced documentation for production, customer support, and the architecture review committee.

A critical activity in all agile projects is the retrospective, and holding a final retrospective at the end of the project is vital in learning what went well during the project, what didn't work well, and how to ensure a smoother project experience for everyone in the future. Invite all stakeholders to this meeting—the results can help the organization identify and implement broader changes affecting the agile rollout and enterprise operations.

Table 4-5 provides a summary comparison of project closeout activities from the traditional and agile perspectives.

Table 4-5
Close Project

Traditional	Agile
Administrative closure (production readiness, final acceptance, staff roll-off)	Administrative closure (production readiness, final acceptance, staff roll-off)
Contract closure (activities and deliverables as outlined in the contract)	Contract closure (activities and deliverables as outlined in the contract)
Final product delivery and hand-off	Final product delivery and hand-off
Lessons learned	Project retrospective

Summary

This chapter made the following points:

- There are two ways to develop a project charter in an agile environment: using the traditional method modified with Alistair Cockburn's "barely sufficient" guidelines, and as informal documentation created during a vision meeting.
- The formal project plan document is no more; instead, this activity is divided into several different visioning and planning exercises done on an iterative basis with the team and informally documented as appropriate.
- Command-and-control project management is replaced with servant leadership and facilitation in order to help the team realize its goals.
- The agile team can be thought of as the equivalent of a change control board and manages change through the use of a product backlog with the customer/product owner having the final say. Process change is managed through the use of team reviews and retrospectives.
- Close your agile project with a project retrospective meeting—these meetings are crucial to helping you identify and implement broader transition changes that affect the entire enterprise.

Table 4-6 summarizes the differences between the traditional and agile approaches to integration management.

Table 4-6
Agile Project Manager's Change List for Integration Management

I used to do this:	Now I do this:
Drive or participate in the preparation of a formal project charter document, obtaining input and feedback on the contents via individual and group meetings.	Invite the team and interested stakeholders to a visioning meeting where the project objectives are discussed and defined based on the needs presented by the customer.
Obtain project approval via submittal of formal documentation and/or a presentation.	Obtain project approval using Cockburn's "barely sufficient" means.

(continued)

Table 4-6

Agile Project Manager's Change List for Integration Management *(continued)*

I used to do this:	Now I do this:
Prepare a project plan.	Understand and communicate the agile process and framework the team is following; facilitate and informally document team working agreements; facilitate planning, demo, review, and retrospective meetings; informally document results and make them highly visible and accessible to all stakeholders.
Manage a separate change control process.	Integrate change control into the iterations using the selected agile method.
Close the project with a lessons learned meeting and document the results for historic purposes.	Close the project with a project retrospective meeting, and use the results in determining broader organizational change and agile transition strategies.

Endnotes

1. Rob Austin and Lee Devin. *Artful Making: What Managers Need to Know About How Artists Work.* (Upper Saddle River, NJ: Pearson Education, Inc., 2003), 37.

2. Alistair Cockburn, "Balancing Lightness with Sufficiency," http://alistair.cockburn.us/index.php/Balancing_lightness_with_sufficiency.

3. Michele Sliger. "Bridging the Gap." *Better Software,* July/August 2006, 28–29.

4. Geoffrey Moore. *Crossing the Chasm.* (New York: HarperBusiness, 1991), 154.

5. Jim Highsmith. *Agile Project Management: Creating Innovative Products.* (Boston: Pearson Education, Inc., 2004), 93–95.

6. Ibid.

7. *PMBOK® Guide,* 128.

8. Stacia Broderick. "A Change in Plan." *Agile Development,* Summer 2006, 28–31.

Chapter 5

Scope Management

Project Scope Management includes the processes required to ensure that the project includes all the work required, and only the work required, to complete the project successfully.

—PMBOK® Guide

It is not the strongest of the species that survive, nor the most intelligent, but the ones most responsive to change.

—*Charles Darwin,* The Origin of Species

Next week there can't be any crisis. My schedule is already full.

—*Henry Kissinger*

"Scope creep" has always been the bane of traditional project managers, as requirements continue to change in response to customer business needs, changes in the industry, changes in technology, and things that were learned during the development process. Scope planning, scope definition, scope verification, and scope control are all processes that are defined in the *PMBOK® Guide* to prevent scope creep, and these areas earn great attention from project managers. Those who use agile methods believe these deserve great attention as well, but their philosophy on managing scope is completely different. Plan-driven approaches work hard to prevent changes in scope, whereas agile approaches expect and embrace scope change. The agile strategy is to fix resources and schedule, and then work to implement the highest value features as defined by the customer. Thus, the scope remains flexible. This is in contrast to a typical waterfall approach, as shown in Figure 5-1, where features (scope) are first defined in detail, driving the cost and schedule estimates. Agile has simply flipped the triangle.

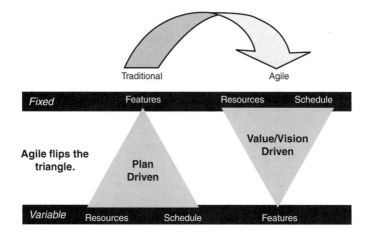

Scope Planning

The *PMBOK® Guide* defines the Project Scope Management Plan as the output of the scope planning process.[1] This document defines the processes that will be followed in defining scope, documenting scope, verifying and accepting scope and completed deliverables, and controlling and managing requests for changes to the scope. In agile, the iterative and incremental process itself is what manages scope. Unless documentation is required for auditing purposes, no additional document outlining procedures for scope management is needed. Scope is defined and redefined constantly in agile, as part of the planning meetings—in particular, release planning and iteration planning—and by the management of the product backlog. Remember, resources and time are typically fixed in agile approaches, and it's the scope that is allowed to change. However, when fixed-scope projects are required, it is the number of iterations that will change, in order to accommodate the need for a full feature set prior to release. Additionally, one of the success criteria in traditional projects is the extent to which we can "stick to the scope"; in agile, it is more important to be able to efficiently and effectively respond to change. The success criteria in agile thus changes to "Are we providing value to our customer?" The primary measure of progress is working code.

Table 5-1 provides a summary comparison of scope planning from the traditional and agile perspectives. In agile projects, scope planning is referred to as "managing the product backlog."

Table 5-1
Scope Planning

Traditional	Agile
Prepare a Project Scope Management Plan document.	Commit to following the framework as outlined in the chosen agile process.

Scope Definition

The *PMBOK® Guide* practices of scope definition, work breakdown structure (WBS) creation, and scope verification occur iteratively in agile. A traditional WBS for software projects is usually divided at its highest level into phases of analysis, design, coding, testing, and deployment activities. Each of these phases is then decomposed into tasks or groups of tasks, referred to as work packages in the *PMBOK® Guide*. Traditional project planning begins top-down and relies on the elaboration of detailed tasks with estimates and dependencies to drive the project schedule via use of critical path analysis. Even though the *PMBOK® Guide* goes into great detail about scope decomposition by way of WBS (work breakdown structure), it also warns that "excessive decomposition can lead to nonproductive management effort, inefficient use of resources, and decreased efficiency in performing the work."[2]

In agile, we approach these practices differently in that we define features at a high level in the product backlog and then place features into iterations during release planning. One can think of the iteration—or even the feature itself—as the agile equivalent of work packages. The features are estimated at a gross level in the product backlog—no detailed tasks or resources are defined at this point in time. Once the iteration begins, the features slated for that iteration—and only that iteration—are then elaborated into tasks that represent a development plan for the feature. Think of it as just-in-time elaboration, preventing a wasteful buildup of requirements inventory that may never be processed. The *PMBOK® Guide* supports this idea of "rolling wave planning":[3] As the work is decomposed to lower levels of detail, the ability to plan, manage, and control the work is enhanced because the short timeframe of the iteration reduces the amount of detail and the complexity of estimating. The agile approach assumes that because things change so often, you shouldn't spend the time doing "excessive decomposition" until you're ready to do the work.

Let's look at how scope is defined throughout an agile project by examining five levels of planning common to most agile projects: the product vision, the product roadmap, the release plan, the iteration plan, and the daily plan.[4]

Product Vision

At the outset of a project, it is typical to hold a kickoff meeting. Agile is no different; however, the way the agile vision meeting is conducted is unlike what a traditional project manager might be accustomed to. Although the vision is defined and presented by the customer or business representative, it is the team that clarifies the vision during the discussions and subsequent exercises. Therefore, the team is heavily involved, and group exercises are a big part of determining the final outcomes. See Chapter 4, "Integration Management," for more detail on vision meetings.

The vision meeting is designed to present the big picture, get all team members on the same page, and ensure a clear understanding of what it is that they've been brought together to do. The vision defines the mission of the project team and the boundaries within which they will work to achieve the desired results. The project's goal should be directly traceable to a corporate strategic objective.

Here the scope is defined at a very high level. It is not uncommon to leave the vision meeting with only a dozen or so features identified, such as "provide online order capabilities," "enable international ordering and delivery," "create data warehouse of customer orders to use for marketing purposes," and "integrate with our current brick-and-mortar inventory system." Clearly these are all very large pieces of functionality with little-to-no detail—and this is what is appropriate at this stage of the project. The farther away the delivery date, the broader the stroke given to feature details.

Product Roadmap

A product roadmap shows how the product will evolve over the next three to four releases or some period of calendar time, typically quarters. The

product roadmap is a high-level representation of what features or themes are to be
delivered in each release, the customer
targeted, the architecture needed to support the features, and the business value
the release is expected to meet. The customer or product manager, agile project
manager, architect, and executive management should meet on average two to
three times a year to collaborate on the
development and revision of the product
roadmap. Figure 5-2 shows a sample roadmap template made popular by
Luke Hohmann in his book *Beyond Software Architecture*.[5]

> **Note**
>
> In agile, the word "release" does not solely mean a product release to the end customer—it can also mean an internal release to fulfill integration milestones and continue to confirm that the product is "potentially shippable."

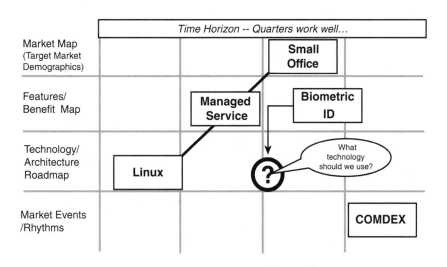

Figure 5-2
Product roadmap template, courtesy of Enthiosys and Luke Hohmann, from his book *Beyond Software Architecture*

Because the customer is responsible for maintaining and prioritizing the
backlog of work, the customer also owns the product roadmap. In large corporations or on projects with multiple customers or product owners, the
customer assigned to the project will often first work with others in his business unit to create a roadmap straw man as part of working out the priorities
of deliverables with the business. Then this straw man is presented to key
project team members (agile project manager, architect, and so on) for further revision. Finally, the roadmap is presented to the entire team and interested stakeholders, usually as part of the vision meeting and/or release

planning meeting. Feedback is encouraged at all sessions because it helps to better define a reasonable approach to product deliverables.

In addition to the vision plan and product roadmap, the end result of the product vision and product roadmap discussions should be the prioritized product backlog. These are all inputs into the next level of planning: release (or quarterly) planning.

Release (or Quarterly) Planning

In a release planning meeting, the team reviews the strategies and vision shared by the customer and determines how to map the work from the prioritized backlog into the iterations that make up a release or that make up a period of time such as a quarter. Figure 5-3 shows a typical release plan agenda, and Figure 5-4 shows the release plan done using a whiteboard and sticky notes, as is common in agile meetings when the team is co-located. The release plan is divided up into iterations (usually one flipchart page per iteration), with associated high-level features. The release plan also includes any assumptions, dependencies, constraints, decisions made, concerns, risks, or other issues that may affect the release. Again, documentation of these additional items can be as simple as posting the flipchart that they were originally recorded on or taking a picture of it and posting it on a shared website.

Last Responsible Moment Decision Points

Note that one of the items on the release planning meeting agenda is the identification of "Last Responsible Moment (LRM) decision points." LRM decision points identify points in the release where a decision must be made on an issue so as not to allow a default decision to occur. In other words, they identify "the moment at which failing to make a decision eliminates an important alternative".[6] Up until this point, the team can continue its momentum and gather additional information that will help in the decision-making. For example, one team knew it would have to make a decision between going with a Sybase database and an Oracle database. But the team did not have to decide this before they could start on the project—indeed, the team realized that it could develop code that was database-independent until the third iteration, when integration and reporting were required. Therefore, the team set the end of the second iteration as its LRM on the database decision, giving the architect and the DBA time to experiment with the work being developed concurrently.

Figure 5-3
Release planning
meeting agenda

Release Planning Meeting Agenda

- Introductions, ground rules, review of purpose and agenda (Project manager)
- Do we need to review our current situation and/or existing product roadmap? (Project manager, architect, customer/product owner)
- Do we remember the product vision? Has it changed? (Customer/product owner)
- What is the release date? How many iterations make up this release? (Project Manager)
- What is the theme for this release? (Customer/product owner)
- What are the features we need for this release? (Customer/product owner)
- What assumptions are we making? What constraints are we dealing with? (Team)
- What are the milestones/deliverables expected? Do we have any LRM decision points? (Team)
- What is the capacity of the team (iteration velocity)? (Team)
- Can we move the features into the iterations? Do we need to break them into smaller features so that they can be completed in a single iteration? (Team)
- What issues/concerns do we have? (Team)
- Can we commit to this release as a team, given what we know today? (Team)
- Close: empty parking lot, action items, next steps (Project manager)

Figure 5-4
Release plan

Teams that are not co-located should make every effort to bring everyone together for this meeting. Agile emphasizes face-to-face communication because of its benefits. However, balancing this with the realities of geographically dispersed teams means that budget constraints force teams to be selective about when they can gather together as a group. The vision and release planning meetings should receive high priority, because the information shared and decisions made in these meetings guide the team throughout the remainder of the release.

Iteration Planning

Traditional scope definition and many of the practices defined in the *PMBOK® Guide* knowledge area of Project Time Management are done as part of iteration planning. Here, features are elaborated (creating the equivalent of *PMBOK® Guide* work packages), tasks are identified, and the time needed to accomplish the tasks is estimated (see Figures 5-5 and 5-8). At the beginning of each iteration, the team should hold an iteration planning meeting to conduct this work. The team reviews the release plan and the prioritized items in the backlog, reviews the features requested for the current iteration, and tasks out and estimates those features. See Figure 5-6 for a typical iteration planning meeting agenda. In keeping with the agile practice of just-in-time design, it is here that the details of the features are discussed and negotiated.

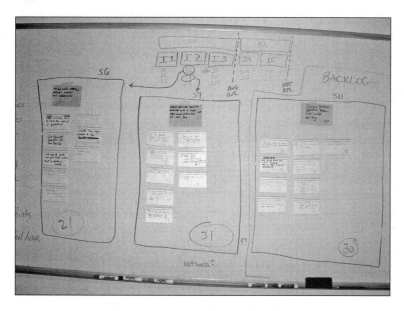

Figure 5-5
Iteration plan

Figure 5-6
Iteration planning
meeting agenda

Iteration Planning Meeting Agenda

- *Introductions, ground rules, review of purpose and agenda (Project manager)*
- *Do we know our iteration start and end dates? (Project manager)*
- *Do we know the team's velocity? (Team)*
- *Do we know what "done" means? (Team)*
- *What are the features we need for this iteration? What is the acceptance criteria for each feature? (Customer/product owner)*
- *Do we have enough information about the features so that we can task them out? (Team)*
- *Can we estimate the time it takes to complete the tasks? (Team)*
- *What assumptions are we making? What constraints are we dealing with? Are there dependencies that affect our prioritization? (Team)*
- *Are we within our velocity limits? (Team)*
- *What issues/concerns do we have? (Team)*
- *Can we commit to this iteration as a team, given what we know today? (Team)*
- *Close: empty parking lot, action items, next steps (Project manager)*

Again, planning and design work is done only for the pieces that are being readied to code in that iteration, not for the entire system. It's often discovered during iteration planning that the sum of the task efforts exceeds the size of the iteration timebox. When this occurs, some of the work needs to be shifted either into the next iteration or back into the backlog. Similarly, if a team discovers that it has chosen too little work for the iteration, it will consult with the customer, who can then give the team an additional feature or two to make up the difference. This allows the team to make a realistic commitment to the scope of the work being defined.

Daily Stand-Up

One of the key heartbeats of agile development involves the practice of daily stand-up meetings. It is just what it sounds like: a daily meeting, where all team members attend, and while remaining standing, they each relate their status to the other team members and their plan for the day based on the progress that they've made. Standing helps keep the meetings short—stand-ups should run only 5 to 15 minutes. Its primary purpose is for the team members to inspect and adapt its work plan (iteration backlog) by quickly sharing information about the progress (or lack of) being made by each individual regarding the tasks that were committed to during the iteration planning meeting. These stand-ups help the team to remain focused on the agreed-to scope and goals of the iteration.

Summary Comparison

Table 5-2 provides a summary comparison of traditional and agile approaches to scope definition. In agile projects this is called "multilevel planning."

Table 5-2
Scope Definition

Traditional	Agile
Prepare a Project Scope Statement document that includes items such as the following: Project boundaries and objectives, product scope description...	Conduct a vision meeting to share the product vision; confirm and clarify the boundaries, objectives, and product scope description using exercises such as the elevator statement and design the box.

Traditional	Agile
And major milestones and project deliverables…	Conduct a planning meeting to prepare the product roadmap, as well as release or quarterly planning meetings that also include milestones and deliverables at an iteration level.
And product specifications and acceptance criteria…	Conduct an iteration planning meeting that results in the detail around each feature, and the tasks needed to complete the feature according to the team's definition of "done" and the acceptance criteria defined by the customer.
And assumptions and constraints.	All planning meetings identify and/or review assumptions and constraints.

Create a WBS

Agile teams do not tend to create formal WBSs (work breakdown structures). Instead, flipcharts and whiteboards are used to capture the breakdown of work. You've seen examples of these in Figures 5-4 and 5-5. So at the end of release planning, the agile equivalent of a WBS—a feature breakdown structure—would look like the sample release plan feature breakdown structure in Figure 5-7. If having iterations as work packages is not sufficient for your organization/billing needs, then breaking the work down further into smaller work packages would look like the results of an iteration planning meeting, as illustrated in Figure 5-8.

Table 5-3 compares the traditional and agile approaches to work breakdown. In agile projects, the work breakdown structure is captured in the release plan and the iteration plan.

Table 5-3
WBS Creation

Traditional	Agile
Create a work breakdown structure diagram.	Conduct planning meetings and give the team the responsibility for breaking down the work into smaller work packages (features and tasks), displayed as the release plan at the high level, and the iteration plan at the more detailed level.

Figure 5-7
Release plan feature
breakdown structure

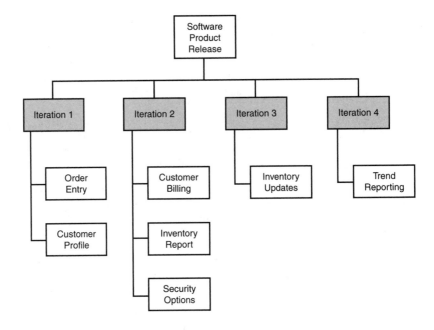

Figure 5-8
Iteration plan (partial)

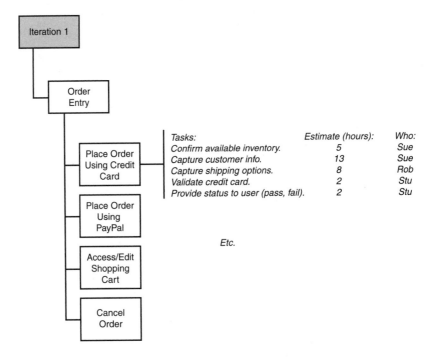

Tasks:	Estimate (hours):	Who:
Confirm available inventory.	5	Sue
Capture customer info.	13	Sue
Capture shipping options.	8	Rob
Validate credit card.	2	Stu
Provide status to user (pass, fail).	2	Stu

Etc.

Scope Verification

Scope verification is accomplished within the iteration, as the customer gets to review, test, and accept the implemented features. Ideally this happens throughout the iteration, but it can also happen at the end of the iteration, during the demo of the working code. Those features that were not accepted (either because they weren't ready or weren't right) move back into the backlog or into the next iteration at the discretion of the customer. Scope change control is handled by the management of this backlog, as discussed in the previous chapter on integration.

Table 5-4 makes the comparison between the traditional and agile approaches to scope verification. Scope verification is captured by the agile practices of acceptance testing and customer acceptance.

Table 5-4
Scope Verification

Traditional	Agile
Document those completed deliverables that have been accepted and those that have not been accepted, along with the reason.	Documentation of accepted features may be done informally (by moving the sticky notes to the "done" pile) or formally.
Document change requests.	Customer updates the backlog.

Scope Control

Controlling scope in agile projects consists of two things: managing the product backlog and protecting the iteration. Whereas the customer maintains the backlog, it is the agile project manager who protects the team and helps prevent scope changes from occurring during the iteration.

When a team commits to the iteration at the end of the iteration planning meeting, the delivery team is effectively saying, "Given what we know today, we believe we can deliver this work using our definition of 'done' within this iteration," and the customer is effectively saying, "Given what I know today, this is the work that I am expecting by the end of the iteration, and during that time I will not mess with the iteration backlog" (that is, scope). The iteration backlog is thus locked in.

It is important to set the length of your iteration accordingly, because the customer must wait until the next iteration to make changes. If there happens to be lots of "requirements churn" (that is, requests for changes are coming in very frequently), you may want to discuss shorter iteration cycles with the team in order to enable more frequent changes. Maintenance teams may have iteration lengths of only one week, whereas larger system developments with known requirements may have an iteration length of four to six weeks. If the customer keeps trying to interrupt the team with changes, the iteration length may be too long.

There will always be exceptions, and in those cases a discussion between the customer and the agile project manager should help identify potential resolutions. Iterations can be aborted and restarted, but this should be the rare exception.

Given the short duration of iterations, it is easy to protect the iteration backlog from change. However, changes in the product roadmap and the release plan are expected and therefore should be reviewed regularly.

Table 5-5 lists out the differences between the traditional and agile approaches to scope control. Agile users refer to scope control as "managing the product backlog."

Table 5-5
Scope Control

Traditional	Agile
Use a change control system to manage change.	The customer manages the product backlog; once the team commits to the work to be done in an iteration, the scope is protected for that duration.
Update all documents as appropriate with the approved changes.	The team revisits release plans and product roadmaps regularly, making changes as needed to better reflect the team's progress and changes requested by the customer.

Summary

The main points of this chapter can be summarized as follows:

- "Scope creep" doesn't exist in agile projects, because scope is expected to change.
- Scope management in agile is primarily a function of "rolling wave" planning and the management of the product backlog.
- Scope is defined and redefined using five different levels of planning that take the team from the broad vision down to what team members plan to complete today.
- WBSs are not created per se; instead, release/quarterly plans and iteration plans serve to break down the work into smaller work packages, referred to as "features and tasks."
- Scope is verified by the customer, who is responsible for accepting or rejecting the features completed each iteration.
- Scope is controlled through the use of the backlog, rolling wave planning, and the protection of the iteration.

Table 5-6 presents the differences in project management behavior regarding scope management in traditional and agile projects.

Table 5-6
Agile Project Manager's Change List for Scope Management

I used to do this:	Now I do this:
Prepare a formal Project Scope Management plan.	Make sure the team understands the framework and process structure of the chosen agile approach.
Prepare a formal Project Scope Statement document.	Facilitate planning meetings—vision, release, iteration, daily stand-up—and arrange for the informally documented plans to be highly visible to all stakeholders.
Create the WBS.	Facilitate the release planning meeting so that the team can create the plan showing the breakdown of work across several iterations.

(continued)

Table 5-6
Agile Project Manager's Change List for Scope Management *(continued)*

I used to do this:	Now I do this:
Manage the change control system and try to prevent scope creep.	Step away from the backlog; it is owned by the customer. If needed, remind the customer that during the iteration, the team is protected from scope changes.
Manage the delivery of tasks to prevent or correct scope creep at the task level.	Allow team members to manage their daily tasks and facilitate conversations with the customer to avoid unnecessary work or "gold plating."

Endnotes

1. *PMBOK® Guide*, 107.

2. Ibid, 114.

3. Ibid.

4. Mike Cohn. *Agile Estimating and Planning* (Upper Saddle River, NJ: Pearson Education, Inc., 2006), 28.

5. Luke Hohmann. *Beyond Software Architecture* (Boston: Addison-Wesley, 2003), 287.

6. Poppendieck. *Lean Software Development*, 57.

Chapter 6

Time Management

*Time management includes the processes required to accomplish
timely completion of the project.*

—PMBOK® Guide

*Time is neutral and does not change things. With courage and
initiative, leaders change things.*

—Jesse Jackson

*A predictable organization does not guess about the future and call it
a plan; it develops the capacity to rapidly respond to the future as it
unfolds.*

—Mary Poppendieck

Physicists, scientists, mathematicians, and philosophers have debated the
idea of time for thousands of years. Is it an unchanging presence in our uni-
verse, or is it a separate entity somehow entangled with space? Is it merely a
measurement imposed by man, an illusion?

What we know in the project management realm is that time is an
important element to be managed. But can we really manage time? Can we
stop time, engage time, elongate time, or shrink time? Can we reward time
so that it performs better for us? Can we report on time in order to better
understand its quality? Time, then, in project management, is an imposed
constraint by the business or the customer; managing time really means that
we manage the activities and deliverables that occur within that given constraint in order to produce the best possible results. This means that the

business can decide to extend or bring in dates, depending on the project's progress, market conditions, or other internal or external factors.

Many software projects traditionally have been managed by what we call a skill/phase-based approach; first, analysts analyze the problem, designers design a solution, coders code, testers test, and then the product is released. That is, the collection of people with skills equates to the different phases of the project; project controls are put in place to manage each group of skilled people, among other things. In this waterfall approach, the analysis and design phases provide an end date for the project; the assumption is that by understanding the work and breaking it down into small enough pieces (tasks), the tasks can be estimated and the end date of the project can be calculated. This approach to managing software project schedules is flawed for several reasons.

First, the "industrial making approach," or serial handoff of a deliverable from one set of skill groups to the next, works well for a repeatable process with a predictable outcome.[1] In other words, if I am a deck builder and I offer a prepackaged solution for a 12'×12' wooden deck, I know when to schedule permits with the township, when to schedule the backhoe and post setter, if needed; I know exactly how many pieces of wood and the number of screws I need, as well as how many hours and men that each job requires. Bad weather not withstanding, this kind of project schedule is easy to create in a prescriptive fashion. In fact, my ability to predict milestones, dates, and hand-offs would be quite reliable.

Although some forethought and insight is necessary to discover points of synchronization, procurement deadlines, and funding milestones, among other events in software development projects, the actual day-to-day crafting of software is much too complex to predict and control. What happens in one day—in one hour, even—can impact dependent tasks significantly, and the thousands of permutations of outcomes are impossible to capture in a project schedule. The tasks involved with building software, day to day, cannot be predicted and certainly are not repeatable. From one software project to the next, requirements change, technology may or may not be stable, and people bring another level of complexity to the table. Attempting to predict task-level detail in such mayhem is waste, and formulating a date off of this flawed prediction is setting up a project team for failure.

Finally, change happens. Whether the customer asks for a new feature or simply a change to a screen color, many teams have realized that software developed in a series of empirical trials in collaboration with the customer is best to address these changes. Build, learn, build again, learn more. Through these attempts, teams make the right product. Thus, this "artful making"[2] approach to software development suggests that a project end date is very difficult to perfectly predict because we cannot perfectly predict the features. We simply cannot know today exactly how the system will be built; sure, we have a vision, a general direction, but we cannot say exactly how it will operate, or look, or feel to the user. Only by developing in repeated trial-and-error passes can we begin to see the system evolving and how we need to carry it forward. Agile builds these checkpoints into the iterative process.

The flawed thinking that we can predict a system and its capabilities, coupled with frequent and necessary change, should cause us to reconsider our estimation processes and date commitments. This chapter illustrates how to "manage time" by providing visibility into project results so that the team and the customer can negotiate an outcome. We'll call it forecasting instead of prediction. And we'll think of estimates—whether at the strategic or tactical level—as forecasting tools, not commitments written in stone.

So, how do we forecast in an agile project, then, while simultaneously delivering on the dates that are important for the customer? First, we must recognize that delivery is a partnership between the customer and the delivery team. Then, we start top-down. The customer provides the team with a product vision and a roadmap, which are standard practices, agile or not. The team then determines a release date based on a given set of features, or alternatively decides which subset of features it can deliver within a given timeframe. Time management is then a negotiation between the customer (or the business) and the team from one iteration to the next, based on product feedback, changing market conditions, and insight into how rapidly a team can create working features (known as "velocity"). As agile project managers, we make project progress visible at the iteration and release levels, and as you'll discover in this chapter, we allow the team of experts—Drucker's famous "knowledge workers"[3]—to manage themselves on a day-to-day basis.

This chapter differentiates between strategic and tactical planning and provides you with ideas about how to plan an agile project using this paradigm. Additionally, we give you the context in which detailed activity decomposition and estimating occurs, while helping you understand how you can leverage the team's results to report project status, thus enabling the business or the customer to make educated decisions about the emerging product. As you will see, combining high-level release plans with detailed iteration plans addresses complex project planning with the right amount of detail at the right time.

Strategic Versus Tactical Planning

We've concluded that time management really is a factor of managing the activities and deliverables that occur within a given time constraint in order to produce the best possible project results. There are ways that we can more intelligently plan our agile projects so that we can set realistic milestones and facilitate negotiation between the business/customer and the delivery team.

There is a common analogy in business management that is referred to as strategic and tactical planning. As you may know, a strategy is a long-term plan of action designed to achieve a particular goal. A tactic is a method employed to achieve a certain goal. The goal pursued by strategic planning is at a higher level of abstraction than the goals pursued by tactics. Strategic planning in agile projects, then, occurs at the release/feature level upfront and throughout the project, whereas tactical planning at the task level occurs during iteration planning and is adjusted as needed, on a daily basis, throughout the iteration by the team.

Thinking in terms of strategic and tactical planning is certainly not a new concept, but we feel that explicitly adding both sets of planning practices into your project planning toolkit is something that can help you better manage time expectations with your customers and organization.

Think of an agile software project consisting of multiple boxes made of steel; we stop dropping in feature bricks when each box is full (see Figure 6-1). We then close the box, padlock it for that iteration, and work the features through to acceptance. Then, we move on to the next box. This is different from software projects that follow the traditional approach where there is only one big box into which we stuff (and often overstuff) feature bricks. The duration of an agile project is measured by how many steel boxes of bricks are necessary to complete the vision for the product. It's the steel box that we're putting our features into, and steel is not bendable and cannot burst at its seams. Furthermore, because we are collaborating with our customers and have the opportunity to release working code faster, customers don't feel the need to overstuff the box. There can always be another box if necessary. Strategic planning happens at the "how many steel boxes do we need to complete our features" level. The team engages in tactics when figuring out how it's going to build each feature within a timebox.

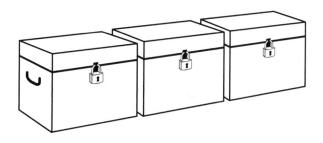

Figure 6-1
The software project as multiple steel boxes

The imposed time constraint in a project is a stake in the ground; it represents the business or customer's need. Ultimately, the customer may decide that more iterations of development are necessary or that rebudgeting for more resources is possible. It is the agile project manager's responsibility to balance the business needs against the delivery team's capabilities, keeping progress visible so that collaborative decision-making about managing time is possible.

We'll start with developing and controlling a project plan at the strategic level (the release plan), and then illustrate how the team plans its tactics for an iteration.

Release Planning: Developing the Schedule at the Strategic Level

The *PMBOK® Guide* refers to schedule development as "an iterative process [that] determines planned start and finish dates for project activities. Schedule development can require that duration estimates and resource estimates are reviewed and revised to create an approved project schedule that can serve as a baseline against which progress can be tracked."[4] The traditional project schedule is the primary tool to measure time and other project performance; the agile equivalent is the agile release plan. Instead of an iterative process that determines start and finish dates for activities, as is done in traditional project schedule planning, the agile release plans determine finish dates for features, which correlate to an iteration's end date.

As you learned in previous chapters, agile release planning is a process in which we gain an understanding of the features that will comprise a collection of iterations. We achieve this knowledge via top-down (or strategic) planning. We do this because we embrace the fact that change will occur in the course of our project, and we save ourselves the weeks (or sometimes months!) identifying every detail upfront. Many teams have found agile release planning to be at the right level, in between prescriptive, plan-driven project schedules and the inappropriate "you'll get it when you get it" mantra of some freshman agile teams. Moreover, because the release plan is expressed as a timeline of which features will drop into each iteration, the customer more easily understands project schedule and progress much more readily; it is exactly the depth of information they're interested in, because features represent value. Tasks, which represent *how* something is built, usually aren't interesting to the end consumer of the project's product.

The Release Plan: Schedule Development at the Strategic Level

The agile release plan helps us focus on a three- to six-iteration window of time. If you have a year-long project, for example, you may want to consider release planning on a quarterly basis, with a high-level project roadmap to guide the overall initiative. Once the project is underway, updates to the release plan should be made at the end of each iteration based on the actual progress and the remaining work for the release. See Chapter 5, "Scope Management," for additional details about how to conduct release and roadmap planning meetings.

Additionally, consider the way agile teams estimate at the strategic level. Because we've dispelled the myth that we can predict long-term complex initiatives at the task level, creating a strategic plan in hours and days is not the appropriate level of estimation. Rather, many agile teams will use abstract measurements to estimate product backlog items for strategic planning.

The most common abstract measurement is story points, which can follow the Fibonacci sequence: 1, 2, 3, 5, 8, 13, 21 (another common expression is an exponential scale of 1, 2, 4, 8, 16, 32, 64...). It is common for features in the product backlog to be written as "user stories," which is a format for writing requirements from a user's perspective.[5] For example, rather than stating "the system shall…," a user story would say "as a <type of user> I want to be able to do <feature/function> so that <I get value>."[6] These features or user stories are then estimated in a unit of measure called "story points"; assigning a story point "estimate" to a user story says, "We think it's about this complex." All other user stories are then assigned story points in relation to the first one that's estimated. This relative complexity is a way of giving an indication of difficulty at a very high level. A sense of how many story points a team can complete in one iteration lends the ability to forecast the number of iterations a set of features will take to implement.

Regardless of your unit of measure, the team's iteration length, or the involvement level of the customer, the agile release plan has a fundamental, critical assumption: that the functionality delivered every iteration is of the highest quality possible. If the team is delivering code that's not tested and integrated every iteration, there remains an indeterminable amount of work due to the unknown product quality, which is risky. However, if the team frontloads as much testing work as possible during the iteration, so that the incremental deliveries are all of the highest quality, the team may only need a short hardening iteration at the end of the release in order to release the product to production. Additionally, it has mitigated the risk of the unknown by testing early and often.

While we're on the subject of different iteration types, many teams schedule an Iteration 0 (zero) at the beginning of the project, and an Iteration H (hardening) as the last iteration in a release (to production) cycle. Iteration 0 is used for project approvals, environment setup, ramp-up, discovery and initial overviews, and design discussions. Iteration H is used at the end to prepare for delivery, and it includes activities such as finalizing training and marketing materials and preparing the golden master or installation/download files. Iteration H is not used as a testing cycle; in fact, analysis, design, and testing should happen continuously throughout the iterations themselves, verified by the customer once he signs off on a story as being "done" for the iteration. Rather, Iterations 0 and H are used as minimal bookends for work that is not explicitly new development. Additionally, and very importantly, we firmly believe in asking our teams to deliver at least one feature in Iteration 0 because we've seen many teams revert to form, utilizing Iteration 0 as purely a design or analysis phase.

Figure 6-2 illustrates two release possibilities—internal and external—when thinking about release plans. When teams stay disciplined in delivering working product every iteration, the organization theoretically has the ability to package up and "release" what's been built. Whether or not the package is actually released to customers depends on a number of factors, but it could just as well be released internally to training or support services or externally to a partner for a limited user-acceptance testing cycle. Regardless of the use, sticking to quality increments of product will provide the organization the agility it desires for whatever need is most pressing.

Figure 6-2
A release plan is a high-level plan for a series of iterations. Releases can be internal or external.

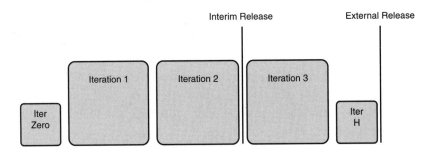

Table 6-1 provides a summary comparison of traditional and agile approaches to schedule development at the strategic level. Agile schedule development at the strategic level is referred to as "release planning."

Table 6-1
Schedule Development at the Strategic Level

Traditional	Agile
Create the final project schedule (usually in a tool that shows bar charts, milestones, and a network diagram) and baseline.	Facilitate the collaborative creation of the release plan, resulting in a quarterly high-level plan indicating release goals, features to be completed, and timeboxes.
Update the activity attributes, resources, project plan, etc., as appropriate.	Assist the team in updating the release plan as needed, based on iteration results.

The Release Plan: Schedule Control at the Strategic Level

Schedule control is carried out by knowing the current status of the project schedule, and managing changes in the plan that might impact the schedule. The agile release plan is managed in a similar fashion, except that the plan remains high level instead of containing detailed tasks from beginning to end; additionally, the agile project manager facilitates the customer and the team in making schedule changes, if necessary, based on project visibility. We will tell a story to illustrate this concept.

During a release planning meeting, our fictitious team, whom we'll call "GERT," analyzed its previous work and determined that it could reasonably commit to a pace of ten points per iteration, each iteration being four weeks in length. The product owner really needed the release six months later, and he was interested to know about how many features he would receive in the release. The team went through a collaborative exercise of placing user stories into iterations by using sticky notes and flip chart paper, "filling up" each iteration (or steel box) with no more than ten points' worth of stories in each. The GERT team stopped once it filled the final iteration with features, and realized that it had chosen a subset of the product backlog equal to roughly 60 points (10 points × 6 iterations = 60 points). This set of features, called the "release backlog," can be used as a baseline by which project progress is measured. Remember, however, that we want to allow appropriate change as the customer provides product feedback. Thus, "managing" the project schedule in an agile setting is really about making progress visible so that the customer can balance the original product vision along with the necessary changes in scope that arise out of natural product evolution.

Back to our team. After the first iteration, the team only completed seven story points; velocity was lower than initially expected because the team ran into some unexpected environment setup issues. The project manager, team, and customer discussed the situation and decided to extend the release plan to seven total iterations, versus the six originally predicted, in order to account for the lower velocity. At this point, the customer could have just as well reduced the amount of scope in the release backlog, but he decided that he had a little wiggle room in the overall release end date and could float another iteration. When discovering that actual velocity is higher or lower than expected, the product owner can decide if he wants to reprioritize user stories, drop user stories from the release backlog, or extend the release by n iterations.

The GERT team completed 12 story points of work in the second iteration. The customer was delighted! Even though the team and the customer were happy about the increase in velocity, they decided to keep the extended date just in case they needed the buffer. Figure 6-3 shows how the team began with a commitment to 60 points over six months using four-week iterations and baselined this. Then the burndown of what the team delivered each iteration was noted, resulting in the decision to commit to a new baseline.

Figure 6-3
This release burndown chart represents the GERT team's progress through iterations 1 and 2 of its project.

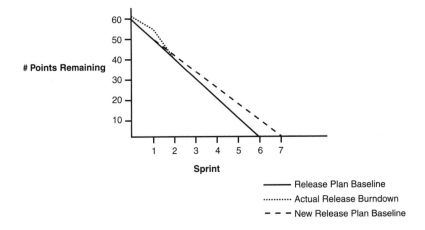

Managing a number of iterations in a release plan is dependent on the real-time status of the working product, as well as on the collaboration and negotiation between the customer and delivery team. The agile project manager facilitates this discussion and makes certain that both sides have the information each needs in order to reach a collaborative decision about the release.

As new discoveries are made about the system, any changes that need to be made can be done by adding an item to the product backlog. In Agile, it is expected that these changes are necessary in order to build the right product. The product and release backlogs therefore function as a natural change management system.

Table 6-2 provides a summary comparison of schedule control at the strategic level for the traditional and agile approaches to project management. In agile terminology, schedule control at the strategic level is referred to as "agile release plan management."

Table 6-2
Schedule Control at the Strategic Level

Traditional	Agile
Update the schedule based on approved changes and re-baseline.	Facilitate the review meeting where the team updates the release plan based on the team's velocity and changes in the backlog.
Calculate schedule variance and schedule performance index.	Remind the team of its duty to update the work remaining in the iteration backlog; at the end of every iteration, the release burndown chart is updated. The team also measures its velocity.
Track and document requested changes.	The customer updates the product and/or release backlog.
Identify and analyze recommended corrective action to get the project back on track.	Facilitate a discussion between the customer and the team to discuss any corrective action that should be taken (i.e., add another iteration, add a team, drop features, terminate the project, etc.).

Iteration Planning: Developing the Schedule at the Tactical Level

Iteration planning brings us inside the steel box. It is the meeting in which the team breaks down the items from a prioritized product or release backlog into small tasks and assigns estimates and owners sufficiently so that the team can agree to the iteration plan. It is in this meeting that the activities (tasks) are defined, sequenced, and estimated by the team. Like the steel box, the iteration end date is fixed and padlocked; the team, based on its past performance (that is, velocity) will choose enough work to fill up the box. The iteration planning meeting can take up to eight hours for a month-long iteration, or up to four hours for a two-week iteration.

An iteration planning meeting includes the delivery team, the project manager, and the customer (or customer's representative, often referred to as the "product owner"). Others may attend the meeting if they wish to observe or contribute supplemental information about the features to be built.

The output of this meeting is the iteration backlog, which is a list of the team's tasks and other information necessary to manage its day-to-day tactics in turning product backlog items into working product increments for the iteration. A main difference between the release backlog and the iteration backlog is its unit of measure for the estimates: release backlog items—or features—are measured in story points or other high-level estimates, whereas iteration backlog items—or tasks—are estimated in hours.

Because the timeframe is so narrow—one to four weeks—teams become quite proficient at predicting the work within the iteration. Teams perform the traditional planning processes of activity definition, sequencing, and estimation in the planning meeting and throughout the duration of the iteration as needed, leveraging the daily stand-up meeting to gain valuable insights that may affect the tactics.

Activity Definition

The *PMBOK® Guide* classifies activity definition as "identifying and documenting the work that is planned to be performed." [7] In traditional project planning, a project manager would think about all the tasks that might ever happen during the course of the project as part of documenting the expected work to be performed. In fact, project managers often have at hand their methodology templates or project structures used previously that contain the work breakdown structure and subsequent tasks; the project manager simply inserts the new project name and makes a few adjustments. This reuse of a previous project plan is in line with traditional thinking, that new product development can be predicted and repeated. As we know, planning in an agile project should account for the change that will happen and involves teams working as a cohesive unit, task-sharing their way to iteration success.

Thus, activity definition happens in an agile project when the iteration has arrived in which the feature will be worked on; this breakdown occurs in the iteration planning meeting by the team, not the project manager. The iteration planning meeting occurs on the first day of every iteration; it is supported by the *PMBOK® Guide* and is referred to as "rolling wave planning."[8]

To prepare for the iteration planning meeting, the customer brings the list of highest-priority features and no more. The team should have already looked ahead at this list in order to estimate the complexity of the high-priority items. The customer will discuss what the requirement is all about, how he or she will consider it is sufficiently implemented (known as acceptance criteria), and answer any questions that the team has about the intent and purpose of the requirement. Think of this first part of the meeting as the "What" and "Why" of iteration planning. This detailed understanding of the business case or user intent is imperative for accurate and reliable activity definition.

During the second part of the meeting, the team will determine all of the tasks necessary to complete the requirements that the product owner considers highest priority—the "How." The team will discuss details such as, What stored procedure do we need to write? What user interface changes are necessary? Do we need another table in the database? Will performance be impacted? As the team members flesh out the answers to these questions, they will begin to make note of their tasks, as well as how long each of the tasks will take. A very popular way to record this information is on sticky notes arranged on a task board. Sometimes, electronic tools are used, but remember the simplest, most visible solution is often best.

The ultimate goal of iteration planning is to have a set of activities (or tasks) that the team will perform within the boundaries of the padlocked timebox (or iteration). This resulting list of tasks, regardless of the means by which it's captured, is referred to in agile as the "iteration backlog." Most importantly, the team derives its own tasks and its own sense of what it can accomplish by the iteration end date. Figure 6-4 depicts a team's task board, a community location in which cards representing tasks are placed on the board and moved to the column that represents the feature's status. Task boards are very popular with co-located teams.

Table 6-3 presents a summary comparison of traditional and agile approaches to activity definition. In the agile vernacular, activity definition is referred to as "defining and tasking out user stories." It is done by the team as part of developing the schedule at the tactical level.

Figure 6-4
An iteration
task board

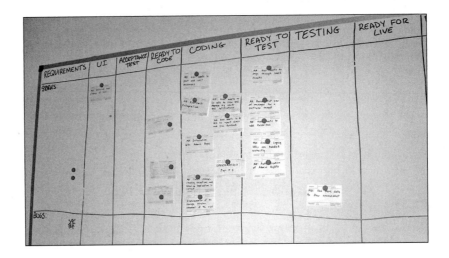

Table 6-3
Activity Definition

Traditional	Agile
Prepare an activity list showing all scheduled activities to be performed on the project.	Each iteration, the team will break down the selected features into a list of tasks that become part of the iteration backlog, or iteration plan.
Define activity attributes such as task owner, predecessors, successors, constraints, assumptions, level of effort, etc., and include in the project schedule.	Activity attributes such as task owner and estimate are defined during the iteration planning meeting and included in the iteration plan.
Milestones are defined for the entire project and inserted into the project schedule.	Themes are identified for each iteration during release planning; often, project managers refer to the increment of working code delivered at the end of each iteration as a milestone.
Requested changes resulting from the activity definition exercise are put through the change request process.	If new requirements are discovered during iteration planning, the customer should capture this information by adding the item to the product backlog. Sometimes the new requirements are included in the iteration that is being planned, but only if the customer agrees to remove lower-priority features from the iteration and place them back into the product backlog, so that the steel timebox is not compromised.

It is important to note that the *PMBOK® Guide* also explains that activity definition "will identify the deliverables at the lowest level in the work breakdown structure, which is called the work package. Project work packages are decomposed into smaller components called schedule activities to provide a basis for estimating, scheduling, executing and monitoring and controlling the project work."[9] In an agile project, this is done on an iteration-by-iteration basis, and for the most part, the work package equates to the feature, not to individual tasks.

Activity Duration Estimating

Agile project managers don't track duration of activities. In fact, duration is removed from the activity altogether. Duration is represented by the padlocked iteration timebox; it has definitive start and end dates that do not change. The team, then, decomposes features into tasks, which are then estimated in terms of work effort hours, and doesn't plan for more tasks than what it can do during the timebox. The estimates are aggregated and the team members compare this to the amount of work they estimate they can do (their capacity based on hours). They also make sure that the total number of story points doesn't greatly exceed what they've completed in previous iterations. Newer teams usually also compare their task hours to each team member's individual capacity; more mature teams have embraced role-sharing and thus have devised ways of thinking about capacity as a whole. In fact, for some advanced teams, the high-level product backlog estimate alone suffices to answer the question, "Is it in or out for this iteration?" Many teams work through the product backlog of features, in order of priority, and do not move to the next feature until the current one is finished— by the entire team!

Sometimes, the team discovers during iteration planning that the sum of the task efforts exceeds the size of the iteration timebox. When this occurs, some of the work needs to be shifted either into the next iteration or back into the backlog. After adjustments are made to the iteration's scope, the team can commit to the iteration—the agreement to padlock the timebox.

Estimates Get Better with Experience

I had to drive to Ensenada, Mexico, one summer. To get there, I crossed the border in San Diego and headed due south. Not having driven in Mexico much, and in fact, not at all in any country that uses kilometers as the measure of distance, I was quite interested in the sign that read "Ensenada, 90km." Now, when driving in the States, if I see a sign that says "35 miles," I know that at my current rate (which is normally around 70 mph), I can reach my destination in 30 minutes. In Mexico, however, I didn't know what 90km "feels" like, and I couldn't quickly do the math to convert distance to time. So I had to just say, "Well, it's 90 and it will take me however long it will take me to get there." Once I saw the next sign that said "Ensenada, 40km," I could begin to predict my arrival based on how far I had come and how long it had taken. This "speaking in kilometers" exercise occurred to me to be similar to how we measure feature complexity in story points. Story points are a measure of complexity. Based on our "burn rate"—or in this case "driving rate"—through creating functionality, we can predict within a normal range of certainty how long our requirements will take us to complete. And the *huevos rancheros* after driving a long day through a product backlog are worth it!

After a series of iterations, a team's ability to predict the amount of work it can accomplish becomes more precise. This is because the team has established an average velocity, has figured out how to work together, and has learned about the emerging system.

Table 6-4 provides a comparison of the traditional and agile perspectives on activity duration estimating. Activity duration estimating is referred to in the agile world as "task estimating," as part of developing the schedule at the tactical level.

Table 6-4
Activity Duration Estimating

Traditional	Agile
Estimate activity durations.	Team members provide estimates for tasks during iteration planning and throughout the iteration when new tasks are needed or when existing tasks change.

Activity Sequencing

Activity sequencing "involves identifying and documenting the logical relationships among schedule activities." [10] Activity sequencing in a traditional project can be quite complicated, with "relationships" between activities ranging from finish-to-start, to finish-to-finish, to start-to-finish, to start-to-start. These relationship types are used in traditional project scheduling to keep track of what happens first, second, and simultaneously, and is especially useful in creating automatic project schedules. Knowing when one activity can start as well as knowing if certain conditions must be met for another activity is important. This is relevant for managing projects by both traditional and agile methods. The difference in agile is that we don't worry about this level of detail until the iteration is at hand.

The trouble with pinpointing activity sequence before the project starts is that a software project's tasks are numerous and are subject to change; once requirements or tasks change, we have to try to mirror these changes in the project schedule. This takes an incredible amount of time and is often inaccurate. The main difference with agile activity sequencing is that it is performed by the team in iteration planning, and changes throughout the iteration based on daily team synchronization as it discovers more details about building the feature, based on ad-hoc discussions or new information.

During iteration planning, the project manager and the team are aware of the iteration start and end dates, and they also keep in mind other important dates or milestones (beta program, training, and so on). They can then plan their activity sequencing based on this high-level information. Sometimes the team will discover a technical dependency in the product backlog during iteration planning, at which time the team will let the customer know about it. At the task level, however, the team will figure out the dependencies and the order in which work needs to happen. A great litmus test is to have a round-robin exercise before committing to the iteration in which each team member answers two questions: First, what are you going to work on tomorrow when you come in? And second, what's the next thing you're going to work on and with whom do you plan to work? This exercise helps by kick-starting the first few dependency discoveries; after that, the team will discover more during the iteration.

It is also helpful if the project manager brings a visual to help during planning. Often, we have found that just simply drawing a calendar on the whiteboard to show the days during the iteration is helpful. It serves as a memory jog; this information helps teams think about not only the work, but other things to consider as well. Another example of this is shown in Figure 6-5, which is an actual project manager's rendering of the iteration calendar that he would draw on the whiteboard to remind the team of important milestones or meetings. This would sometimes cause a reordering of tasks.

Figure 6-5
Timeline for iteration task sequencing

It is important to note that there are two types of dependencies in agile projects: overall project dependencies and task dependencies. The team members, because they know more than the managers about the details of the work they are performing, can best manage the task dependencies. The project manager can bring the overall project dependencies to the table. For example, if I know that my project team is awaiting a third-party code drop by the end of December, I can help manage that external dependency and shield the team from the burden. However, the fact that Bob is waiting on Joe to make the database schema changes is something that I will entrust the both of them to handle. As long as Joe does this in time for Bob to finish coding and testing by the end of the iteration, that is all I am concerned with.

Table 6-5 compares activity sequencing from the traditional and agile perspectives. There is no specific agile term for activity sequencing. It is simply part of developing and finalizing the schedule at the tactical level.

Table 6-5
Activity Sequencing

Traditional	Agile
Define activity sequencing for the project for display in project schedule network diagrams.	Facilitate iteration planning, where the team will determine how to handle task sequencing. The team and customer together determine how technical and external dependencies might affect the order of the items in the product backlog.
Updates to activity lists, attributes, and change log are captured and processed accordingly.	Updates to the iteration backlog in response to discovered or resolved dependencies are maintained by the team.

Activity Resource Estimating

Resource estimating in traditional project management is often determined after the activities have been defined.

This is reversed in agile. That is, a team's members (resources) are determined upfront and are dedicated to the project. The stray resource coming in and out of the project team is an exception (think DBA or third-party integration specialist). This is because qualitative studies have shown that individuals are ultimately more effective if dedicated and not time-sliced across multiple endeavors; subjectively, the dedicated teams we have worked with display much higher morale than their time-sliced colleagues.

Teams experience an increase in efficiency and productivity when allowed to work in a dedicated fashion toward delivering the iteration's features. Additionally, most teams that are together for a series of iterations will begin to think like an organic group. Instead of thinking linearly, as in "I'll code and you test and Pat will write documentation," it becomes "Let's do this together." You'll see team members jump in and start learning new skills. It's a switch from linear thinking to team thinking. It's a big jump here for the project manager to not think in terms of loading resources into the tasks of a project schedule and instead having teams that are cross-functional and dedicated and "loaded" into iterations.

Human resources, then, are not estimated to fill the timebox; rather, the team comes along with the timebox, and the team chooses however many features it can fit within its allotted time for the iteration.

There are material resources to consider as well—such as servers, credit card readers, switches, and so on. In agile, we can discover these items during the iteration, but there's also another time for this discovery—in agile release planning. Taking a high-level look at the expected or desired functionality over a series of iterations allows us to know when certain material resources will be necessary. For example, a team I was working with knew it would need a data architect as well as two new servers for a new data warehouse, but this wouldn't be necessary for another four months based on the release plan. The team was able to forge ahead while the project manager made the necessary decisions to procure the contractor and the equipment in time for that stage of the project.

Table 6-6 provides a summary comparison of activity resource estimating from the traditional and agile perspectives. There is no specific agile term for activity resource estimating. It is simply part of developing the schedule at the tactical level as a dedicated cross-functional team.

Table 6-6
Activity Resource Estimating

Traditional	Agile
Identify the resources required for each work package.	The team is dedicated to the iteration and is known before the iteration begins. Other resources can be planned for at the agile release planning level.
Create a calendar showing resource availability and needs.	Remind teams to think of the times when they won't work on features during the iteration—that is, holidays, training, leave of absence, and so on.

The Iteration Plan: Schedule Control at the Tactical Level

Although our release (or series of iterations) can be managed by watching the release burndown chart (refer to Figure 6-3) and facilitating the customer's decisions, the primary tools to measure iteration progress are the iteration backlog (or plan), iteration burndown chart, and the daily stand-up meeting.

The iteration burndown chart, shown in Figure 6-6, is a graph that represents the team's remaining work in the iteration. Each day, team members update their tasks in the iteration backlog with the remaining hours for each task; these daily numbers are summarized and charted on the iteration burndown chart, which plots remaining work over the length of the iteration. As the team starts to work through their tasks, the idea is that the line will start to "burn down"; that is, the graph line will begin to follow a downward trend, representing a decreasing amount of work over the course of the iteration.

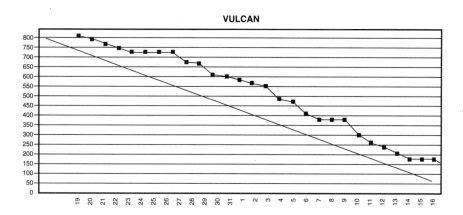

VULCAN

Figure 6-6
An example of a team's iteration burndown chart. The project manager and the team can tell early on that the team's velocity is not as high as originally thought. This will impact what is planned for the next iteration in the agile release plan.

Progress of the iteration can be determined from this graph line. A flat line means that either the team is not updating its remaining work hours, or there is an obstacle preventing progress. An upward spike means that new work was discovered. In Figure 6-6, the team should have approached the product owner around the sixth day of the iteration, as it is clear that the team had overcommitted its work for the iteration. The agile project manager's goal is to remove obstacles that get in the way of completing the functionality that the team committed to in iteration planning. The burndown chart is a first indicator that the iteration is either on or off track, and if the team recognizes that it overcommitted to the iteration, it will discuss this with the customer to determine which low-priority feature should be dropped from the iteration; likewise, if the team undercommitted, the team and customer will figure out which feature to add to the iteration.

The second tool for gauging progress of the iteration is the 15-minute daily stand-up meeting. Team members report their status and impediments to their progress to each other; the agile project manager is on hand to listen for these impediments and take ownership if the team needs his help. External project members, such as stakeholders and managers, are encouraged to attend these daily meetings as observers, but only the team members are allowed to discuss their work. The team members outline the results of inspecting where they are in the iteration and making adaptations to their work plan based on real results.

By synchronizing in the daily stand-up meetings and working together in an ad-hoc fashion throughout the iteration, a team manages its tasks. Sometimes this means that a team member might change the order of his work or delete a task because it is no longer relevant. He will update his team members verbally in case their tasks are related to his, as well as update his tasks in the team's iteration backlog. It's a proactive, team-based approach to managing work within the timebox.

Once the iteration has concluded, the team will provide a high-level report to stakeholders at the iteration review meeting regarding which features it completed, as well as which features it did not complete. This is also a great time to apprise attendees of the status of the release based on the results of the iteration. After the team demonstrates the working features in the iteration review meeting, the team will hold an iteration retrospective to discuss details and actions to take regarding the planning processes in the next iteration planning meeting. Following are some examples of the types of questions that might be asked during an iteration review in order to focus on how the release might be impacted overall:

- What features did the team(s) complete this iteration?
- Was the iteration accomplishment more or less than what was expected?
- Is the team able to fully test the features? If not, what work remains, and how does that impact our release plan?
- What is the team's observed velocity?
- Is this velocity increasing over time? Decreasing?
- What are the factors bringing about the increase or decrease?
- How might this impact the other iterations in the release?

- Should we ask for more iterations? Do we need an iteration to integrate or run performance tests? Or should we remove the lowest-priority features from the release and put them back into the product backlog?
- How does the team feel about the plan based on observed results?

The answers to these questions may indicate a need for a re-baseline and communication of the updated release plan.

In Chapter 7, "Cost Management," we discuss the use of Earned Value Management (EVM) techniques to control costs; there you will also find information about schedule variances should you choose to employ these techniques on your agile project.

The most important thing to remember about managing the release plan and the iteration plan is that "project status" is real time, based on complete increments of functionality. There is a basic assumption that the features being delivered at the end of the iteration are of high quality; that no "technical debt" is carried over from one iteration to the next. Agile release planning management brings the stakeholders and team together in the iteration review meeting to communicate, in person, around the real status of the project: the capability to run tested features.

The idea that the team manages its tasks on a day-to-day basis can be frightening for new agile project managers because they feel a loss of control. Sometimes we meet project managers who feel that their team members cannot be trusted. Letting go and empowering a team can be a challenge, especially when a manager is not accustomed to working in that manner.

Many agile project managers have found that managing the project at a macro—or release—level, is a considerably more valuable use of time. In fact, many project managers we have spoken with say that by allowing the team to manage the day-to-day tasks, they have more time to work on contract negotiation and procurement, manage buy-versus-build decisions, remove obstacles for the team, work on agile reporting (in a program or project portfolio situation), as well as educate and help others understand and work within the iterative and incremental process.

Table 6-7 provides a summary comparison of the traditional and agile approaches to schedule control at the tactical level. In agile parlance, schedule control at the tactical level is simply referred to as "teamwork."

Table 6-7
Schedule Control at the Tactical Level

Traditional	Agile
Update the schedule based on approved changes, and re-baseline.	No changes are allowed in the iteration once the iteration has been planned, so that the team can work the features through to completion without distraction. However, the customer can decide to terminate the iteration if changes are such that they negate the value of the current iteration.
Calculate schedule variance and schedule performance index.	Remind the team of its duty to update the work remaining in the iteration backlog on a daily basis. The team also measures its velocity.
Track and document requested changes.	The customer updates the product and/or release backlog.
Identify and analyze recommended corrective action to get the project back on track.	Facilitate a discussion between the customer and the team to discuss any adaptive action that should be taken—that is, add another iteration, add a team, drop features, terminate the project, and so on.

Summary

This chapter makes the following points:

- An agile release is made up of a series of iterations. Releases can be internal or external, or just simply a period of time (usually quarters).
- We plan strategically for a release and tactically for each iteration.
- We estimate items in the product and/or release backlog at a high level, using "story points"; we estimate tasks in the iteration backlog at a detailed level, using hours.
- Product and release backlog items are referred to as "items," "requirements," "features," or "user stories." Any term is acceptable. However, do note that user stories have a defined format: " As a <type of user> I want to be able to do <feature/function>".

- The agile release plan progress is reviewed at the end of every iteration and adjusted based on conversations between the customer and the team.
- The agile release plan is used to help manage resources. However, agile assumes that the team is fully dedicated for the duration of the project.
- An agile release plan is communicated with the understanding that response to change is expected and built in. It is never meant to be prescriptive or locked down.
- Release and iteration burndown charts provide a first look into the status of the release and iteration, respectively.
- A team's average velocity and the burndown chart are two of the most important measurements of progress against the release backlog.
- Iterations can be thought of as padlocked steel boxes, where work should fill the boxes but not cause it to burst at the seams. This allows the team to work at a sustainable pace and establish a rhythm.
- Features that go into the padlocked boxes are negotiated by the team and the customer based on priority; we work on a "fixed-time, variable scope" model.
- Activity definition is done during iteration planning, where the team defines the tasks required to implement the features selected for the iteration.
- Agile processes do not track duration, because the duration is always the same—it's the length of the iteration. Only work effort is tracked, at the task level.
- Dependencies are discussed and addressed by the team in the iteration planning meeting; task dependencies are managed by the team and project dependencies are managed by the project manager.

Table 6-8 runs down the differences between a traditional and an agile project manager's time management behaviors.

Table 6-8

Agile Project Manager's Change List for Time Management

I used to do this:	Now I do this:
Determine the requirements for the project before developing the project schedule.	Facilitate discussions with the customer and team in order to define the features in detail that are appropriate to the horizon. Help the customer create a product backlog that is easy to maintain.
Work with a resource manager to determine when I would need what types of skill sets, based on the detailed project schedule.	Enjoy the consistency of a dedicated team where resources no longer come and go; continue to work with resource managers on the remaining exceptions based on the needs outlined in the release plan.
Ask for estimates of the tasks required to complete the requirements.	Ensure that the team is providing high-level estimates for the items in the product and/or release backlog and then more granular estimates for tasks as they are defined in the iteration planning meeting.
Identify all task dependencies and adjust the schedule to show the relationships and how best to manage them.	Trust in the team to manage its task dependencies; focus on the broader project dependencies and work with others to ensure proper coordination.
Create the project schedule.	Facilitate release and iteration planning meetings, where the team creates the high-level strategic release plans and the more detailed tactical iteration plans.
Update the project schedule; work diligently with change control to prevent scope creep.	Help the team in updating the burndown charts that indicate iteration and release progress; remind the customer of the need for adjustments in the release and product backlog and product roadmap based on team performance and deliverables accepted each iteration.

Endnotes

1. Ogunnaike. *Process Dynamics, Modeling, and Control.*

2. Austin. *Artful Making.*

3. Coined by Peter Drucker in 1959, a knowledge worker is "one who works primarily with information or one who develops and uses knowledge in the workplace." http://en.wikipedia.org/wiki/knowledge_worker.

4. *PMBOK® Guide*, 143.

5. Don't get confused by the naming conventions for items in the backlog! A feature, user story, and requirement are often the same thing—what distinguishes a user story is the format in which it's written. In this book, we'll refer to requirements, stories, and features and use them interchangeably. For more information on user stories and story points, read Mike Cohn's *User Stories Applied and Agile Estimating and Planning*.

6. Originated by Mike Cohn. For more information, see his book, *User Stories Applied*. (Boston: Addison-Wesley, 2004).

7. *PMBOK® Guide*, 127.

8. Ibid., 128.

9. Ibid., 130.

10. Ibid.

Chapter 7

Cost Management

Project cost management includes the processes involved in planning, estimating, budgeting and controlling costs so that the project can be completed within the approved budget.

—PMBOK® Guide

Fast, cheap, good: you can have any two.

—*Author unknown*

For a project manager, overruns are as certain as death and taxes.

—*Author unknown*

Like beauty, value is in the eye of the beholder. What is priceless art to some is worthless to others. What each of us buys in a store differs based on our individual needs and desires, and value is that internal discussion or decision that tells us that what we are about to purchase seems like it is worth at least the price we will pay at that particular moment in time. Great value is when what we think we get far exceeds the price we pay, such as when we find the best discount on a set of golf clubs or a seller eager to move out of a beautiful home. Sometimes we purchase items hoping that value will increase over time; like wine, the true value isn't apparent today. It is merely speculated on for the future. Often, in the technical world, objects lose value over time because newer items are introduced quickly into the market (such as when I purchased a small MP3 player a few years ago, only to be envious when the iPod came out a month later).

When it comes to value in software, we are looking for features and functionality that make our jobs easier, perhaps more automated, and certainly less complex. We don't want to be overwhelmed by bells and whistles, yet we don't want the design to be so simplistic that we feel that we are missing out on something. We don't want to be forced to think too much about the software that we use; we want to get started "out of the box," with minimal training and instruction. In this fast world that we live in, we'd rather not spend the time to read a user's manual.

What we've learned in building software is that we cannot maximize customer value without working closely with the customer. All of the questions surrounding a customer's subjective interpretation of value, price points, market timeliness, and product "coolness," for example, must be considered in product development, whether built for the internal or external customer. Often an internal product manager works with the external customer and/or users to understand what new features are necessary or which existing features may be merely refined, all with careful consideration of not overstuffing the product or overwhelming the user. As project managers, by estimating, budgeting for, and managing a project's cost we can help the customer see the point at which he will receive the most value.

The first step in determining a project's cost is to understand the time constraint and the circumstances necessary to deliver the product. Employing agile methods on a project does not mean that the agile project manager or team no longer has to estimate and stick to a budget. A project manager must pay attention to the project's delivery cost, as well as additional life-cycle costs, the cost of poor quality, and other indirect costs, just like he does in a traditional setting.

This chapter explores the building blocks of agile project cost management—top-down cost estimating and whole team involvement—in order to help you understand how to estimate and manage cost within your agile project. Although every budgeting process will be different from one organization to the next, we give you some ideas about budgeting for and funding projects based on preliminary cost estimates. This chapter also talks about how to enable the business (or customers) to control its costs by giving insight into the project's progress. In doing so, agile project managers can teach the customer how to maximize value. Product returns in the U.S. amount to over 100 billion dollars per year; half of the products returned have nothing wrong with them—customers cannot figure out how to use them because of feature creep![1] Although this book doesn't delve too deeply into this complex subject, we do hope to get you thinking about what it means to deliver business value, and we provide you with some additional resources. In agile projects, the agile project manager does not make decisions about cost; he or she facilitates the team and the business/customer to collaborate and negotiate these decisions.

Cost Estimating

It's very difficult, if not impossible, to predict costs for a complex situation. I can't drive into the next state to visit my in-laws without encountering some unforeseen cost, whether it's the two cents difference in gasoline or the coffee stop halfway through the trip. This is exactly why estimating is called estimating; a quick Google search on the Web for definitions of estimating returns results such as "an approximate calculation of quantity" and "a statement indicating the likely cost of some job." None of the definitions returned indicated that the word **estimate** means to exactly predict the future.

Although it's easy to estimate the cost of adding a 12'×12' wooden deck on the back of my home, it's very difficult to estimate the cost of building a software system. Why is this? Well, the very act of building software is artistic in nature; based on perfecting a series of run-throughs, it is never finished.[2] Software systems *emerge* due to information acquired throughout the development lifecycle, as well as frequent customer changes. The intricacies of software systems are never accurately predicted up front, and many shops have given up on the idea of big design up front (BDUF) because it's an expensive exercise in a sea of constant change.

Therefore, we can only estimate what we know and build in allowances for change. We must estimate costs for the period of time the team thinks it will need to create the software or enhancements, and then keep the customer informed of the project's progress so that he or she may make important value decisions along the way.

Agile Project Costs Are Best Calculated by the Delivery Team

In traditional project planning, the project manager is responsible for estimating project costs. In agile projects, the team indirectly estimates costs by first providing feature estimates to aid in release planning. As you saw in the previous chapter, an agile release plan, the output of the release planning meeting, represents team ownership of estimates and consensus to the plan. This release plan—a number of iterations—can be converted into cost estimates, as we show later in the chapter.

For the most part, team members are dedicated to the agile delivery team throughout the life of the project; therefore, estimating the human resources costs for an agile project should be much less complicated than in traditional projects. The project manager takes the fully loaded cost for the team members and multiplies that by the number of iterations projected by the team in the release plan. Of course, the project manager factors in all of the other direct and indirect costs that are typically considered in the project cost estimate; the team can help supply this information as well.

Because the team may not have any experience with or understand the project lifecycle in its entirety, an experienced project manager can contribute by educating the team about cost topics such as labor, materials, equipment, services, and facilities. Spreading this knowledge to the team members will help them identify areas of additional costs at the beginning and during the life of the project.

Many agile project managers choose to shield team members from this administrative burden and listen for cost impacts during the daily stand-up and other meetings. However, don't rule out the idea that some on the team may want to be involved in these details. Having a "Budget Task Force" staffed by you and volunteers from the team can ease the burden on the project manager, increase visibility into the cost structures, and allow team members to become full participants in their work environment.

Many experiences have shown that the estimates provided by a team during release planning are far better than what one or two people can provide. By engaging the team members to provide estimates for features, as well as empowering them to plan their release, they will construct a plan that they can commit to, live with, and feel empowered to carry out.

Agile Projects Are Estimated Top-Down Rather Than Bottom-Up

In traditional project planning, a project manager will create a work breakdown structure (WBS) and then create tasks to support each lowest-level WBS. The estimates on each task, combined with "loading" resources onto tasks, provide a total cost for the entire project. This is known as "bottom-up estimating" and usually occurs by using a project management tool.

Agile projects are estimated top-down because it is impossible to accurately predict the work at the task level, along with task dependencies, for a software development project up front. Additionally, we estimate top-down in order to make comfortable room for the requirements changes that come from collaborating with our customers about the emerging product. The top-down approach allows teams to estimate with detail appropriate to the time horizon by using a just-in-time elaboration of details. For example, a team should only plan one release at a time: *this release*. Likewise, a team should only task out one iteration plan at a time: *this iteration*. Estimating top-down and relative to the horizon lowers the upfront planning costs as well as the cost of change later in the project.

As we have mentioned previously, the first best time to estimate costs for an agile project is when the team has agreed on a release plan after a release planning meeting. This initial cost estimate will be revisited by the customer every iteration once functionality has been delivered. Cost estimating in agile is another representation of the "interactions of the individuals" (the team) working together with the customer to determine which features will be completed in the release and how long the release will take.

Table 7-1 is a cost-estimating worksheet based on the discoveries of the team in release planning. First, the team members estimated that it would take three one-month iterations to finish the release. They also assumed that, for the most part, they were dedicated throughout the release. They discovered that Misha wouldn't be available for Iteration 3 because she is going out on maternity leave, so they know they'll have to get a contractor to take her place. Additionally, the team remembered that they have a training session to attend during Iteration 2. The project manager was able to factor in all of these assumptions and known events, as well as additional costs related to equipment, software, and other items, to derive the total release cost estimate. This is a very simplistic view, of course, but we hope that you see with dedicated teams it is much simpler to aggregate resource costs based on the estimated number of iterations by the team in release planning.

Table 7-1
Agile Cost Estimation Worksheet (Based on Output of Release Planning)

Release A							
Sprint *n*		**Sprint *n*+1**		**Sprint *n*+2**			
Bobby	10,000.00	Bobby	10,000.00	Bobby	10,000.00		
Jeanne	8,000.00	Jeanne	8,000.00	Jeanne	8,000.00		
Ted	11,000.00	Ted	11,000.00	Ted	11,000.00		
Liam	7,500.00	Liam	7,500.00	Liam	7,500.00		
Nellie	10,000.00	Nellie	10,000.00	Nellie	10,000.00		
Misha	9,000.00	Misha	9,000.00				
		Eric	4,000.00	UI Contractor	16,000.00		
Total	**55,500.00**	**Total**	**59,500.00**	**Total**	**62,500.00**	**Total Human Costs**	**177,500.00**
Server	25,000.00			Server-Alpha	25,000.00		
Environment	30,000.00	Training	10,000.00				
Testing tools	40,000.00	Testing license	2,500.00	Testing license	2,500.00		
PM tool	5,000.00	PM tool	2,000.00	PM tool	2,000.00		
Total	100,000.00	Total	14,500.00	Total	29,500.00	**Total Other Costs**	**144,000.00**
						Total Est. Cost	**321,500.00**

Teams Can Present Alternatives during Release Planning

Agile projects have the ability to always be on time, and within budget, if the scope is flexible. Teams plan releases with customers based on what's in the product backlog and their average velocity. Difficult trade-offs still have to be made from time to time, but the delivery team begins to build credibility with the rest of the organization through reliable iteration deliveries so that the panic button isn't pressed every time a feature doesn't make a release. These situations are also diffused because the team has focused on delivering the most important features first; often these scope negotiations occur around low-level, "nice-to-have" features. The organization learns that there can always be another release if desired or necessary, either until the customer is satisfied, the priorities of the business change, or the money runs out.

Likewise, the team will present alternatives along the way. These alternatives may translate to cost savings or increased expense. It is up to the project stakeholders or customers to make the final decision regarding cost and up to the project manager to make sure information is bubbled up from the team so that timely decisions can be made.

How can stakeholders or customers make this decision? Well, if you look at the aggregated project costs as determined in Table 7-1, the release decision could be made when the delivered business value equals or surpasses project costs.

Cost Estimates Become More Refined throughout the Life of the Project

Initial cost estimates from the release plan can be updated at the end of each iteration based on information about what was completed and what is remaining in the product backlog. Costs can be recalculated in terms of a recalculated number of iterations based on the team's velocity. Finally, as teams are dedicated and stay together for an extended duration, their iteration estimates become increasingly more accurate. The combination of established velocity, an increase in the level of estimation accuracy, and knowing what's done after every iteration makes it very easy to understand the cost performance of the project.

Realistic Estimates

I conducted a 100-person release planning session one August for 11 teams who were all to deliver a legacy rewrite. Each team had a particular module of the system in its charge. After a lengthy two days of planning with breakout sessions and lots of product owner involvement, the teams determined that the project would take around eight months to deliver all 50 features in the product backlog. Senior management wanted a delivery in December—in four months, or half the time! Teams started working in two-week iterations, and by the time November came, teams were meeting with product owners to drop functionality, as predicted in the August release planning. In fact, the December release was severely scaled back, and only released in limited availability. After the new year, the team resumed work on the lower-priority features, and eventually delivered the entire release in May, nine months after release planning! The team's original projection—based entirely on complexity estimations—was off by only one month.

Through focusing on top-down estimation techniques and a team approach to release planning, agile project costs can be estimated within generally accepted boundaries.

Table 7-2 provides a summary comparison of traditional and agile approaches to cost estimation.

Table 7-2
Cost Estimating

Traditional	Agile
Activity cost estimates are prepared in both detail and summary form using techniques such as bottom-up estimating for review by management and finance.	Cost estimates are prepared by the agile project manager and/or the volunteer budget task force, using top-down techniques and output from the release planning meeting.
Requested changes are processed for review using the formal change control process.	The release backlog is updated to reflect new and changing requirements. From these updates, the team can determine how the release plan will be impacted (which may then impact the cost estimates).

Cost Budgeting

The *PMBOK® Guide* has this to say about cost budgeting: "Cost budgeting involves aggregating the estimated costs of individual schedule activities or work packages to establish a total cost baseline for measuring performance."[3]

In traditional project planning, work by the team is not authorized until after cost budgeting has taken place. In agile, some work must be authorized prior to project kickoff so that the team can at least engage in release planning; the resulting release plan will then establish the cost baseline and subsequent budget. Once the team comes to consensus on the release plan, and the other associated costs are known, the project manager and/or the budget task force can aggregate the cost per iteration to get the cost baseline. The idea is that the estimates will be better by having the entire team involved in planning, potentially offsetting these costs with higher-quality estimates and team consensus on the plan.

Aggregating the total costs for iterations creates the cost baseline. In Table 7-1, the cost baseline for the project is $321,500. This number will be revisited every iteration and recalculated based on the changes to the release plan. Let's imagine that the customer sees the product increment at the end of the first iteration and thinks of three new features he would like to have. The team estimates the features with story points and determines that the additional features would take one more iteration to build. This translates to an added cost of $62,500. If the customer decides to authorize spending for these additional features, then the new cost baseline becomes $383,000, considering no other expenses are involved. The customer may decide that the additional $62,500 is too much to spend for three features, and change his mind to add only one of the features, Feature A. The team can figure out a cost for this one feature based on its average velocity. Let's say our team has an average velocity of ten points per iteration, and it estimated that Feature A is two points. Because the feature estimate is 20% of the velocity, the team determines that Feature A would cost the customer about $12,000. The customer has new data to work with and can make a decision to extend the team's work by a small iteration, or trade Feature A for another feature in the original set that hasn't been worked on yet.

Reserve Analysis and Funding Limit Reconciliations

A buffer iteration in the last release of the project may be a practical way for new teams to allocate a contingency in which to address some final finishing features. An example of this would be if our team had estimated four iterations of work right away because it knew that the customer always adds features once he sees emerging product. A buffer iteration is not the same as a hardening iteration. A hardening iteration is strictly for readying the product for production—capturing screenshots for marketing materials, training the help desk, and other small tweaks and final tests that couldn't be conducted within the regular iterations.

The *PMBOK® Guide* also mentions funding limit reconciliations. Organizations are not too keen on huge variances in the amount of budget expenditures from work package to work package. Thankfully, in agile projects, dedicated teams help stabilize the costs throughout the lifecycle of the project. Variances in expected costs can be noted early (such as in Misha's case earlier) and reevaluated on an iteration-by-iteration basis. Regardless of the process you use, you will need to verify the budget against funding requirements within your organization.

Table 7-3 presents a summary comparison of traditional and agile approaches to cost budgeting.

Table 7-3
Cost Budgeting

Traditional	Agile
Prepare a cost baseline for the entire project and derive funding requirements for the project from this baseline.	The team provides the release plan; from this release plan, the cost baseline can be derived by aggregating the costs of all iterations.
Update the cost management plan with updates from the approved changes.	Update the release plan cost baseline after every iteration.

Cost Control

The *PMBOK® Guide* characterizes cost control in the following way: "Project cost control searches out the positive and negative variances and is part of Integrated Change Control."[4] The same holds true for an agile project; the agile project manager makes visible the team's velocity. A higher-than-expected velocity could mean a lower number of iterations than initially planned; conversely, a lower-than-expected velocity could mean more iterations to implement the release backlog. With this information visible to the customer, the customer can then negotiate scope, authorize an increase in budget, or change the project's release date in response to what's happening.

The *PMBOK® Guide* specifically states that controlling costs "includes influencing the factors that create changes to the cost baseline."[5] In other words, a project manager and/or the team may decide that it is worthwhile to contract phases of development in order to reduce project costs; these lower costs would then factor back into the cost baseline, and all actual costs would then be compared against the revised baseline. Another type of cost control is the decision to buy instead of build a solution (for example, a shopping cart). The team may investigate a third-party shopping cart and find that the cost of buying it is much less than building it from scratch. This lower-cost alternative, if approved by the customer, would be reflected in the new cost baseline. Often, the delivery team will identify and suggest reusable technologies in these types of situations; it is another reason why allowing the team to self-manage is so important. Having the ability to go back to the customer with a lower cost for building a feature allows him to spend the found savings on another feature.

As previously mentioned, if the actual velocity is lower than projected in the initial cost baseline, the project will take more iterations to complete. Sometimes there are ways a team can improve its velocity (co-location and using XP practices, for example), and you can help facilitate this knowledge in the team's retrospective and help team members make improvements for future iterations. The bigger task for the project manager is creating awareness in the customer and other stakeholders that output isn't as high as originally estimated by the team. It's a difficult message to communicate, but it is reliable information upon which stakeholders can make timely, informed decisions.

Managing the Release Backlog

Changes to the cost baseline in agile projects are handled through proper utilization of the prioritized backlog. Adding or reprioritizing a feature in the product backlog constitutes what we traditionally know as scope change (or scope creep); it's called "expected change" in agile terminology. Affixing estimates to these changes enables us to truly understand how the change impacts the bottom line (our cost baseline), and the customer can make changes appropriately. This is a bit easier in agile projects; the team can assign a complexity rating (story points) to the new feature/user story and determines whether this will add or remove iterations from the initial determination, at which point the cost baseline can be updated.

The project manager and the team can then negotiate with the customer to either spend more, spend less, or attempt to equalize spending with the baseline. The agile project manager facilitates the team and the customer being able to discuss alternatives and make the best decision based on cost and benefit.

Locking Down the Iteration

The agile project manager, along with the team, shares ownership to "prevent incorrect, inappropriate, or unapproved changes from being included in the reported cost or resource usage." [6] In other words, the agile team will lock down the iteration once it has completed iteration planning in an attempt to prevent unapproved changes that might have a downstream effect on the overall agreed-upon budget for the release. Any changes requested by the customer once the iteration has begun must be negotiated by the customer and team; there might be budgetary considerations that will affect the cost baseline and release plan, not to mention derail a team's planning effort and hard-won consensus.

Similarly, when the team discovers that an estimate has either been greatly over- or greatly underestimated, it has the responsibility to alert the customer so that proper decisions can be made. It is not the team's responsibility to decide how to spend the budget of the project; nor is it the project manager's. Rather, both must discuss with the customer the implications of such changes and make the best decision based on the knowledge they have.

Informing Stakeholders of Cost Changes

Cost control also means "informing appropriate stakeholders of approved changes."[7] The way an agile team can go about this is to provide an iteration delta table (see Chapter 10, "Communications Management") to stakeholders at the iteration review and demo meeting. Of course, if faster communication of changes is necessary, the project manager should take on this administrative burden.

AgileEVM (Earned Value Management) to Measure Cost Performance

Another tool used in traditional project execution (especially within the government) is Earned Value Management (EVM). As it turns out, EVM can be utilized for agile projects, too. A 2006 study and whitepaper titled "AgileEVM—Earned Value Management in Scrum Projects"[8] explores this technique on agile projects. We are including an excerpt from the whitepaper to help you understand the mapping of EVM terms and calculations, as well as the basic set of assumptions for each method.

A basic set of assumptions is necessary when using AgileEVM:

- Measure progress at the release level, not the iteration or product level.
- Measure progress at the end of each iteration, when actual iteration velocity and actual iteration costs are known.
- Functionality is "done" at the end of each iteration.

Table 7-4 is a comparison of AgileEVM to traditional EVM terms. We encourage you to read the whitepaper for more details on AgileEVM as a way to measure cost performance. In the excerpts from the whitepaper, the Scrum term "sprint" is used. You can consider this term to be, for all intents and purposes, synonymous with the general agile term "iteration."

Table 7-4

Comparison of AgileEVM (Earned Value Management) and Traditional EVM Terms (©2006 IEEE)[9]

Performance Measurement Baseline (PMB)	
Traditional EVM	The sum of all work package schedule estimates (duration and effort).
AgileEVM	Total number of story points planned for a release (PRP).

Schedule Baseline—Often Integrated in PMB	
Traditional EVM	The sum of all work packages for each time period calculated for the total duration.
AgileEVM	The total number of planned iterations (PS) multiplied by sprint length.

Budget at Complete (BAC)	
Traditional EVM	The planned budget for the release or project.
AgileEVM	The planned budget for the release.

Planned Percent Complete (PPC)	
Traditional EVM	What percentage complete did we expect to be at this point in the project? Can be a subjective estimate or a calculation of the dollar value of the cumulative tasks planned to be complete by this point in time divided by the performance baseline.
AgileEVM	The number of current sprint (n) divided by the total number of planned sprints.

Actual Percent Complete (APC)	
Traditional EVM	The dollar value of work packages actually completed divided by total dollar value of the budget at completion.
AgileEVM	The total number of story points completed (potentially shippable increments) divided by the total number of story points planned.

What AgileEVM, like traditional EVM, does not provide is the actual amount of business value delivered to the customer. Calculating business value is a complex task; we want to understand the answers to questions such as, "If we implement the feature, how much revenue will the business gain?" "When will we recognize that revenue?" "Is it a seasonal gain or yearly?" "How timely is the feature?" "Can we build it in an intuitive, simplistic fashion?" "Does the user desire a simple interface, or does he like complexity?" "How will implementing this feature impact the overall supply chain—our customers' customers?" "How will our business benefit from that impact?" "Should we invest in the feature today given that we know the product will be retired early next year?"

As you can see, determining the true value of delivering a feature is tricky. Trying to assign a dollar amount is difficult given the subjectivity of value. It is beyond the scope of this book to help you determine how to valuate product backlog items from the business or customer's perspective, but we encourage you to talk with your product owners and customers about what value means to them and how they'll know it when they see it. At the end of the day, Earned Value Management (whether traditional or AgileEVM) simply measures how much the customer has spent relative to the point in time of measurement in the project. "Without the need to manage cost performance, AgileEVM does not add significant value above traditional burndown methods."[10] We urge you to consider the deeper meaning of value and engage your customer and project team in conversations about this topic.

Table 7-5 provides a summary comparison of traditional and agile approaches to cost control.

Table 7-5
Cost Control

Traditional	Agile
Update the cost estimates and cost baseline based on approved changes, new forecasts, and performance measurements such as EV.	Update the release plan cost baseline using the team's iterative learning (as well as other tools you may choose to use, such as AgileEVM).
Take corrective action and/or submit change requests to a formal change control process in order to bring costs back into alignment with the original plan.	The team refines its forecast each iteration, updating the release plan, the release backlog, and cost estimates.

Summary

The chapter can be summarized as follows:

- Estimating costs for an agile project is a team activity and starts with the release planning meeting.
- Inviting volunteers from the team to be a part of the budget task force ensures the team's ownership of the project as a whole and leads to better estimating and control.
- Educating the team on different costs associated with the project will help mitigate the risk of "unknown unknowns."
- All projects, including agile projects, carry the difficulties of making tough tradeoffs between cost, schedule, and scope.
- Agile projects are estimated top-down with detail and accuracy appropriate to the time horizon: the farther away the deadline, the grosser the estimate; the closer the deadline, the more detailed the estimate.
- Cost estimates become more refined throughout the project's life-cycle.
- Cost control occurs at the release level; cost baselines are updated based on the deliverables of each iteration, velocity, and customer changes to scope.
- AgileEVM is a valuable technique when cost performance must be measured.

Table 7-6 compares the cost management behaviors of project managers managing traditional and agile projects.

Table 7-6

Agile Project Manager's Change List for Cost Management

I used to do this:	Now I do this:
Resource load a schedule in order to derive costs.	Dedicate teams and facilitate release planning to create a forecast and derive costs.
Get resources after the cost budget is established.	Have the team engage in estimating the items in the backlog and release planning in order to establish the cost budget.
Try to predict every task cost upfront using bottom-up estimating.	Plan top-down and establish reserves in order to plan for the unknown.
Use EVM as part of my regular budget reporting.	Use AgileEVM if there is a need for this type of performance reporting.
Take responsibility for the budget and the delivery of the project's product.	Invite the team, including the customer or product owner, to take responsibility for the budget as part of the budget task force; the team remains responsible for the delivery of the project.

Endnotes

1. James Surowiecki. "Feature Presentation." *The New Yorker Magazine,* May 28, 2007, 28.

2. Austin, *Artful Making.*

3. *PMBOK® Guide*, 167.

4. Ibid., 169.

5. Ibid., 171.

6. Ibid.

7. Ibid.

8. Brent Barton et al. "AgileEVM—Earned Value Management in Scrum Projects." (paper presented at the annual Agile conference, Minneapolis, MN, July 23–28, 2006), 9.

9. Ibid.

10. Ibid., 15.

Chapter 8

Quality Management

Project Quality Management processes include all the activities of
the performing organization that determine quality policies,
objectives, and responsibilities so that the project will satisfy the
needs for which it was undertaken.

—PMBOK® Guide

A product is not 'quality' because it is hard to make and costs a lot of
money…. 'Quality' in a product or service is not what the supplier
puts in. It is what the customer gets out and is willing to pay for.
Customers pay only for what is of use to them and gives them value.
Nothing else constitutes 'quality'.

—Peter Drucker

Making quality certain means getting people to do better all the
worthwhile things they ought to be doing anyway.

—Philip B. Crosby

Quality always seems to be the last phase in traditional plan-driven projects,
going against the *PMBOK® Guide* ideal of prevention over detection. Many
divisions labeled "quality assurance" (QA) are really quality control (QC)
organizations designed solely to find bugs, not prevent them from being
coded in the first place. QA staff in these organizations know to expect
shortened timeframes for testing, specs that don't match the product delivered, and little interest in their input until the last few weeks of the project.

As one of our QA colleagues used to say, "We must be done testing because today is the release date!"

Agile software development gives these disenfranchised QA personnel the opportunity to fulfill their original mission: the prevention of defects and the fostering of continuous improvement. You'll recall that agile teams are cross-functional, meaning the team is made up of coders, testers, technical writers, and anyone else who contributes to the delivery of running, tested features. Therefore, QA is brought back into the analysis and design of the product, keeping these team members heavily involved in decision-making throughout the entire lifecycle. Because incremental code is being developed each iteration, QA is now testing at the very beginning of the project lifecycle instead of waiting for something to be "thrown over the wall" at the end. And because throughput is increased as a result of agile's iterative and incremental development, QA is finding itself with a need to become more technical as it must automate much of its current manual testing activities in order to keep up with the rest of the team.

This chapter begins with a discussion of quality planning and then moves on to cover both quality assurance and quality control.

Quality Planning

According to the *PMBOK® Guide,* "Quality is planned, designed, and built in—not inspected in."[1] Typically, quality planning demands that a plan should be defined that covers how to perform quality assurance and quality control activities as they relate to standard practices and to organization policies and procedures. Agile team members still address this need and determine what tools and technology they will use in writing, running, and reporting tests and results. They also determine what metrics will be tracked in each iteration. It is important to engage developers in this definition, because they will be contributing to testing by writing unit tests and helping with the framework for automating regression and acceptance testing. Customers or product owners must also be involved, because they should be helping to define acceptance criteria and create and run the acceptance tests. In agile, everyone contributes to defining, maintaining, reviewing, and enhancing the quality of the product and the process.

Table 8-1 provides a summary comparison of the traditional and agile approaches to quality planning. There is no formal term for quality planning in the agile framework. It is part of the planning discussion held during release planning and/or iteration planning meetings.

Table 8-1
Quality Planning

Traditional	Agile
Meetings with QA to determine how to implement quality policies and standards.	Ask the customer and the team to determine appropriate quality policies and standards.
Results in a formal document outlining the quality management plan and process improvement plan.	Results in team working agreements and coding/testing standards that are usually documented informally.
Advise the team of the metrics that will be tracked during the project.	Gain consensus from the team on what metrics it feels will be helpful in determining quality and discuss the use of metrics that are helpful to management.

Quality Assurance

Quality assurance, with its focus on preventing defects, is translated into the agile practice of having committed QA resources on the development team that participate in decision-making on a daily basis, throughout the lifecycle of the project. The QA team members' input during elaboration and design helps developers write better code. More "what-if" scenarios are considered and planned for, as the collaboration between coders and testers gives the coders more insights than if they were to have planned the work on their own. Likewise, the testers gain added insight into the expected functionality from the coders and the customer and are able to write more effective test cases for the product.

Another purpose of quality assurance is continuous improvement. The agile principles of constant feedback and responding to change support this idea, and stopping points to inspect and adapt are built in to all agile frameworks. Owned by the team, continuous improvement is practiced in planning meetings, daily activities, and in particular, during iteration reviews and retrospectives.

Demo, Review, and Retrospective

At the end of each iteration, a demo of the working code is provided to interested stakeholders as well as a review and a retrospective on how the iteration went. This is the team's opportunity to collect and share feedback and recommend changes both in the process and in the product. Although the demo is open to everyone, the review and retrospective portions of the meeting are limited to the team. This is the team members' opportunity to acknowledge what they've learned in the iteration and make changes to improve their ability to deliver in the next iteration. You can see an example of a demo, review, and retrospective meeting agenda in Figure 8-1.

The review allows a team to review the facts collected in the iteration; the team essentially conducts an audit on the process and team productivity. In the review, the team analyzes its metrics in order to understand its performance and to see if there are any changes that need to be made in order to help improve performance. Items commonly reviewed include the burndown chart, features committed to versus features accepted, number of times the build broke, number of defects found (and fixed) in the iteration, and number of outstanding defects remaining. Teams should track metrics that they find helpful in their quest for continuous improvement. For example, a team just starting out with little-to-no test automation may decide that tracking the number of regression tests that have been automated is a necessary metric to maintain; then, once automation of the old manual tests is complete, this metric can be dropped.

Demo, Review, and Retrospective Meeting Agenda

- *Ground rules, review of purpose and agenda (Project manager)*
- *What are all the features we committed to completing in this iteration? (Team)*
- *Of these, which ones did we actually complete? (Team)*
- *Were there any additional features that we completed in this iteration? (Team)*
- *What happened to the stories we did not complete? (Team)*
- *Demo of the working code. (Team member)*
- *What feedback do we have about the product? (Product owner)*
- *How does this feedback affect the product backlog and our goals for the next iteration or release? (Product owner)*
  - *End of the Demo –*
- *What metrics should we review? What have we learned from these metrics? (Team)*
- *Are there any additional metrics we should begin tracking? (Team)*
  - *End of the Review –*
- *What worked well for us in this iteration? (Team)*
- *What did not work well? (Team)*
- *What recommendations do we have? (Team)*
- *Of these recommendations, which ones do we want to act on for the next iteration? (Team)*
- *Of these recommendations that we will act on, what are those actions, and how will we know when we've succeeded? (Team)*
- *What decisions have we made here today? (Team)*
  - *End of the Retrospective –*
- *Close: empty parking lot, action items, next steps (Project manager)*

Figure 8-1
Demo, review, and retrospective meeting agenda

A qualitative approach is also used in auditing the process, and this is referred to as the retrospective. A recognized exercise in the iteration retrospective is to engage the team in answering what went well in the iteration, what did not go well, and based on this information, what changes should be made going forward in the next iteration. Other retrospective activities may include conducting a root cause analysis, defining team working agreements, and recording decisions and identifying action items. You can see the results of a retrospective in Figures 8-2, 8-3, 8-4, and 8-5.

Figure 8-2
What went well?

What Worked Well

- We stayed focused the entire iteration.
- Visibility into what everyone was doing.
- Stand-ups kept us all on the same page.
- Liked being involved from the very beginning.
- The product owner loves the team!
- Liked having smaller, fewer, well-defined tasks.
- I had the sense we were actually making progress.
- Having the list of tasks in front of me every day was great.
- Getting prioritization and information from the product owner so I knew I was doing the right thing.
- Liked seeing what we could really accomplish.
- Great information sharing!
- Liked not having to constantly repeat things.

Figure 8-3
What didn't go well?

What Didn't Work Well

- Dev. tasks done late in the iteration made test and acceptance difficult.
- Don't like the structure of the planning meeting.
- There were more support issues than expected.
- We bit off more than we could chew.
- We didn't account for external work.
- Planning meetings ran too long.
- Time-slicing is killing me.
- Too much "new": new methodology, new tool, new team, new branching structure.
- Our definition of "done" is too hard to achieve.
- We didn't get to see the GUI until late in the iteration.
- I had my own tasks, but I spent more time helping others with their tasks.
- I didn't get all my tasks done.
- Felt tremendous pressure to unblock tasks.
- Had to work overtime.

What Recommendations Do We Have?

- *Need to find a way to dedicate the resources.*
- *Need to condense these meetings.*
- *Take into account the extra things that are expected of you when estimating.*
- *Need to figure out what to do with unfinished features.*
- *We need to do release planning.*
- *Define communications standards for communicating outside our team.*
- *We need to have a code freeze date so we can get our testing done.*
- *We need to start investigating tools to automate our testing.*
- *Training on how to write better user stories.*
- *We can't commit to as much work in the next iteration.*

Figure 8-4
What recommendations do we have?

What Decisions Have We Made? What Actions Will We Take?

- *Decide what to do with unfinished stories as part of Monday's iteration planning meeting.*
- *Set a code freeze date before the end of the iteration.*
- *At Monday's iteration planning meeting, share the things that are pulling you away from this project.*
- *Remember: We committed to 56 points in this iteration and only did 40 points, so on Monday we will commit to no more than 40 points worth of stories.*
- *Action item: Jay to meet with the CEO on Monday afternoon regarding time-slicing issues.*

Figure 8-5
What decisions have we made? Action items?

The *PMBOK® Guide* states that audits may be conducted by third parties.[2] Typically it is the agile project manager who performs this iterative review and retrospective facilitation function, but in more formal quality audit environments a third-party facilitator could be brought in.

Swapping Roles

An organization that wanted its agile project managers to focus more on participating in the reviews and retrospectives rather than on facilitating decided to "swap" project managers during these meetings. Project Manager B would come to Team A's meeting and facilitate, allowing Project Manager A to take off her facilitator hat and put on her developer, architect, analyst, or tester hat and voice concerns and observations. Once Team A had completed its meeting, Project Manager A would then head to Team B's meeting and facilitate its review and retrospective, giving Project Manager B the opportunity to focus on participation.

I've also seen a team actually use a hat—the Project Leader would wear the hat when in facilitation mode, but take it off when he wanted to contribute as part of the team. It was an immediate visual reference for the team, who could literally see what role the individual was playing at any given time.

Keep in mind that there is a clear difference between agile review and retrospective meeting facilitation by the agile project manager, and an audit performed by an external party. The former requires full involvement and participation of the team, whereas the latter is often a series of interviews with individuals reviewing documented proof that a defined process is being followed, and that the product is being created in a valid and verifiable fashion. Even though agile audits, or reviews and retrospectives, provide proof of these things through the use of informal documentation and team consensus, your organization may require something more formal (for example, in keeping with FDA or Sarbanes-Oxley audit requirements).

As an agile project manager, you will have to work with your auditors to provide them with the

Balancing Product Features with Audit Requirements

As an agile project manager on a corporate financial project, I had to pass a Sarbanes-Oxley audit. I met with our internal auditors and together we determined the minimal documentation required in order to pass the audit. Some of the items I could produce myself, thereby enabling the team to continue to focus on the work at hand. But other items required their participation and meant some changes in our process. Therefore, during a discussion in our review meeting, we created audit-specific items and added them to the release backlog. Our product owner immediately moved them to the top of the list to be worked in the next iteration, because she needed the project to pass the audit in order to put the application into production. It meant fewer features were completed (we lost almost an entire iteration of features in order to focus on documentation) but we did pass the audit—on our first review, no less!

information they need, with the least amount of disruption to the team as possible and with a minimum of waste. See Chapter 14, "How Will I Work with Other Teams Who Aren't Agile?" for more information.

Table 8-2 provides a summary comparison of the traditional and agile approaches to quality assurance. In agile terminology, quality assurance is referred to as the "demo, review, and retrospective."

Table 8-2
Quality Assurance

Traditional	Agile
	Include quality personnel as part of the project team and involve them from the beginning, encouraging their input in all product development activities
Conduct audits	Conduct iteration demos, reviews, and retrospectives
Conduct process analysis	Conduct process analysis
Identify requested changes and recommended corrective action	Identify recommendations for change obtained during the review and retrospective meeting and corresponding action items needed to implement the change

Quality Control

Traditional quality control places its emphasis on finding defects that have already slipped into the system and working with developers to eliminate those defects. In agile, this bug-checking is done within the iteration, using techniques such as daily builds and smoke tests, automated regression testing, unit testing, functional and exploratory testing, and acceptance testing. And everyone participates—no one is exempt from the tasks of ensuring that the feature coded meets the customer's expectations. The goal is to find and fix all the bugs in order to have the feature accepted by the customer by the end of the iteration.

Understanding precisely what constitutes acceptance is determined during the iteration planning meeting. Here the team not only defines what "done" means for the iteration overall but also listens as the customer defines acceptance criteria for each feature in the iteration backlog. This way, the team members have a clear vision of the work that needs to be performed and how they will know when they're done.

If the feature is found to still have defects at the end of the iteration, then that feature should not be accepted by the customer. It is up to the customer to decide next steps, and there are many to choose from. Some examples include the following:

- The feature could be pulled and given a lowered priority, meaning that it may be revisited in a later iteration.
- The feature could remain in the code base, while the defects are entered into the backlog and given a high priority so that they are worked in the next iteration.
- If the defect is a minor flaw, the customer may go ahead and accept the feature, while adding the defect to the backlog as a lower -priority item to address in a future iteration.
- Portions of the feature may work and be acceptable, indicating that perhaps the feature was too large for the iteration. Here, the item can be split so that the piece that is working is accepted, while the piece that is not acceptable is returned to the backlog as a new and smaller item.

Paying on Technical Debt

If teams aren't careful, they can build up what's called "technical debt." Technical debt occurs when the system isn't functioning properly and yet the team continues to add new features rather than fix existing problems. We've seen many teams fall into their old habits of thinking that the bugs can be fixed at the end of the project and just keep adding new features and dropping the defects (with a lower priority) into the backlog. Naturally they end up with the same problems they had with their old methodology: At the end of the project they scramble to get the product into an acceptable state, working long hours and often having to scrap the delivery due to product flaws. To prevent this, the team must pay attention to their velocity and reduce what they can commit to in each iteration until they are able to complete the features through to acceptance by the customer. If the product is in bad shape, the team must stop adding new features and work to make the existing product one that is stable and potentially shippable. We've had many teams have up to three iterations where they've done nothing but fix bugs and refactor code. Technical debt is like credit card debt—it builds up and is harder to pay down each billing cycle.

The *PMBOK® Guide* lists a variety of tools to use in monitoring quality levels, such as cause-and-effect diagrams, control charts, flowcharting, histograms, and others. Although it is not common to see them in use in an agile software development project, this does not mean they cannot be used, particularly if it makes sense in your environment. Common quality monitoring tools used in an agile team include burndown charts (see Figure 8-6), root cause analysis, and automated testing tools. (Agile teams may also elect to use a defect tracking tool, especially if they are new to agile and have a backlog of defects. But teams should work to find and eliminate defects within the iteration, so that any outstanding bugs are few and can be simply added to the existing product backlog as an item to be worked.)

As you recall from our discussion of burndown charts in Chapter 6, "Time Management," an iteration burndown chart tracks what is left to be done. As you can see in Figure 8-6, the days in the iteration are on the horizontal axis, whereas the task hours are on the vertical axis. As the iteration progresses, the amount of work left to do should "burn down." Monitoring this graph provides insight as to whether or not the team is on track to meet its commitment, giving the team a daily opportunity to adapt as needed.

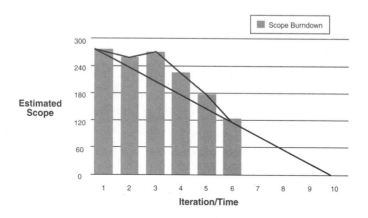

Figure 8-6
Iteration burndown chart

In some agile practices, quality drives the entire software development process in an approach called test-driven development (TDD). In this approach, tests are written and automated first, before the functional code is written. As stated in one of the FAQ responses at testdriven.com's website: "Write a small test, write enough code to make the test succeed, clean up the code. Repeat."

Table 8-3 presents a summary comparison of the traditional and agile approaches to quality control. In agile terminology, quality control is referred to as "acceptance, review, and retrospective."

Table 8-3
Quality Control

Traditional	Agile
Test code for bugs at the end of the project.	Test the code for bugs every iteration.
It's okay if manual testing is how we do the bulk of our testing.	It's not okay if manual testing is how we do the bulk of our testing because then testing becomes a bottleneck—instead, we automate as many tests as possible in order to maintain quality controls and increase speed to delivery.
Refer to documentation that tells us what to test and what to expect (i.e., how the system should function).	As part of the team, QA works with developers and the customer to understand what to test and what to expect, and what the acceptance criteria is for each feature.
Record defects in a log.	The tester tells the developer about the bug found and offers to walk through the steps to re-create it with her. Record outstanding defects (those not fixed in the iteration) as items in the backlog.
Monitor product quality using a variety of tools (*PMBOK® Guide's* "seven basic tools of quality").	Monitor product quality using the primary tools of passing tests and customer acceptance.
Monitor process quality using a variety of tools that include an audit.	Monitor process quality by using the primary tools of burndown charts, metrics, and root cause analysis that are reviewed at the end of each iteration in the review and retrospective meeting.

Summary

This chapter can be summed up as follows:

- Quality assurance becomes a reality in agile software development, because the quality staffers are an essential part of the agile team from the very beginning of the project.
- The customer and the team define the quality policies and standards they will use in the project.
- Quality in the product is monitored by automated tests and confirmed by customer acceptance; quality in the process is monitored by metrics and confirmed by the review and retrospective "audit."
- Burndown charts and root cause analysis are standard quality control tools used by an agile team.

Table 8-4 provides a comparison of traditional and agile project managers' behavior as it pertains to quality management.

Table 8-4
Agile Project Manager's Change List for Quality Management

I used to do this:	Now I do this:
Prepare a formal quality management plan.	Invite the team to define the specifics around ensuring quality (automated testing tools, frequent and accessible builds, testing environment, metrics to track, definition of "done," etc.) and record decisions informally using flipcharts, whiteboards, wikis, etc.
Arrange QA audits.	Facilitate demo, review, and retrospective meetings at the end of every iteration, and track actions and results around the recommended changes to examine at the next iteration review and retrospective meeting.
Track defects; organize and assign bug fixing activities.	Assist the team if needed as it works to find and fix defects within each iteration; make sure the customer is aware of defects found in previously accepted features.
Maintain a change control log.	Be available to answer questions from the customer as he works to keep the backlog updated.

Endnotes

1. *PMBOK® Guide*, 184.
2. Ibid., 189.

Chapter 9

Human Resources Management

Project Human Resource Management includes the processes that organize and manage the project team.

—PMBOK® Guide

Groups become great only when everyone in them, leaders and members alike, is free to do his or her absolute best. The best thing a leader can do for a Great Group is to allow its members to discover their greatness.

—*Warren Bennis and Patricia Ward Biederman,* Organizing Genius

(The annual review) nourishes short-term performance, annihilates long-term planning, builds fear, demolishes teamwork, nourishes rivalry and politics.... It leaves people bitter, crushed, bruised, battered, desolate, despondent, dejected, feeling inferior, some even depressed, unfit for work for weeks after receipt of rating, unable to comprehend why they are inferior. It is unfair, as it ascribes to people in a group differences that may be caused totally by the system that they work in.

—*Dr. W. Edwards Deming*

The traditional approach to human resource management focuses on the planning, acquisition, development, and management of the project team. Roles and responsibilities are identified and assigned; appropriate skill sets and competencies of each individual team member are developed, tracked, and assessed. Contrasted with this, the agile approach is to establish cross-functional teams with mutual accountability, and allow them to self-organize within a framework that requires regular team retrospection.

Establishing a cross-functional team means that the development team is no longer made up solely of programmers. Instead, the agile development team consists of all the key players needed to create an increment of working code: coders, testers, analysts, architects, technical writers, and so on. These individuals bring with them a particular skill set, but as the team matures, each individual will learn more about others' tasks and efforts, and will gradually become more willing and able to pitch in and help in areas outside the individual's normal expertise. Having a cross-functional team eventually comes to mean that you have a group of individuals so committed to delivering the promised features that they will chip in and help do whatever needs to be done in order to meet their commitment and successfully finish the iteration.

The team becomes self-organizing as a result of the regular check-ins on the product and process, where the team collaboratively examines what it has accomplished and makes decisions about how it wants to continue. This total ownership by the team of the planning, execution, and review of both the product and the process leads groups to a high level of self-directed performance maintained by continuous reflection and improvement.

These concepts of self-organizing cross-functional teams often lead to increased nervousness on the part of project managers, because they begin to wonder what their role will be if they're no longer directing a team's efforts. Here is where the shift from being a command-and-control manager to what Robert Greenleaf described in his 1970 book *The Servant as Leader* as a "servant leader" must occur. Team dynamics don't change overnight, and teams new to agile methods need strong leadership to help them learn how to make group decisions. Becoming a servant leader involves learning how to foster collaboration and reflection as a means to allow your team to do the best work it possibly can. Ongoing servant leadership in maturing teams includes responsibilities such as mentoring, guidance, facilitation, and roadblock removal. All of these are soft skills involved in the development and management of the project team.

In the following sections, we'll look at how an agile project manager must address the issues of planning, acquiring, coordinating, and managing human resources on an agile team. You'll see how the agile principle of having dedicated cross-functional teams fundamentally changes the way project human resource management is handled on an agile project.

Human Resource Planning

A goal of human resource planning is to create a staffing management plan for the project. Because traditional plan-driven projects have already defined all the features and tasks necessary to implement the product, resource planning is a matter of identifying roles and inserting resources to fit those roles into the project schedule. If resource leveling pushes the delivery date out, you add resources until the date becomes attainable. Using this method, you can also see when particular skills, such as those of an Oracle DBA, will be needed and can procure that individual for that timeframe only.

The problem with this type of staffing plan is that it never works out the way you originally define it. New features are requested, the amount of time to implement a feature takes longer than expected, team members transfer out or take time off, third-party tools don't work as expected, late deliveries from external sources push out the schedule, and so on. For the same reasons that agile teams do not invest in "big design up front," they also do not attempt to create a staffing plan that outlines who will be needed at specific time periods. Instead, agile project managers create cross-functional teams that are fully dedicated to the project for the duration of the project.

Table 9-1 provides a summary comparison of the traditional and agile approaches to human resource planning. In the agile framework, there is no formal terminology for human resource planning (although agile practitioners tend to refer to themselves as "people" rather than "resources"). It is just done as part of release planning.

A Human Resource Caveat

It's not always possible to expect a resource such as an Oracle DBA to be available for the duration of the project, particularly in large matrixed organizations where agile adoption is in its early phases in the organization. One team in this predicament used its release plans to determine when it might need a DBA and someone from Operations to participate in an iteration. The team planned out quarterly releases, noting which features it planned on implementing in the iterations that made up that release. Then the team would go back over its release plan, putting a blue dot on those items where external skills would be required. Based on this information, the team could then put in a request for these folks, and provide a date range where their services would be needed (the full duration of that iteration).

Table 9-1
Human Resource Planning

Traditional	Agile
Identify skill sets needed and timeframes for individual involvement with the project, based on the detailed project plan and schedule.	Create a fully dedicated cross-functional team; identify specialists needed that the team does not have and the timeframes these individuals will be needed based on the release plan.
Record results in a formal document outlining the staffing management plan.	Record results in informal documentation (the release plan).

Acquiring a Project Team

Agile team size generally ranges from five to ten team members. Pulling together a cross-functional team means selecting not only developers, but also testers, analysts, technical writers, architects—all the people who are needed to implement the features of the product. Because people are accustomed to being highly specialized, this may make for a large team when assembling staff in a waterfall organization. Keeping the team to a reasonable size means selecting "generalized specialists"[1] who are willing to do additional work outside what has been traditionally expected of them given their job title. In an agile team, for example, developers can assist with the technical writing of the help screens; technical writers can assist with the creation of functional test cases; testers can help with the code reviews.

A great agile team consists of people who do not expect nor need to be told what to do. Dennis Bakke, former CEO of AES Corporation and author of *Joy at Work*, said that at AES they "focused on finding self-starters who would take responsibility for their own actions."[2] Candidates are vetted by asking, "Did they have the courage to make decisions? Did they understand what it meant to serve their colleagues, other stakeholders, and the company as a whole?"[3] Although this is a great way to build a team, it may be more difficult to find these risk-taking generalized specialists in large bureaucratic companies. Indeed, it may take some coaxing on the part of the agile project manager to bring out these characteristics in team members who are not accustomed to being given the freedom to make decisions.

Once team members are identified, there are other issues to grapple with. One of the biggest impediments to success in agile projects is that of team members who are being "time-sliced," or having to devote portions of their time to multiple concurrent projects. Researchers from the Federal Aviation Authority and the University of Michigan published a study that showed productivity actually declines when working on multiple tasks.[4] Much of this time is lost in having to mentally change gears between task items (that is, losing focus and then rebuilding focus as individuals are forced to stop without being able to complete task A, then picking up task B and trying to remember where they left off and what they need to do next). In fact, the term "multitasking" is actually a misnomer—human brains can only focus on one task at a time, and the act of trying to switch between too many tasks can actually cause serious health issues (increased stress resulting in a higher risk of stroke, heart attack, and brain damage!).[5] So when negotiating for team members for an agile project, make every effort to get fully dedicated team members who can give your project their full attention.

Ideally, the agile team should be co-located. Unfortunately many agile project managers find themselves having to work with virtual teams instead and therefore must pay close attention to tools and techniques that will help the team effectively communicate. A variety of options exist, and the team will have to experiment to find the methods that work best for their environment and culture. Remember that in agile software development, teams must communicate daily—throughout the day, every day—in order to share information and plan work. Some examples of tools used to facilitate this communication include the use of shared sites such as wikis where commentary and photos are published, web conferencing tools and online whiteboards, videoconferencing, instant messaging (IM), and third-party agile

Virtual Stand-up Meetings

One team with an offshore group located in Egypt found that the best way for team members to conduct their daily stand-ups was by using IM—although the Egyptians' spoken English was difficult to understand, their written English was flawless. Another team had amazing facilities and no budgetary constraints, so they took advantage of their videoconferencing for their daily stand-ups and planning meetings. Yet another team would include their colleagues from the other coast by using conference calls and NetMeeting (a web conference tool) and assigning a scribe who copied everything down in real time on the virtual whiteboard so those on the phone could still follow along.

project management tools. Teams must have working agreements in place that define how best to use these tools. See Chapter 10, "Communications Management," for more detail.

Table 9-2 provides a summary comparison of the traditional and agile approaches to acquiring project teams.

Table 9-2
Acquiring the Project Team

Traditional	Agile
Acquire team members based on the staffing management plan and update documentation as appropriate.	Create a cross-functional team where all members understand that they equally bear responsibility for the delivery of the product.
When negotiating for team members, provide the dates and/or the percentage of time they will be needed on the project.	Negotiate for fully dedicated team members.
Save money by using virtual teams.	Save money by using co-located teams, which increases productivity and reduces costs associated with miscommunication and communication lag time.

Develop the Project Team

The development of the agile project team is not dissimilar to that of any team whose purpose is to achieve a common goal through collaborative decision-making and mutual accountability. It is the agile self-organizing team that is responsible for its own development, however, rather than the project manager. The agile project manager's role in this process is to facilitate the activities that lead to team cohesion and high performance, provide the environment in which the team can do its work, and remove roadblocks that prevent the team from reaching its objectives.

Despite the progress we've made in so many areas that affect our lives, several team management practices still seem to be stuck in a paradigm of Theory X management, refusing to shift to Theory Y. Douglas McGregor, a management professor at MIT, coined the phrases Theory X and Theory Y to represent the motivational styles of management in the workplace.

In Theory X, employees are assumed to be lazy and shiftless and will avoid work and responsibility if they can. Theory Y proposes that people want to do well and are self-motivated to succeed if given the opportunity. Theory Y is far removed from Frederick Taylor's early work in which he asserted that extrinsic motivators (rewards and punishments) were required to extract any effort beyond the minimum allowed for continued employment. Taylor failed to recognize what others like McGregor, W. Edwards Deming, and Peter Drucker have noted: The unique qualities of human behavior such as self-expression, creativity, curiosity, self-esteem, and sense of community are also forces that affect motivation.

Unfortunately, much of the prevalent management practices in use today still focus on Theory X drivers (that is, the use of rewards and punishment and annual performance appraisals to "motivate" employees). McGregor noted that although it is possible to get people to do something, no one can force another to *desire* to do something: "Strictly speaking, the answer to the question managers so often ask of behavioral scientists—'How do you motivate people?'—is, 'You don't.'"[6] The agile project manager must instead focus on providing team members with the environment in which they can find their own intrinsic motivation, and thus their own sense of satisfaction in achieving objectives. The best teams are those where each person truly wants to achieve the goals laid out before him or her.

This has been proven with a variety of studies, one of which resulted in salary being ranked sixteenth out of a list of 20 reasons for deciding whether or not to take a job, far below such items as "open communication," "stimulating work," and "control over work content."[7] Therefore, an agile project manager's responsibility in the development of a project team is to "set up certain conditions that will maximize the probability of their developing an interest in what they are doing and remove the conditions that function as constraints."[8] Part of setting up these conditions includes the facilitation of clearly defined team values.

Values in Agile

Agile software development is noted for being value-driven instead of plan-driven. Agile novices often believe this is limited to business value (that is, focusing on completing features that have the most importance to the customer early in the project, before adding on features of lesser importance).

However, agile processes were not created with only business value in mind but also with consideration for values regarding the ethical and sustainable ways in which we work.

This is not to say that non-agile projects have no values or are unethical. The difference between the two kinds of projects is simply the difference between implied values in traditional approaches, and explicitly stated values in agile approaches. Most traditional methodologies focus on the practices and disciplines for developing good software and then stop there with expectations that people will now perform according to plan to meet the objectives laid out before them. Agile approaches, on the other hand, went a step further and explicitly defined a set of values (the Agile Manifesto and its guiding principles) in order to help guide behaviors.

Some agile frameworks have already explicitly defined a set of team values. For example, Scrum has five values that drive and support its practices: commitment, openness, focus, courage, and respect. Extreme Programming also has five values: communication, feedback, simplicity, courage, and respect. These values are easy to remember, they are short (one word), and they are few. But even when the values are defined for you, is it enough? Does the team agree with the values? And is one word without context enough? Where does that leave us on interpretation?

From Values to Behaviors

It isn't enough to have a few words that represent the values we wish to embrace. Teams, and companies, must take these values and weave them into the fabric of their organization. Their values must become things that guide decisions and not just empty platitudes. They must become things that inspire and not simply posters in the hallways. They must become an intrinsic part of the corporate culture and not solely a good soundbite for PR material. In order to do this, you have to add a construct around the value to turn it into an actionable tenet. Doing so will force the team to think through exactly what is meant by the value and the best ways to explain it. And it's as straightforward as stating what you believe in and what you will do about it. Using a simple template such as, "We believe in <value>; therefore, we will <do something>," allows us to consider the behaviors we will see as a result of embracing the value.

Let's use Scrum's values as an example. As the team's coach, or Scrum-Master, I would want to have a conversation with my team to discuss what we think is meant by each of the Scrum values. After facilitating some brainstorming and visualization exercises, the team arrives at the following consensus:

- "We believe in Openness; therefore, we will share project status in the highest visible way possible, and we will deliver the unvarnished truth in all our communications."
- "We believe in Respect; therefore, we will treat one another with courtesy and fairness and focus on problem-solving instead of finger-pointing."
- "We believe in Courage; therefore, we will not shy away from difficult conversations and we will say 'no' when we must."

Actively Defining Goals and Values

We were once members of a team that was tasked with defining its goals and values. Our facilitator asked us to visualize ourselves at a huge awards ceremony where we were receiving a prestigious honor. (We did this in silence, each of us creating our own imaginary awards ceremony.) She directed us by saying, "First the master of ceremonies gives a short speech. What is he saying about your team? Why is your team receiving the award? Then imagine your manager making a speech. What did she say? Then one of your customers steps up to the mic. What did they say? Then your colleagues go up and speak. What did they say?" For each of these vignettes we were given plenty of time to imagine what was being said, and write down our impressions.

We then broke into small groups and shared the results of our visualization. We recorded thoughts that occurred more than once (that is, more than one person "heard" the same speech item). Then we grouped these items and labeled the groupings.

We then created a goal statement for each labeled grouping using one of three verbs to start the sentence: Promote, Provide, or Maximize.

Finally, based on our discussions of our vision of the future and our newly stated goals, we defined what our core values were. We used the format "We believe… therefore we will…." This was actually quite easy because of all the work done around the visioning.

We hung the flipcharts that contained our values and our goals in our team area, and referred to them often in the months that followed.

- "We believe in Focus; therefore, we will organize our work into that which is part of the sprint (iteration) and that which is not, and give priority to that which is part of the sprint."
- "We believe in Commitment; therefore, when we promise to do something, we will assume the accountability and authority we need to get it done and deliver."

You can see how we've now transformed a word without context into something we can all own and rally around. Now when voices are raised in frustration or anger, the team can ask, "Is this in keeping with our value of Respect? How do we want to behave instead?" When the customer asks for more features than the team members can deliver in the next iteration, the Courage value should drive their decision to announce that "We cannot commit to this; we must face the unvarnished truth and admit that we do not have the people to deliver all these features in the next 30 days." The values, *as defined and agreed to by the team,* are now the glue that guides the team in its decisions and behaviors. In the same way, we need a vision to define what we will and will not do with regards to the product; we need a set of values to define how we will and will not behave as individuals and as members of the team.

Table 9-3 runs down, in summary comparison fashion, the traditional and agile approaches to developing the project team. The agile terminology for developing the project team is simply that of self-organizing teams.

Table 9-3
Developing the Project Team

Traditional	Agile
Master important "soft skills" such as empathy, listening, addressing issues, and facilitation.	Master important "soft skills" such as empathy, listening, addressing issues, and facilitation.
Co-location of the team is a good strategy, and the use of virtual teams will reduce the frequency of gathering together.	Co-location of the team is the preferred strategy; unfortunately, the use of virtual teams will often limit the frequency of gathering together.
Provide team-building activities that build trust and establish good working relationships.	Team-building activities that build trust and establish good working relationships are part of the agile framework.

HUMAN RESOURCES MANAGEMENT

Traditional	Agile
Establish ground rules for the team in order to define team values and set clear expectations.	Facilitate the creation of ground rules and working agreements by and for the team in order to define team values and set clear expectations.
Recognize and reward desirable behavior.	Provide an environment that fosters a motivated team by providing the members with opportunities: to learn new skills, to experience variation in tasks, to develop and demonstrate competence, to rise to meet a challenge and experience success.[9]
Conduct assessments to evaluate team performance.	Facilitate retrospectives to assess team performance and determine ways to improve.

Manage the Project Team

Managing a project team traditionally involves observing, tracking, and correcting performance. Because agile frameworks provide frequent opportunities for teams to reflect and refine, the project manager's responsibility centers on providing the forum and facilitation for this continuous feedback. Iteration reviews and retrospectives allow the team to inspect the work it has done and the processes it has followed, and make changes as needed to improve performance. You can read more about iteration reviews and retrospectives in Chapter 8, "Quality Management."

Often in a traditional setting, the project manager is also responsible for conducting annual performance reviews of individual team members. This tends to be true even in matrixed environments, where at a minimum the project manager is asked for his or her input as part of preparing the appraisal. In agile environments, having the agile project manager conduct individual performance appraisals is considered an unhealthy conflict of interest. Because the agile project manager exists in service to the team, suddenly taking a position of "superiority" as the team members' appraiser undermines the agile project manager's work as the team's mentor. Indeed, because the agile focus is on mutual accountability and team performance, the idea of emphasizing hierarchies and individual rankings disenfranchises teams, leaving them feeling that there is a ranking within the team and that they are not all equally important to the delivery of the product. The team that was so cohesive and high-performing only yesterday can quickly fall into disarray when confronted with this unspoken message.

It is important to address the issue of annual performance reviews and the alternatives in an agile environment. Unfortunately, there are no clear-cut answers as to what those alternatives may be; instead, it varies depending on the corporate culture and level of agile adoption in the organization. There are guidelines, however, for setting new policies, in books such as *Abolishing Performance Appraisals* and *Punished by Rewards,* as well as works by W. Edwards Deming. Alfie Kohn, author of *Punished by Rewards,* suggests simply, "Pay people generously and equitably. Do your best to make sure they don't feel exploited. Then do everything in your power to help them put money out of their minds...the problem is that money is made too salient...it is pushed into people's faces...moreover it is offered contingently. What I attempt to do in other words, is decouple the task from the compensation."[10]

Changing the performance evaluation process in your organization won't be as easy as Kohn makes it sound; it is an ongoing discussion that is often uncomfortable and offers no black-and-white solutions. We offer no clear solutions here either, but encourage you to do your own investigation and research,[11] involve your teams in solving this problem, and experiment with alternatives.

Even though we recommend avoiding the tradition of the annual performance appraisal, we are not recommending a total lack of assessment feedback. On the contrary, it is important to the individuals on the team that they have a forum to work privately with their agile project manager, one on one, where they can discuss and resolve issues and concerns. They need to know what they are doing well, how their actions are impacting the team, and what they need to work on in order to continue to grow and

The Value of the Human Being

The General Electric plant in Durham, North Carolina, created an alternative appraisal environment. In its facility, everyone knows what everyone else makes because employees are graded and paid on a specific set of skills. There are only three grades of technicians at the plant—tech-1, tech-2, and tech-3—and one wage rate for each grade. Because each employee has the freedom to do the jobs that interest him or her, the grades, or labels, are intentionally vague. There are no performance incentives. And yet turnover is very low— less than 5% per year—because people are working for no reward other than their own personal satisfaction. Quotes from their employees include: "I'm much happier here. I can change what goes on." "I couldn't wait to get to work every day...I was never valued that much as an employee in my life." "I think what they've discovered in Durham is the value of the human being."[12]

improve. Simply put, they need to be coached. Annual performance reviews never served these goals well—waiting until the end of the year to learn how your work is perceived often meant discovering that you've been doing something wrong for months and no one bothered to tell you! Can you imagine how unhelpful it would be for a football coach to provide guidance to his players only after the season ended?

The agile project manager, or "coach," will conduct these one-on-ones with team members, giving feedback about how the individual's actions affect the team in both positive and unfavorable ways. It's important to have these informal one-on-ones with some frequency so the team members can make changes that will ensure their success. Agile project managers are not "seagull managers"—those who "aren't around until something goes wrong, and then they fly in, make a lot of noise, dump on people, and then fly out."[13] Instead, agile project managers coach their team members to perform according to their potential, often exceeding what the individual themselves thought they could do.

And even these scheduled one-on-ones are not meant to prevent the team's coach from helping the team when he or she sees a clear need. Don't wait for a one-on-one if you see an action occur that needs redirection. Employ real-time feedback and address the issues as they arise; try to provide the feedback as close to the event as possible so it is more meaningful and corrections can be made quickly.

Table 9-4 compares and summarizes the traditional and agile approaches to managing project teams. In agile parlance, this is called "coaching a team."

Table 9-4
Manage Project Team

Traditional	Agile
Observe work and attitudes of team members; have conversations to "stay in touch."	Sit with and coach the team, helping the members stay focused on the goal and make course corrections as needed, and conduct regular one-on-ones with each team member to share feedback and address concerns.
Conduct performance appraisals for team members.	Avoid giving individual performance appraisals; instead, coach team members using one-on-ones and real-time feedback.

(continued)

Table 9-4
Manage Project Team *(continued)*

Traditional	Agile
Take preventive or corrective actions such as cross-training or additional training for personnel, staff changes, disciplinary actions, and recognitions and rewards.	Facilitate iteration reviews and retrospectives where recommendations to improve performance are gathered, assessed, and implemented by the team.

Summary

This chapter can be summarized in the following way:

- An agile team is a cross-functional group of people fully dedicated to the project and mutually accountable for its success.
- Agile teams work best when co-located; however, communication tools exist for those who must deal with geographically dispersed teams.
- Agile teams are self-organizing, and the agile project manager facilitates and guides the team in its efforts at continuous improvement.
- An agile project manager should attempt to shift to a Theory Y approach to build a group of people intrinsically motivated to do their best.
- In order for an agile team to do its best work, the agile project manager must provide an environment that supports the team in its efforts, provide opportunities for the members to contribute and learn, and remove roadblocks to success.
- Agile is value-driven not only with regard to providing business value but also in the way people work; therefore, the Agile Manifesto, its guiding principles, and values that the team explicitly defines, are critical to team development.
- Agile project managers should avoid giving performance appraisals, because the judgment of individuals sets up a conflict of interest with their role as servants to the team.

- Finding an alternative to the annual performance review is an important issue to resolve, and it is recommended that those creating and enacting new policies make every effort to separate compensation from tasks.
- One-on-ones and real-time feedback are important to the growth of the team members and the team.

Table 9-5 compares the human resources management behaviors of a project manager as a traditional project manager and as an agile project manager.

Table 9-5
Agile Project Manager's Change List for Human Resource Management

I used to do this:	Now I do this:
Prepare a staffing management plan based on the detailed project plan and schedule.	Gather a cross-functional team that is preferably co-located and fully dedicated to the project for its duration.
Negotiate for percentages of people.	Negotiate for people who can be full-time contributors; generalized specialists are preferred.
Plan team-building activities to build unity and boost morale.	Adhere to the agile framework; constant participatory decision-making results in team unity and high morale.
Conduct regular assessments of team performance.	Facilitate iteration reviews and retrospectives.
Provide motivators such as individual recognition, rewards, and punishment.	Provide an environment where the team is free to do its best work, intrinsically motivated by its own interests.
Visit with the individuals on the team regularly to stay in touch.	Following the agile framework means daily interaction with everyone.
Conduct annual performance reviews of team members.	Coach the team and its members in the behaviors that will lead to success through the use of one-on-ones and real-time feedback.

(continued)

Table 9-5
Agile Project Manager's Change List for Human Resource Management *(continued)*

I used to do this:	Now I do this:
Take corrective action when the team or its members fail to perform to expectations.	Facilitate the team in its retrospective at the end of each iteration, where the team identifies areas that need improvement, recommendations, and the actions to be taken to implement the improvement plan.

Endnotes

1. This phrase was coined by Scott Ambler.

2. Dennis W. Bakke. *Joy at Work.* (Seattle: PVG, 2005), 95.

3. Ibid.

4. Joshua S. Rubenstein et al. "Executive Control of Cognitive Processes in Task Switching." *Journal of Experimental Psychology: Human Perception and Performance,* Volume 27, Number 4, 2001.

5. Melissa Heally. "We're All Multitasking, But What's The Cost?" *Los Angeles Times*, 19 July 2004, 1–5.

6. Douglas McGregor. *Leadership and Motivation: Essays of Douglas McGregor.* (Boston: M.I.T. Press, 1968), 208.

7. Alfie Kohn. *Punished by Rewards.* (New York: Houghton Mifflin, 1993), 266.

8. Ibid., 181.

9. Ibid., 189–190.

10. Ibid., 182–3.

11. Additional work on this subject specific to agile teams is explored in articles by Mary Poppendieck and Esther Derby and can be found at their websites, www.poppendieck.com and www.estherderby.com, respectively.

12. Charles Fishman. "Engines of Democracy." *Fast Company*, September 1999, 174.

13. Ken Blanchard and Don Schula. *The Little Book of Coaching: Motivating People to Be Winners.* (New York: HarperCollins Publishers, 2001), 69.

Chapter 10

Communications Management

Communications management employs the processes required to ensure timely and appropriate generation, collection, distribution, storage, retrieval and ultimate disposition of project information.

—PMBOK® Guide

If you want to build a ship, then don't drum up men to gather wood, give orders, and divide the work. Rather, teach them to yearn for the far and endless sea.

—Antoine de Saint-Exupéry

Tell me and I'll forget. Show me and I'll remember. Involve me and I'll understand.

—Author unknown

Projects are executed by humans. And humans must interact. There is no doubt that communicating frequently and often is necessary throughout the life of any project. For any number of people on any given project, there are multiple permutations of communication paths, and any missed path at an inopportune time constitutes project communication failure. A 2000 Pennsylvania State University study found that "project abandonment is often a result of poor leadership and communication among project team members, and between the project team and top management."[1]

What is communication, exactly? Communication is "a process by which information is exchanged between individuals through a common system of symbols, signs, or behavior."[2] We like to take the definition one step further: Effective communication involves not only the exchange of information, but it is an exchange that results in both parties *understanding* the information. From our point of view as receivers of messages, making sure that we truly understand another project team member means that we must listen, capture the data, run it through our own filter, and either store or act on that information. One way we may have to act on the information is to provide feedback to the sender of the message about our interpretation of it, to see if we interpreted it as intended. From our point of view as senders of messages, making sure that we truly provide understandable information to another project member means that we must attempt to take the perspective and knowledge of the project member into consideration and create and present a message that he or she is likely to interpret in the way we intended. We may have to act further to ensure that the project member understood the message by eliciting feedback that helps us to assess whether he or she interpreted the message as we intended.

It is easy to cite poor communication as a project failure point, but what, exactly, causes poor communication? One author contends that it can be distilled to seven factors: fear, misaligned expectations, confusion, loss of momentum, dissatisfaction, lack of commitment, and unconscious incompetence.[3] Agile project teams, as we have experienced, don't encounter as many of these issues as non-agile project teams. This is because agile project managers work hard to create trust within the team unit, so that team members are not afraid to approach each other for information. Additionally, the acts of release and iteration planning keep the team aligned to the goals for the appropriate time horizon, and daily synchronization eliminates confusion in knowing what to do next. The iteration demos keep the team focused on its deliverables, so that team members experience satisfaction in delivering on their commitment every single iteration. The unconscious incompetence of inexperienced team members can be thwarted by the close working nature of agile teams. These newbies are usually paired with a senior team member to learn the ropes; daily synchronization and check-in mitigates the risk of a newbie wreaking havoc on a project.

As you read this chapter, think about the traditional *PMBOK® Guide* "communications management" as agile "communications facilitation." This distinction is important because of the emphasis that agile places on self-organizing teams, as well as the emphasis on the leader, the agile project manager, who brings the right people together to make the right decisions. Because teams are autonomous within the bounds of the iteration, an agile project manager, then, facilitates the communication between the project team and top management/stakeholders at specific points throughout the project, above and around these iteration boundaries. Agile project managers do not "manage" communication; rather, they facilitate and understand the power of people connecting to making decisions about events in the project.

Agile projects emphasize the instant exchange of information via face-to-face communication, whereas more traditional methods tend to rely on the exchange of documentation. This chapter explains how agile project managers plan for and distribute information within the project, how they are involved in communicating basic project information, as well as how they report performance and manage stakeholders.

Communications Planning

According to the *PMBOK® Guide*, "The analysis of the communications requirements results in the sum of the information needs of the project stakeholders."[4] Stakeholders require accurate and timely information as a basis for accurate and timely decisions. Just as in traditional project communications planning, it is very important to determine who needs the information, how often it is needed, and what methods are best to communicate it. However, in agile approaches, formal documentation of the communications plan is not required, because much of the foundation for communications is included as an integral part of the agile frameworks. The Agile Manifesto lists "individuals and interactions" and "customer collaboration" as two key areas of focus, and all agile approaches support these principles in their processes.

Communicating Basic Project Information—The Who, What, When, Where, and How

After the team has met for roadmap and release planning, information about the project should be made visible to stakeholders. The team and customer will have decided upon the number of and dates of the project's iterations as well as assumptions and will have established an initial risk log for the project. This basic information, along with the vision, theme, and targeted release date from the customer, is pertinent information of which all stakeholders should be aware. Often, this occurs in the form of a project kickoff or vision meeting, with results posted on a wiki or share site; sometimes, teams post this information just outside the war room. It is up to the team to devise the best way to communicate these project basics.

Most stakeholders are primarily interested in when they will recognize ROI, or delivery of value. Communicating the basic information about the project is pertinent because it sets the project's heartbeat and advises stakeholders early on regarding the project's important iteration review dates. After iteration planning meetings, we have observed many teams communicate an iteration goals update to alert stakeholders as to what functionality has been committed to for the iteration. Although not mandatory, this is another example of the types of communication in which some teams feel it is important to engage.

Here are a few bits of information your stakeholders may be interested in:

- The project manager or agile team leader
- The delivery team, with photo, team name, and mission
- Team war room and location
- Daily stand-up time/location or conference bridge
- Demo, review, and retrospective meeting dates/times/locations and conference bridge
- Release planning meeting date/time/location
- Iteration planning meeting date/time/location
- The iteration task board (or other tool in which the team tracks its tasks)
- The current release plan

- Backlogs: product, release and iteration
- A pointer or link to the project's information (SharePoint, wiki, and so on)

Although it is important to plan how you and the team will communicate during the course of the project, keep in mind that agile values the "individuals and interactions" over the tools and processes that you might employ. It is often helpful to remember this first line of the Agile Manifesto; it is a good litmus test to find out if you're putting too much effort into the communications plan—effort that could be better spent in simply communicating. It is also helpful to keep an agile mindset in your communications planning: Something that you planned for today might become obsolete in the future, so plan to reevaluate decisions with the team, and always include communications as a topic for your retrospectives.

Table 10-1 provides a summary description of the traditional and agile approaches to communication plan development.

Table 10-1
Communication Plan Development

Traditional	Agile
Determine important information about when, how, and who will be communicating about the project.	Determine important information about when, how, and who will be communicating about the project.
Prepare a Project Communications Plan document.	Determine as a team the best method for constant real-time communication (wikis, war rooms, other tools) and continue more formal communication during all planning meetings (vision, release, iteration, daily).

Information Distribution

According to the *PMBOK® Guide,* information distribution is essentially the execution of the communications plan. You and the team share the responsibility to figure out which information should be distributed, and just as importantly, determine the most effective means of distribution.

Additionally, help the team identify hours of overlap between locations and utilize more effective forms of communication. According to the *PMBOK® Guide,* "Face-to-face meetings are the most effective means for communicating and resolving issues with stakeholders."[5] That's because face-to-face communication is high bandwidth; the idea is that telling and showing are more valuable than writing down and expecting a group of people to read and, more importantly, comprehend the intention. You have all the richness of opportunity that face-to-face communication provides to achieve effective communication. To the extent that we can replicate face-to-face communication in agile projects, the better and more valuable it is because it increases the probability that the intent of the message is *understood.*

Figure 10-1 illustrates the hierarchy of effective communication. Notice that documents requiring sign-off are at the bottom; that's because these types of documents represent one-way communication. As you move up the pyramid, the types of communications become increasingly more effective. Think about ways you can utilize face-to-face communication more in your projects.

Figure 10-1
Communications effectiveness pyramid

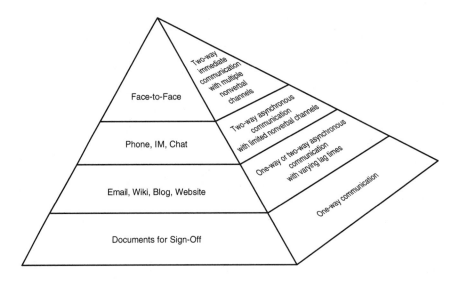

Iteration Demo and Review Meeting

Consider the traditional project status meeting: A number of people gather in a meeting room, some participants may have dialed in and are thus "invisible." Everyone looks at a printed piece of paper or a projected spreadsheet that shows percent complete, reflects an issue/risk log, so forth, and so on. The project manager reviews task status, one by one, but the numbers reflect more of a subjective hopeful reality. Even though the information contained in the project status report is not very reliable, everyone believes in it anyway. This is the proverbial security blanket in traditional projects—the *representation* of a project's status via a document.

In agile projects, the "status meeting"—or iteration review—is much more meaningful because, instead of reading a document that tells stakeholders the progress of the project, they can actually look at working software! Of course, from time to time, your project situation may call for other types of documentation, but these documents should be considered secondary and supplemental in nature, and on an as-needed basis by you and the team. For example, if your team has focused on performance improvements during a particular iteration, the team may decide to demonstrate the performance increases via automated tests, and then publish before-and-after metrics to substantiate the progress made during the iteration. Because progress is demonstrated at the end of each iteration by reviewing working software, this could be considered the most valuable agile meeting in terms of information distribution.

Next, we'll take a look at how project information is distributed on a daily basis.

Face-to-Face with Multiple Teams

In one situation where there were multiple teams creating software for a single application attempting to move toward a single solution, all of the teams decided to hold their iteration reviews at the same time because it was far too difficult to get the stakeholders to show up for separate review meetings for all ten teams. The teams decided to utilize a "science fair" style: All teams gathered in a large room, and each team had a workstation or two on which to demonstrate. The 40–50 stakeholders divided themselves into groups of three to five people, and each group visited a team for fifteen minutes. At the sound of a whistle, the stakeholder groups would rotate to the next team's review, visit for fifteen minutes, until the whistle blew again. This way, within two hours, the stakeholders were able to visit all of the teams. How did we get feedback on the emerging product? Stakeholders were each given a feedback form so that they could record their thoughts about the product. At the end of the review, the stakeholders remained for thirty minutes afterward to present their feedback to the team. Product owners were on hand to capture anything that should be added to the backlog, and to explain why some items would not be added to the backlog. This was a very effective use of time for both the team and the stakeholders, and it also had a very celebratory feel, which lifted morale. The project managers were on hand to make sure that the meeting was well facilitated, that all voices were being heard, and that the proper information was being communicated.

Daily Communication via the Daily Stand-up Meeting

Another meeting that is very useful is the daily stand-up, where each team member syncs up with each other, voices his or her dependencies or issues, and takes action to resolve any outstanding issues. The daily stand-up is reported by the team, for the team, while the project manager is in attendance to remove obstacles, help the team communicate effectively, nudge the team to resolve conflicts, and remind the team to not problem-solve in the meeting. This is an important distinction, and one that many project managers struggle with when transitioning to agile.

In the agile world, you are primarily concerned that a team meets its goals on an iteration-by-iteration basis, and you are to remove any obstacle that prevents this from happening. So, at a macro release level, you are rightly concerned that the project is "on track." At the micro daily level, the team manages its dependencies, assumptions, and start/finish dates. For example, if Mary had intended to finish her task on Friday, but finished it today (Tuesday) instead, she can mention that information in today's daily stand-up and then volunteer to take on another task or help someone else with his or her task.

Have the team determine the best location for its daily stand-up meeting. Invite others to observe the information to provide transparency and visibility into the project's status. Observers can also view the team's burn-down chart to gain an understanding of how the team is tracking for the iteration overall (see Chapter 6, "Time Management," for more information).

Retrospectives

Another source of project information is the iteration retrospective, which we discussed in detail in Chapter 8, "Quality Management." Often overlooked, it is perhaps the single most powerful meeting you can encourage your team to engage in. The purpose of the retrospective is to gather important knowledge from the iteration—what worked well and what didn't—in order to adapt the process to execute the next iteration more efficiently and effectively. The retrospective encourages honest feedback from team members on the process, team dynamics, and the product itself.

The agile retrospective differs from the traditional "lessons learned" or "postmortem" in that it happens after every iteration throughout the project, whereas a traditional project postmortem occurs after the entire project has come to an end. Agile teams realize that waiting that long to learn lessons would give them no time to make corrections; therefore, iterative improvements require iteration retrospectives.

The team will form action plans around identified areas of improvement. Other improvements, especially those that fall under the "organizational change" label, may need to be escalated by the project manager as a way of removing the obstacles. This information may need to be gathered into notes for discussion or, if need be, a formal document for discussion with management or other parties who may help with resolutions. Figure 10-2 is an example of a retrospective summary that was brought to management meetings for discussion of the topics with which the team needed assistance. (Notice that this example uses the Scrum methodology, hence the use of "sprints" instead of "iterations.") Through retrospectives, the team will identify actions for team, product, and process improvements on an iterative basis.

Sprint 1 Issues

1. Group too big. Lots of storming in weeks one and two. Group finally started Performing end of week three. Lots of progress around 6/20-6/24. Group demo on 6/24 @ 3pm.

2. Very difficult to get team to update the sprint backlog. Once they saw the trend line (around 6/17), participation was better. Two groups were consistent in updating hours.

3. There seemed to be a definitive line in the sand between design and testing. I found this a bit troubling at times when overhearing certain conversations. The situation got better around the week of 6/23. Definitely an ownership perception. Design not wanting to let go; testing wanting a faster understanding. Mary really "got it" when it came to Scrum practices.

4. Helpful when Mary announced there would be a design Scrum team that will be in charge of nailing down requirements with marketing. Once those requirements were nailed down, the high-level design will go to the team for further detailed design/coding/testing. I think that design will be much better at handling this concept for the second sprint iteration.

Figure 10-2
A real-world retrospective log

As you can see, agile information distribution means getting the right people in the room at the right time to hear project information and make decisions. Sometimes, it is necessary to produce documents or reports to support this communication and decision making, but remember that this documentation should be secondary in nature to face-to-face communication. Always start with the top of the communications effectiveness pyramid, and work your way down only when you must.

Highly Visible Information Radiators

We've identified specific points in the project where communications are most efficient and effective. However, open communication throughout the project in agile environments demands more than just point communications. Real-time communication occurs throughout the project via the use of what is called "highly visible information radiators." This concept was derived from Lean Manufacturing's use of a signaling system called "kanban,"[6] which provides a way for production lines to observe and respond to demand levels; the word literally means "signal" or "sign." In Agile, kanbans are represented by graphs, tables, burndown charts, task boards, or other displays that show the current status of the project. For example, after your iteration planning meeting, you'll want to post the results—the iteration plan, the concerns identified, the action items, and so on—in the team's war room or along a wall in the team area (or on your shared website or tool). As the team starts the work of the iteration, team members update the status using a task board (physical or virtual). In this fashion, stakeholders can see at any time how the project is progressing. See Figure 10-3 for an example of a task board, one of the information radiators widely used by agile teams. Notice that this task board has sections for "1 Iteration Out" and "2 Iterations Out"—these sections represent the team's take on release planning.

Information Is Information

A team that was geographically dispersed across several time zones used the benefits of technology to keep its low-tech information radiator (index cards on a task board) highly visible to the whole team and interested stakeholders. The team aimed a web camera at the task board so everyone could see how work was progressing! Because this only provided a rough view—lots of cards in the "accepted" column looks good from a distance—the team eventually moved to an automated tool with a dashboard. But the big-picture view was helpful in the interim, and it is still being used by the team (in conjunction with the tool) as a method of tracking progress.

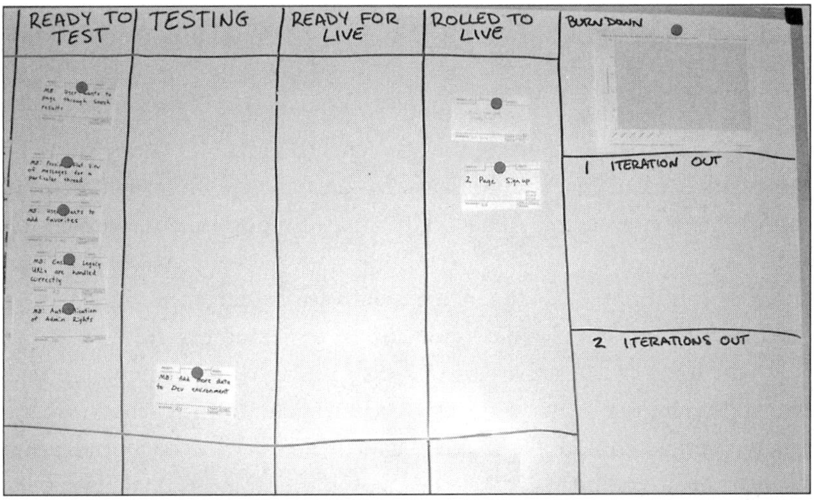

Figure 10-3
Task board example

Table 10-2 provides a summary comparison of the traditional and agile approaches to information distribution.

Table 10-2
Information Distribution

Traditional	Agile
Outline and examine communication skills.	Utilize face-to-face communication as primary method. Educating project team members on its importance and effectiveness is critical.
Define information gathering and retrieval systems.	Information gathering and retrieval should be easy to maintain by the entire team and easy to access by stakeholders. Utilize highly visible information radiators to communicate real-time team status.
Outline information distribution methods.	Keep it simple. Use iteration start/stop dates as natural reporting loops. Work with the team to identify the best means of distributing information by learning stakeholders' needs.
Use lessons learned process to convey information.	Leverage iteration retrospectives at the end of every iteration to provide a means of internal communication resulting in action plans for improvement, as well as communication up the chain for organizational change and removal of obstacles impeding the team's progress.

Performance Reporting

Regardless of the project methodology or process that you use, it is critical to report on the performance of the project. The *PMBOK® Guide* states that performance reporting should consider and include information about scope, schedule, cost, and quality. How do we report on agile project performance?

One of the unique benefits of agile software development is the fact that working software is the primary indicator of project status. Additional project information can be recorded in a task board in the team room. If the team should choose or have the need to formally capture the information gathered in the iteration review meeting, we have provided a couple formats as suggestions. The first is Mike Cohn's example from his book, *Agile Estimating and Planning* (see Figure 10-4).[7]

Figure 10-4
Iteration delta table from Mike Cohn's book, *Agile Estimating and Planning*

Two Weeks Ago

Iteration 1	This is item 1...
Iteration 1	This is item 2...
Iteration 1	This is item 3...
Iteration 1	This is item 4...
Iteration 2	This is item 5...
Iteration 2	This is item 6...
Iteration 2	This is item 7...
Iteration 2	This is item 8...
Iteration 3	This is item 9...
Iteration 3	This is item 10...
Iteration 3	This is item 11...
Iteration 3	This is item 12...
	This is item 13...
	This is item 14...

Today

	Was	
✓	1	This is item 1...
✓	1	This is item 2...
✓	1	This is item 3...
Iteration 2	1	This is item 4...
Iteration 2	2	This is item 5...
Iteration 2	2	This is item 6...
Iteration 2	New	This is item 15...
Iteration 2	2	This is item 8...
Iteration 2	3	This is item 13...
Iteration 3	2	This is item 9...
Iteration 3	2	This is item 7...
Iteration 3	3	This is item 11...
Iteration 3	3	This is item 10...
	3	This is item 12...
	X	This is item 14...

This table is very simple, and yet it is extremely effective in communicating the changes from one iteration to the next. The following legend will help you read the table:

- Check marks indicate stories that were finished in the iteration.
- "Was" shows what iteration the story was originally planned for.

- "New" indicates a story that was added.
- "X" indicates a story that has been deleted.

Figure 10-5 shows another sample iteration report to use if you need something a bit more formal.

Figure 10-5
Iteration status report example

[Project Name] Status Report for Iteration [n] Ending [Date]

Distribution: Insert the names of all recipients of the status report.

Red/Yellow/Green Light Indicator
Indicate using color whether or not the project is green (project is on track), yellow (delayed but course corrections have been identified), or red (project is blocked).

Executive Briefing
Two to three sentences describing overall project status.

Accomplishments
Insert stories, milestones, and so on finished in the iteration.

Work in Progress
Insert stories and activities that have started but have not yet finished. Typically give an estimated completion date for each and reasons why story failed to get to "done" in the iteration.

Upcoming Activities
Insert upcoming milestones, major meetings, and so on with target dates.

Issues
Insert major or new issues. Issues must include a description, next action, next action owner, and next action due date, at a minimum.

Quality, cost, and time performance communications are covered in more detail in their respective chapters. Suffice it to say that the highly visible information radiators and other forms of reporting that the team feels are reasonable will show the status of these areas as part of standard agile practices.

You probably noticed that we did not discuss an agile equivalent for time and cost reporting systems. It is a reality in many organizations in today's world that cost and time must be tracked for compliance and other financial reasons (such as for Sarbanes-Oxley). Those systems live outside of the agile realm, but they may be a reality for you in tracking your projects.

Table 10-3 presents a summary comparison of the traditional and agile forms of performance reporting. In agile, this is referred to as "sharing highly visible information radiators."

Table 10-3
Performance Reporting

Traditional	Agile
Prepare and distribute formal performance reports such as bar charts, graphs, tables, EVA, and status reports.	Make available both formal and informal performance reports to interested stakeholders, such as reviews of working code, release and iteration plans, burndown charts, task boards, the prioritized backlog, and any text reports needed such as iteration summaries and retrospective findings.
Update forecasts based on performance, and submit change requests and suggest corrective action that will bring the project back in line with the original plan.	Facilitate the team and the customer as they review release plans based on performance in the iterations and make changes accordingly, either to the features that will be delivered (standard) or to the release date; the customer should then update and reprioritize the backlog.
Document lessons learned.	Track recommendations and action plans resulting from the iteration retrospectives.

Manage Stakeholders

The *PMBOK® Guide* says the following: "Actively managing stakeholders increases the likelihood that the project will not veer off track due to unresolved stakeholder issues, enhances the ability of persons to operate synergistically, and limits disruptions during the projects."[8] Think of the *PMBOK® Guide's* "managing stakeholders" as agile's "engaging stakeholders." We feel that they are to be engaged and educated, not managed—we'll manage the methods and styles of communication instead.

Because of constant inspecting and adaptation, there are always issues to solve in an agile project. The *PMBOK® Guide* advocates not troubling stakeholders with minutia; in agile, the team is empowered to solve its own problems, yet urged to communicate those obstacles not in its power to resolve up the chain to management, some of whom are usually stakeholders in the project. This gives stakeholders the opportunity for daily insight into issues, if necessary, and on a more regular basis at the end of every iteration.

As we know, it is the minutia of daily obstacles that can derail a project, little by little, one day at a time.

Managers and stakeholders should always be invited to iteration review meetings as a primary means of understanding project status. At the iteration review, the team can also present any changes that have been made through the negotiation process with the customer or product management, as well as any changes it has made within its own team process. Additionally, the reforecast of the release plan can also be presented at the iteration review meeting, thus consolidating the stakeholders' time into one slot. Throughout the project, stakeholders can be called upon more or less, depending on the issues at the time. Establishing this expectation up front will help keep your stakeholders engaged.

Table 10-4 provides a summary comparison of the traditional and agile approaches to managing stakeholders. In agile, this is referred to as "engaging stakeholders."

Table 10-4
Managing Stakeholders

Traditional	Agile
Outline communications methods to be used in the project.	Promote face-to-face communication when possible. Utilize other reports to supplement when stakeholders cannot meet in person.
Use an issues log to communicate issues and their resolution to stakeholders.	Have the team designate issues that cannot be quickly resolved as roadblocks on the task board. These and other issues outside the team's control are managed to resolution by the agile project manager and are communicated via shared tools and planning meetings.
Communicate approved change requests and corrective actions that bring the project back in line with the project plan.	Facilitate the team and the customer as they update release plans and the product backlog appropriately; stakeholders should have access to review these changes at any time or more formally as part of the planning meetings or iteration review and retrospective meetings.
Update documentation, including the project plan.	Update plans and other documentation as needed.

Summary

The following points were made in this chapter:

- The most effective method of communication is face-to-face meetings.
- Stakeholders should be invited to planning meetings and the iteration reviews because these are key points of communication.
- Use highly visible information radiators to convey information about the project, such as the important dates, times, and people in the project, the current status of the project, and roadblocks, issues, or risks that are being worked on.
- Use the end of the iteration as a time to distribute information about the iteration, the product, and the release.
- Use tools such as burndown charts, release plans, iteration plans, task boards, and others as needed to communicate status and forecasts.
- Help facilitate teams to resolve their own issues; escalate bigger issues to management.

Table 10-5 outlines the communication management behaviors of a project manager working on traditional or agile projects.

Table 10-5
Agile Project Manager's Change List for Communications Management

I used to do this:	Now I do this:
Prepare a formal communications management plan.	Work with the team to understand what information is important to distribute and to whom. Utilize face-to-face meetings as main communication channels; support with subsequent forms of communication only when necessary.
Hold a formal project status meeting once a week and then report status to management and other interested stakeholders.	Invite stakeholders to observe daily stand-ups, invite them to planning meetings, and utilize the iteration review as a vehicle for communicating project status.
Hold a project postmortem at the end of the project.	Engage the team in a retrospective at the end of each iteration.

I used to do this:	Now I do this:
Distribute formal project status documents for sign-off and approval.	Keep information high bandwidth and less formal through the use of highly visible information radiators. Encourage face-to-face communication for high effectiveness and to establish trust.
Keep minutia away from stakeholders.	Present stakeholders with issues that the team lacks authority to resolve in order to quickly remove obstacles.

Endnotes

1. Effy Oz and John J. Sosik. "Why Information Systems Projects are Abandoned: A Leadership and Communication Theory and Exploration Study, Oz and Sosik." *Journal of Computer Information Systems,* Fall, 2000, 67.

2. Merriam-Webster Online. http://www.merriam-webster.com/.

3. Sue Dyer. *The Root Causes of Poor Communication.* http://www.myarticlearchive.com/articles/6/143.htm.

4. *PMBOK® Guide,* 235.

5. Ibid.

6. Jeffrey K Liker. *The Toyota Way: 14 Management Principles from the World's Greatest Manufacturer.* (New York: McGraw-Hill, 2004), 23.

7. Mike Cohn. *Agile Estimating and Planning,* 235.

8. *PMBOK® Guide,* 245.

Chapter 11

Risk Management

The objectives of Project Risk Management are to increase the probability and impact of positive events and decrease the probability and impact of events adverse to the project.

—PMBOK® Guide

The business of believing only what you have a right to believe is called risk management.

—*Tom DeMarco and Tim Lister,* Waltzing with Bears

People who don't take risks generally make about two big mistakes a year. People who do take risks generally make about two big mistakes a year.

—*Peter Drucker*

Risk management is a critical component of traditional projects. Those new to agile worry about the lack of defined risk management activities in agile processes. The framework of the agile software development process fosters organic, or naturally emerging risk management by making it an intrinsic part of the project lifecycle. The agile framework both increases positive events and decreases negative events by constantly reviewing the product functionality, the project plans, and the process itself. It is the team that takes on this responsibility—risks are addressed by everybody all the time. Daily stand-ups, iteration planning meetings, release planning meetings, demos, reviews, and retrospective meetings are all venues for risk management activities on an agile project. The agile project manager facilitates the process and makes sure that the results are visible to all.

Let's first look at how the agile framework organically supports risk management, and then discuss specifically how each of the *PMBOK® Guide* Project Risk Management processes maps to agile practices. Along the way we will provide examples of specific overt practices you can ask your team to consider when managing risk in your software development teams.

Organic Risk Management in Agile

Tom DeMarco and Tim Lister identified five core risk areas common to all projects in their book, *Waltzing with Bears*:[1]

- Intrinsic Schedule Flaw (estimates that are wrong and undoable from day one, often based on wishful thinking)
- Specification Breakdown (failure to achieve stakeholder consensus on what to build)
- Scope Creep (additional requirements that inflate the initially accepted set)
- Personnel Loss
- Productivity Variation (difference between assumed and actual performance)

We've all experienced these issues on projects, and in some unlucky cases it's a perfect storm of all five risks hitting at once! Being able to address all of these core risks is what makes an agile framework so appealing. The constant planning, the stopping points built in to handle change, the involvement of all team members in solving the problem—these all successfully mitigate the core risks. The following sections discuss specifically how an agile framework addresses these risks.

Mitigating Intrinsic Schedule Flaw

This is the biggest risk of the five in terms of its impact on planned versus actual performance, and it speaks to a common tendency to underestimate the size of the product being built.[2] Moving to an agile approach won't immediately change that tendency, but it does bring the invalid estimates to light very quickly, enabling the team to resize the release.

This is accomplished by the reevaluation of the release plan at the end of each iteration, to see if the team is still on target. If it isn't, this is the time to re-scope the remainder of the release to more accurately reflect the speed of the team as it deals with the complexities of software development. Preventing much of the wishful thinking that often gets built in to these estimates is accomplished by involving the entire team in the planning process and allowing the team to own its estimates.

As pointed out in this core risk, the estimates may be wrong on day one—but in agile they are not undoable! Instead the plan is corrected and refined as the project moves along, meaning lower-priority features are dropped from the release plan in order for the team to still make its dates. After the team has completed one or two iterations, the plan is much more accurate, because it now reflects reality and uses historic averages in predicting the future (see Chapter 6, "Time Management," for more detail). This is in line with the *PMBOK® Guide* project management process that shows the results of execution feeding back into planning.[4]

> ## When No *I* in Team Isn't So Good: Conformity Pressure
>
> Sometimes the involvement of the team does *not* prevent wishful thinking. In one iteration planning meeting, when the team was asked if it could commit to the iteration plan, the team members responded by holding up three or four fingers, meaning "I can live with and support this" and "this is a good idea," respectively. The facilitator then asked the team members to put their heads down and close their eyes, and vote again. This time the room was full of hands holding up just two fingers, meaning "I have reservations and would have trouble supporting this." In this company, the team members did not feel safe enough to openly voice their doubts.[3]

Mitigating Specification Breakdown

It can be difficult to agree on what to build when each stakeholder may have a different vision of the end product. Disagreements can occur between these stakeholders, leaving the software development team in limbo until the situation is resolved. Disagreements can also occur between the development team and the stakeholder, often leaving one or the other grumbling about the design of the product. Finally, in the absence of business direction the development team may be having its own internal struggle about what to build.

In agile this is resolved by having one customer, or product owner, who makes the decision about what the product should do, what the product should look like, and how it should perform. This product owner defines the features needed in priority order, and owns this backlog of work. Here's how Mike Cohn stated it in his book, *User Stories Applied:*

> "Collectively, the developers have a sequence in which they would like to implement the (features), as will the customer. When there is a disagreement to the sequence, the customer wins. Every time. However, customers cannot prioritize without some information from the development team…"[5] It is up to the development team to "provide information (estimates, assumptions, constraints, alternatives) to the customer in order to help her prioritize the stories."[6]

There can also be a specification breakdown in terms of *how* to build the product—where there are several different approaches available, but no clear answer without extensive analysis, design, and experimentation. In these cases, some agile teams will use a design method called "set-based design,"[7] where a set of possible design solutions are identified and remain in play until learning from each iteration leads the team to begin eliminating choices, leaving the one best choice to move forward with. This is different from the traditional point-based design approach, where one choice is made at each step of the design process to improve the design until it is deemed ready to employ.

Imagine trying to set up a meeting with your colleagues. If you used point-based design, you would start with a specific time: "I'm free at 2 p.m. How about you guys?" "No, 2 p.m. doesn't work for me. How about 3 p.m.?" "I can't do 3:00. Can we meet at 9 a.m. tomorrow instead?" and so on, until a time is finally agreed upon. If you used set-based design, the conversation might go more like this: "I'm free from 10 a.m. to 2 p.m.

Getting to One Product Owner

Just because this is an agile practice it doesn't mean that it is always properly observed. One team I know of is still grappling with the problem of having too many product owners even though they've embraced Scrum. These product owners cannot agree on what features are most important and therefore it's the one who screams loudest or has the most political clout who gets her features put in front of the team. Answering to so many different bosses is unfair to the team and limits their ability to effectively collaborate. They had this problem with waterfall, they have it still with Scrum, yet with Scrum's ability to make roadblocks like these highly visible to all stakeholders, they hope that management will now be forced to eventually take action.

today, or from 9 a.m. to 11 a.m. tomorrow. Are there times in there that would work for you?" "Yes, let's meet at 9 a.m. tomorrow." Where point-based design has us making linear choices, set-based design has us examining a set of options and constraints and making a decision as late as we responsibly can. You've seen this in the retail world already: paint that doesn't have its color mixed in until you pick the palette number at the store, t-shirts customized while you wait, or Dell personal computers loaded with the software of your choice and then shipped to you. It's simply a way of delaying commitment until the number of uncertainties is reduced.

Mitigating Scope Creep

Scope creep is also referred to as "requirements inflation," and the longer the delivery cycle the more likely additional requirements or changes to existing requirements will occur.

In agile, change is an accepted part of software development, and there are stopping points built in to the project to enable the team to address these change requests. At the end of each iteration, the team reviews the work done on the product, the process it followed to get there, and the changes that it may have to make to better accommodate the needs of the customer or changes in the domain. This is the opportunity for the customer to make changes in the backlog, and based on priority, the team will work the next set of features in the next iteration.

> ### Keep That Release Plan Visible
>
> In one instance the customer, delighted with his new-found power, made "Cool! Now try this!" changes three iterations in a row before realizing that playing with the product was not getting the team any closer to a fully functional release. This is why it's important to always have the release plan highly visible and revisit it at the end of each iteration—to remind everyone of the ultimate goal.

Mitigating Personnel Loss

Death march projects tend to experience high turnover, but all projects have to deal with the loss of key personnel at some point. Using an agile framework at least gives the team the ability to self-organize and focus on solving the problem at hand, which in turn leads to higher morale. Additionally, agile teams continuously share knowledge, via face-to-face communication;

therefore, all the team members become experts about the system. This transfer of knowledge to all members of the team helps mitigate personnel loss.

A search for studies done on turnover in agile teams resulted in no findings, but we discovered that there are no studies done on non-agile technical environments either: "A significant amount of research exists in the area of turnover intent but little that deals with turnover intent of technology professionals and none that specifically addresses turnover intent in an IT organization that has implemented the Capability Maturity Model (CMM)."[8] Direct correlations between job satisfaction and turnover have been proven, however, and it is our firm opinion that an agile framework gives team members the best opportunity for job satisfaction as a result of their being full participants in the process.

Mitigating Productivity Variation

Productivity variation is the difference between the assumed and actual performance of the team, but we like to extend it to mean the difference between the assumed and actual performance of the product as well. Again, both are nicely addressed at the end of the iteration in the demo and review meeting. The team reviews how well it did in meeting its commitments, and the demo of the product to the stakeholders illustrates the actual functionality that has been completed. If the team is failing to meet its commitments, it knows that in the next iteration it needs to commit to less work. If the product fails to meet the customer's expectations, those issues are identified immediately and changes are made to correct the issues in the next iteration.

One way to mitigate productivity variation is through the use of a velocity measurement for the team. When a team begins agile development, it takes an educated guess about how much work it can take on in an iteration. After two or three iterations, this guess becomes more solid, and the team begins to confidently pick off the amount of work that it can do. This amount of work is called the team's "velocity." Agile also assumes that a team is dedicated to the work throughout the project. This assumption, coupled with the established team's velocity measurement, helps mitigate the risk of productivity variation.

Now let's look at how each of the *PMBOK® Guide* project risk management processes map to agile practices.

Risk Management Planning

This is the process of "deciding how to approach and conduct the risk management activities for a project."[9] Typically, several planning meetings are held with stakeholders, managers, and/or corporate representatives in order to create a formal document outlining the risk management process. This document generally contains information regarding the methodology, roles and responsibilities, budget, review schedule, risk categories, definitions and measurements, probability/impact matrix, reporting formats, and tracking activities. As outlined in the *PMBOK® Guide*, this risk management plan is a formal document resulting from formal discussions.

However, each company (or each team within a company) may not have a need for such formality. Although the *PMBOK® Guide* recommends the creation of the formal plan as a best practice, it is simply the output of the main goal, which is to agree on how to address risk in the project. Carl Pritchard addressed how to determine the appropriate level of formality in his *The Cutter Edge* article, "Where Do You Start in Building a Risk Standard?" Specifically, he stated that "In more independent, entrepreneurial organizations, fewer steps will likely be seen as appropriate, as individuals grant themselves license to determine how the steps will ultimately be implemented in their areas within the organization. The true heart of establishing the process, however, should be to ensure that the appropriate risks are addressed. While mirroring the organization's culture and needs, the process should integrate with the day-to-day operations of the organization and within the amount of time allocated to accomplish the goals of the process."[10]

It's clear that common sense should dictate that the formality around risk management planning should be context-driven and time-sensitive. Therefore, if your team doesn't need a formal Risk Management Plan document, agile doesn't require you to prepare one. Agile approaches support the idea of managing risk informally without a documented plan because of the way addressing risk is built organically into the agile process, as discussed in the previous section. And yet agile does not prevent teams from inserting more formal plans if their culture or needs require it. This is really the essence of doing risk management planning in agile: determining if we need to do it formally or if we should instead allow risk to be addressed organically as part of the overall process of constant inspection and adaptation. Or perhaps we need to do a blended approach where risk is managed overtly but informally. The organic and the overt practices are covered in the following process sections.

Table 11-1 presents a summary comparison of the traditional and agile approaches to risk management planning. There is no specific agile terminology for risk management planning, but we still plan to manage risk.

Table 11-1
Risk Management Planning

Traditional	Agile
Meetings with managers to decide on the risk management approach.	The team is asked to determine the appropriate risk management approach.
Results in a formal document outlining the risk management process.	Results in less formal or no documentation regarding the process.

Risk Identification

Risk identification is precisely what it sounds like—the process of identifying risks that might affect the project and determining their characteristics.[11] In traditional project environments, risk identification is conducted in meetings with often only a subset of the team, who use checklists, document reviews, assumption analysis, and various other information-gathering techniques to identify project risks and record them in a Risk Register (what we commonly called a "spreadsheet"). Although the *PMBOK® Guide* states that this is an iterative process, oftentimes traditional teams will not perform this exercise more than a few times over the course of the project. And given some of the time constraints we find ourselves in, it's not uncommon to see this exercise done once at the beginning of the project and then never again.

In an agile environment, the whole team does this exercise on an iterative basis during planning meetings, recording results on whiteboards or flipcharts. If the agile team is managing risk overtly, then an agenda item for the team to identify and prioritize risks is included as part of the planning meeting, with the results influencing the work that is being planned for that release or iteration.[12] See Figure 11-1 for an example of an agenda that includes an item regarding the need to identify risks. The results of the risk identification activity may drive changes with regard to which items from the backlog are selected for the iteration or in how they are implemented. Risk-driven teams may wish to use this approach, whereas value-driven teams may be more interested in the next option.

Figure 11-1
Iteration planning meeting agenda with overt risk agenda item

Iteration Planning Meeting Agenda

- *Purpose & Agenda Review*
- *Do we need to review the release plan?*
- *What are our iteration start & end dates?*
- *Do we know what stories we want to complete in this iteration?*
- *Do we have enough information about these stories to be able to task them out?*
- *What are the risks we should be concerned about in this iteration?*
- *What tasks and effort will it take for us to complete these stories? (Do we need to define what "done" means?)*
- *Can we sign up for these tasks now?*
- *How does the total effort we've defined here compare to our expected velocity?*
- *What dependencies might impact the prioritization?*
- *What assumptions are we making?*
- *Given the velocity constraints, dependencies, and assumptions, do we need to reprioritize or move any stories?*
- *Can we now commit to this iteration as a team?*
- *Close: parking lot, action items, communications plan*

Open Space Meetings

One team uses Open Space meetings to resolve risks and cross-team dependencies. An Open Space meeting is a self-organized meeting where the participants set the topic and agenda. Usually several groups form to address the different issues.[13] The team realized that putting the problem—and the right people—together in a room was the best way to solve issues and mitigate the risks in the project. After solving issues such as "agilizing" waterfall testing phases and coming up with creative solutions to an internationalization challenge, the team learned that the value of an Open Space lies within the binding decisions that are made; the people attending are truly interested in solving the *problem*.[14]

If the agile team is managing risk organically, then potential risks are identified as part of the agenda items "What assumptions are we making?" and "What concerns do we have?" Both occur at the very end of the meeting, just prior to asking for team commitment to the iteration or release. See Figure 11-2 for an example. An example of concerns identified by one team is illustrated in Figure 11-3. Some of the items are risks, whereas others are risks already materialized (that is, problems). All of these items remain visible to the team throughout the release, as a constant reminder of what to watch and prepare for.

Figure 11-2
Iteration planning agenda using organic risk management agenda items

Agenda

- *Welcome! Purpose—Agenda—Ground Rules*
- *Do we know what our velocity is?*
- *Do we know what features/req. we want to do for this iteration?*
- *And their priorities?*
- *Do we have enough information to task out the req. & estimate those tasks?*
- *Are all the tasks signed up?*
- *Do we know what dependencies we have & what assumptions we're making?*
- *What concerns do we have about this iteration?*
- *Can we commit to this iteration as a team?*

Figure 11-3
Concerns gathered during an iteration planning meeting as part of organic risk management

Concerns

- *Product managers have 3 roles—will they be available to the team?*
- *The first iteration may be limited due to prior release support.*
- *Will we be able to do a sustainable pace?*
- *16 hrs for the user interface seems small.*
- *Dependencies of defects on this list.*
- *Can we get the defects prioritized soon enough?*
- *Technical deficit for documentation.*
- *Implementation of 1st product will suck our resources.*
- *We're having a really good snow year and no wireless on slopes.*
- *Learning new process.*
- *Will the requirements be detailed enough?*
- *Personnel multitasked, not fully dedicated.*

RISK MANAGEMENT

Risks and problems continue to be identified daily as part of daily stand-up meetings, as do risk triggers, which indicate that a risk has occurred or is about to occur. If the team is conducting risk management organically, then the answer to the stand-up meeting question "What obstacles are preventing me from completing my work?" may reveal new risks or risk triggers. In this organic process, agile project managers will often use sticky notes, whiteboards, or flip charts to keep track of these items.

Ferreting Out the Risks

Sometimes risks are identified as part of the responses to the other two stand-up questions, "What did I do yesterday?" and "What am I going to do today?" Agile project managers must listen carefully in stand-up meetings, because risks may be embedded in otherwise uneventful statements. For example, hearing "Yesterday I finished module XYZ; today I'm going to work with Pat on finalizing component ABC, assuming she doesn't break our appointment again, and nothing is getting in my way" may translate into a risk identified as "Pat is often unavailable to the team, which could lead to a potential bottleneck."

If the team is conducting risk management overtly, then new problems, risks, and risk triggers are identified during the stand-up meeting and placed in a highly visible location, usually the Risk Board (see Figure 11-4 and the "Obstacles" section of the whiteboard later on in Figure 11-5). Items placed here are discussed after the stand-up because the short 15-minute timeframe of the meeting prevents analysis and response planning. Those interested in or affected by the risk are welcome to stay, while other team members are free to get to work.

Figure 11-4
Team doing their daily stand-up at the Risk Board.[15]

Table 11-2 presents a summary comparison of traditional and agile approaches to risk identification. There is no specific agile terminology for risk identification, but we identify risks in all our planning meetings.

Table 11-2
Risk Identification

Traditional	Agile
Identify risks using checklists, document reviews, information gathering, assumption analysis, and diagramming...	Identify risks using information gathering and assumption analysis...
In limited meetings...	In every planning meeting with the whole team...
And formally documented in the Risk Register.	And informally documented.

Risk Analysis

Risk analysis deals with the analysis of identified risks, their prioritization, and determination of which risks warrant response. Traditional projects use both quantitative analysis (assigning real numbers to the costs of safeguards and the amount of damage that can occur) and qualitative analysis (using judgment, intuition, and experience in determining risks and potential losses). Agile projects generally perform only qualitative analysis, agile's short development cycles and constant reviews making this feasible and effective. Again, the *PMBOK® Guide* supports this approach: "Qualitative risk analysis is usually a rapid and cost-effective means of establishing priorities for Risk Response Planning, and lays the foundation for Quantitative Risk Analysis *if this is required* [emphasis mine]." [16]

And *if this is required,* the agile framework does not prevent teams from conducting quantitative risk analysis. If deemed appropriate by the team, time should be set aside for this activity as part of the release and/or iteration planning meetings.

Qualitative analysis in agile projects can be organic, with discussions about the probability and impact of risks emerging during planning meetings. Judgment, intuition, and experience are what agile teams rely on in their analysis. This can also be an overt activity, with daily post-stand-up meetings held at the Risk Board to conduct informal analysis discussion. The end result in both cases is a short list of risks to respond to and risks to watch (Concerns and/or Risk Board). Table 11-3 provides a summary comparison of the traditional and agile approaches to risk analysis. There is no specific term for risk analysis as part of agile terminology. Risk analysis is conducted in planning meetings as appropriate.

Table 11-3
Risk Analysis

Traditional	Agile
Uses qualitative and quantitative analysis…	Uses qualitative analysis…
Prioritizes risks using probability and impact analysis…	Prioritizes or groups risks using probability and impact analysis…
Resulting in risks to respond to and risks to watch…	Resulting in risks to respond to and risks to watch…
And formally documented in the Risk Register.	And informally documented.

Risk Response Planning

Developing options and actions to reduce threats and increase opportunities is performed in both traditional and agile environments, with the key differences being that in an agile environment the entire team participates and it is conducted with more frequency than is common in traditional plan-driven projects. Performed organically in planning meetings, team discussions lead to action items that are often designed to mitigate an identified risk. Response planning is also part of the retrospective, where teams make recommendations regarding how to improve the process and reduce bottlenecks.

Many agile teams doing overt risk management using a Risk Board follow Tom DeMarco and Tim Lister's recommended category breakout as explained in their book, *Waltzing with Bears*. According to DeMarco and Lister, risks can fall into one of four response categories:

- **Avoid**—Don't do the project or part of the project that entails the risk. For example, avoiding an upgrade to a new platform.
- **Mitigate**—Take steps before the risk materializes to reduce the eventual containment costs. For example, moving a feature to an earlier iteration to ensure that it's completed in time for the release.
- **Contain**—Set aside time and money to pay for the risk should it materialize (equivalent to the *PMBOK® Guide* "Plan Contingency"). For example, preparing training on new automated testing software.
- **Evade**—When you do none of the above and yet manage to get lucky (equivalent to the *PMBOK® Guide* "Accept").[17] For example, ignoring the problem of not having a dedicated team for the duration of the project qualifies as evading.

Figure 11-5 shows an example of risks being managed using these categories, which are displayed on a whiteboard. The larger sticky notes indicate an identified risk, and the smaller sticky notes indicate some action being taken to mitigate or contain that risk. Items on the left side of the board are obstacles identified during daily stand-ups. Obstacles tend to be either problems (risks that have already occurred) or risk triggers.

Figure 11-5
Risk response planning using DeMarco/Lister categories.

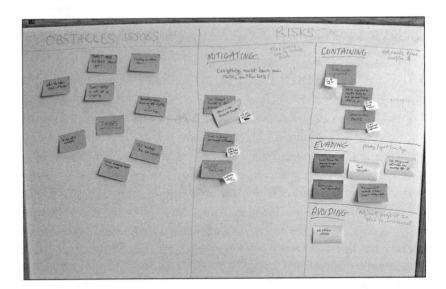

Table 11-4 presents the traditional and agile approaches to risk response planning. Again, this is not a concept for which agile includes specific terms, but it is part of how agile teams self-organize and solve problems.

Table 11-4
Risk Response Planning

Traditional	Agile
One or more people assigned to develop strategies to…	The team brainstorms strategies to…
Avoid	Avoid
Mitigate	Mitigate
Plan contingency	Contain
Accept	Evade

Risk Monitoring and Controlling

Risk monitoring and controlling involves watching for new risks, tracking and validation of identified risks, and tracking and reviewing risk responses. The *PMBOK® Guide* identifies several tools to use when doing risk monitoring and controlling activities: risk reassessment, risk audits, variance and trend analysis, technical performance measurement, and status meetings. All of this is accomplished as part of an agile approach, and is considered to be simply part of the organic process.

The reassessment of risks is conducted constantly in all planning meetings, as well as during the retrospective meetings, where previous risks/concerns are revisited as part of determining changes that need to be made going forward. Risk audits, which examine the effectiveness of risk responses, are also conducted as part of the retrospective meeting.

Burndown charts and other metrics are part of the variance and trend analysis done during iteration review meetings, and a review of the team's velocity is done in keeping with the technical performance measurement.

Risks are monitored on a daily basis by the use of highly visible information radiators such as task boards and burndown charts, which show the current status (see Figure 11-6 for an example of this organic risk monitoring tool). Daily stand-up meetings contribute to the constant monitoring process by exposing potential risk triggers and new risks.

Figure 11-6
Task board with burndown chart[18]

Table 11-5 provides a summary comparison of the traditional and agile approaches to risk monitoring and controlling. In the agile framework, this is simply referred to as "iteration tracking and review."

Table 11-5
Risk Monitoring and Controlling

Traditional	Agile
Risk reassessment in formal risk management review meetings	Risk reassessment in planning and retrospective meetings
Risk audit as a formal audit or as part of risk management review meetings	Risk audit in retrospective meetings
Variance and trend analysis	Burndown chart and metrics analysis in review meetings

RISK MANAGEMENT

Traditional	Agile
Technical performance measurement	Velocity analysis in review meetings
Status meetings	Task boards, burndown charts, and daily stand-up meetings

Summary

This chapter covered the following points:

- Risk management can be both organic (intrinsic in the process framework) and overt (addressed by specific activities)
- Risk management is owned by the team
- The project manager facilitates the process and makes the results visible
- Risks are identified in all planning meetings: release, iteration, and daily stand-ups
- Risks can be analyzed and addressed in all planning meetings, with the focus on qualitative analysis, not quantitative
- Risks are monitored by the use of high visibility information radiators, daily stand-ups, and iteration reviews and retrospectives

Table 11-6 runs down the change list behaviors of the project manager exhibited before and after adopting agile practices.

Table 11-6
Agile Project Manager's Change List for Risk Management

I used to do this:	Now I do this:
Prepare a formal risk management plan.	Educate the team about risk management and invite the team to determine how to best manage risk: formally, organically, or informally but overtly.
Conduct formal risk identification meetings and document results in a Risk Register.	Ask the team to identify risks (either organically as assumptions and concerns or overtly as risk events) in all planning meetings and record them on flip charts, whiteboards, or online tools, making sure they are in a highly visible area accessible to all stakeholders.

(continued)

Table 11-6

Agile Project Manager's Change List for Risk Management *(continued)*

I used to do this:	Now I do this:
Conduct both qualitative and quantitative analysis; determine how to respond and use the results to update the Risk Register.	Facilitate the team in its qualitative analysis, determine how to respond, and post results (see the previous item).
Periodically review the Risk Register and make updates as needed.	Constantly review risks and responses as part of the planning meetings, reviews, and retrospectives, either organically as emergent discussions or overtly as scheduled agenda items.

Endnotes

1. Tom DeMarco and Tim Lister. *Waltzing with Bears.* (New York: Dorset House Publishing, 2003), 101–110.

2. DeMarco and Lister. *Waltzing with Bears*, 102.

3. The display of fingers to indicate commitment is called "the fist of five" and is taken from work done by agile thought leader and certified professional facilitator Jean Tabaka. When asking a team if they agree to a decision, or are ready to commit, they each hold up their fingers to indicate one of the following: (one finger) This is wrong-minded of us and we should not proceed; (two fingers) I have reservations and would have trouble supporting this; (three fingers) I can live with and support this; (four fingers) This is a good idea; and (five fingers) This is a fabulous idea! When looking for commitment in planning meetings, you are looking for three, four, and five fingers from the team members. If anyone holds up one or two fingers, you should ask what it would take to get them from a one to a three, or from a two to a three, respectively. The team cannot commit as a whole without everyone at a minimum being willing to live with and support the decision.

4. *PMBOK® Guide,* 40.

5. Cohn. *User Stories Applied*, 99.

6. Ibid.

7. Poppendieck. *Lean Software Development*, 38.

8. Janet K. Ply. "The Impact of Organizational Maturity on Job Attitudes and Intentions Within Software Development Organizations." (PhD diss., George Mason University, 2004), 15.

9. *PMBOK® Guide*, 242.

10. Carl Pritchard. "Where Do You Start in Building a Risk Standard?" *The Cutter Edge*, March 7, 2006, http://www.cutter.com/research/2006/edge060307.html.

11. *PMBOK® Guide*, 246.

12. Preston G. Smith and Roman Pichler. "Agile Risks/Agile Rewards." *Software Development*, April 2005, 52.

13. Read more about the commonly used agile tool Open Space Meetings at http://en.wikipedia.org/wiki/Open-space_meeting.

14. Constance M.Tartaglia and Prasad Ramnath. "Using Open Spaces to Resolve Cross Team Issues." (paper presented at the Agile2005 conference, Denver, Colorado, USA, July 24–29, 2005).

15. Photo courtesy of Rally Software Development Grp. All rights reserved. Used with permission.

16. *PMBOK® Guide*, 250.

17. DeMarco and Lister. *Waltzing with Bears*, 63–64.

18. Photo courtesy of Mike Cohn, Mountain Goat Software. Used with permission.

Chapter 12

Procurement Management

Project Procurement Management includes the processes required to purchase or acquire the products, services, or results needed from outside the project team to perform the work.

—PMBOK® Guide

The handshake | Seals the contract | From the contract | There's no turning back.

—Depeche Mode lyrics "Everything Counts"

Unless both sides win, no agreement can be permanent.

—Jimmy Carter

Finding contractors and aligning their skills with a project's vision and needs is no simple task. From interviewing, coordinating schedules, and determining a suitable pay scale or price procuring a resource (human or otherwise) can sometimes be fraught with tough negotiations, disappointments, and surprises along the way. From the contractor's perspective, understanding a buyer's requirements and needs can be extremely difficult. Then, there's the contract negotiation aspect for both parties: legalese, lawyer involvement, and the exchange of money. Anyone who has been involved with submitting a request for proposal and negotiating and accepting a contract can understand the daunting nature of this process. Contracts are the legal safety net that corporations put in place to protect their rights, ensure that their interests are being met, and offset risk to the other party. Although certainly a valuable business necessity, the process—from interview, to contract, to closure—can be intense, stressful, rigid, and often very time-consuming.

So how do we reconcile this with what the Agile Manifesto says about "customer collaboration over contract negotiation?" Does this mean that we do not go through procurement or write contracts any longer? Not at all. Procuring vendors and contractors is a necessary part of the business world. A contract is the result of the buyer and contractor collaborating on the needs for the project; collaborating about the best solution often involves the skill of negotiating. The contract is an output of the very important conversations between seller and buyer and serves as a guide for billing and accounting purposes once the project is underway. The communication that occurs to create the document is the most important part of the process. It is through this process that we build relationships that enable us to build the right software, with our customers' help, or as customers, work with our vendors in a way that they can understand our needs.

As we wrote this chapter, we realized that there isn't much difference between traditional and agile approaches in the way to go about procurement—from planning, to selecting sellers, to managing the contract along the way. What we will do in this chapter is give you some ideas to think about for your procurement process from an agile perspective, whether you're a buyer or seller, as well as some ideas for how to write contracts that enable more alignment between the two parties. You'll find additional guidance on vendors and contracting in the "Clearing the Hurdles" section of Chapter 14, "How Will I Work with Other Teams Who Aren't Agile?" This is a relatively new area of focus for agile software organizations; as they practice agile for longer periods of time, it begins to impact the way in which they approach their procurement and contracting processes. Much of this is due to the way in which agile teams work, as well as the need for writing contracts that create more alignment between buyers and sellers.

We begin by looking at planning of purchases and acquisitions and contracting as well. Then we turn to sellers, in terms of their responses and selecting them. Finally, we address contracts: administering them and closing them.

Plan Purchases and Acquisitions

The *PMBOK® Guide* defines plan purchases and acquisitions as the process that "identifies which project needs can be best met by purchasing or acquiring products, services, or results outside the project organization, and which project needs can be accomplished by the project team during project execution."[1] These "make or buy" decisions are weighed heavily by an organization in order to determine cost effectiveness and overall applicability to the project. The administration of these buy decisions is often a project-within-a-project; that is, it is managed separately but in conjunction with the deliverables of the overall project.

We certainly encounter these make-versus-buy decisions in agile projects. An opportunity to purchase services or other technology can occur at any level of planning, but most often these decisions are planned well ahead of time. This is because the contract negotiations must occur between the buyer and the provider of services, and we must allow time for this to happen. The types of things we may want to plan for include the following: services from third-party contractors, hardware, software, hiring resources, and buying other companies. These types of purchases and acquisitions will certainly affect the cost of our project, and this chapter later discusses how we manage costs from contracts in our release plan.

In agile projects, the research into criteria for buying decisions is often expanded to include the team. Teams are empowered to investigate and share knowledge whenever possible. The creation of a "learning culture" in agile teams is valuable from a purchasing perspective in that there is grassroots involvement in both the research and selection of items of purchase.

Certainly, in any contracting situation, technical, financial, and legal expert judgment should be sought and

Buy the Technology, Buy the Company

One company I worked with had a unique way of planning a purchase for version 6.0 of its product. While the majority of the development organization was wrapping up version 5.0, five key team members were allocated to research new technologies that would be used in the enhancement for the 6.0 version. They conducted their research in iterations. While in the midst of their research, they encountered an organization that had just the technology they needed for the 6.0 version; it met every criteria on their checklist. After three rounds of prototypes to prove ease of integration and a couple of key features, it was determined to not only buy the right to integrate the third-party tool but to acquire the company altogether!

considered. Indeed, this can impact the type of contract type that we choose; in fact, most of us abide by these contract types today: fixed-price (lump sum), cost-reimbursable, time and materials (T&M). Some agile companies choose to contract on a T&M basis with built-in checkpoints (iteration demos) tied to compensation. Part of planning for what we need to contract is determining how best to contract for it.

Mary Poppendieck discusses one of Toyota's contracting approaches: creating target cost contracts, where seller and buyer agree to a target cost and share the expense of overruns. Such a contract motivates both parties to try and contain costs. Poppendieck takes a strong stance on the subject: "A fixed price contract with a vendor hoping to profit from changes, combined with rigorous change approval mechanisms to contain cost, may approximately double the cost and time it takes to develop the software, while producing a lower quality result."[2] Toyota's contracting approaches, combined with other supplier programs such as developing capabilities, sharing information, and focusing on continually improving processes, build partnerships in the long run. Although target cost contracts are nothing new from a general procurement management perspective, we are beginning to see many software companies leveraging these types of contracts with their customers.

Although you may have some influence on the way in which your contractors are procured, the contracting process will be largely determined and enforced by the legal influences on your organization. Larger organizations, for the most part, tend to have more rigid controls around contracts, procurement, purchase orders, make-or-buy analysis, and other information pertinent to its particular industry, with separate legal and financial divisions to oversee these contracts. These controls and related information can be found in the organization's procurement management plan. As new ways of contracting are discovered, this procurement plan should be updated for others in the organization.

Table 12-1 provides a summary comparison of traditional and agile approaches to planning purchases and acquisitions.

Table 12-1

Plan Purchases and Acquisitions

Traditional	Agile
Develop a procurement management plan based on information from the WBS, the scope statement, and the project management plan.	Ask for the team's assistance in providing input on the product roadmap and release plan as it relates to possible procurement activities.
Determine the contract type (often dictated by the organization).	Consider alternatives to traditional software development contracts, such as a target cost or T&M contracts.
Create a Contract Statement of Work to outline the work required by the seller.	Create the Contract Statement of Work based on input by the team.
Decide to "Make-or-Buy"—that is, make or buy functionality for the system.	Ask the team to research implementation paths and reach a decision: Do we make the functionality, or is it best to buy it?

Plan Contracting

Plan contracting includes the activities needed to prepare the proper documents for selecting sellers and soliciting seller responses. Whether traditional or agile in nature, your organization will have certain documents that it requires before requesting seller responses in an RFP (Request for Proposal) process. This is also true for contractors who are preparing to respond to an RFP (documents needed to fulfill the requests outlined in the RFP).

When the project manager or the team has identified a buy decision, the project manager will have to begin the plan contracting phase—that is, preparing the documents in order to get seller responses. Organizations that go through procurement often will have standardized documents that can be used. The *PMBOK® Guide* mentions that "procurement documents are rigorous enough to ensure consistent, comparable responses, but flexible enough to allow consideration of seller suggestions for better ways to satisfy the requirements."[3] This is a really important concept, and one that supports the notion of "customer collaboration." Often our customers have ideas at the contracting phase that can make for a better situation for both parties and often a more stable and satisfactory foundation from which to execute the contract.

Evaluation criteria are used to rate or score responses from suppliers. In the story earlier in the chapter, the 6.0 product team had a checklist of items against which it rated each potential supplier. This checklist was then expanded into bullets within the contract; these evaluation criteria served as the first iteration of expectations from the team. We have seen an increase in the number of buyers who request that the contractors from the selling agency act in an "agile fashion." That is, they attend iteration planning, daily stand-up meetings, and demo/review meetings just like the team. In fact, many third-party contractors or contracting agencies act much like an extended part of the team. If this is something you are interested in acquiring, the expected behavior must be identified in the contract and reinforced by the behavior of the procuring team. The IEEE has drafted a standard outlining this relationship that we hope will one day be published: *IEEE P1648 Recommended Practice for Establishing and Managing Software Development Efforts Using Agile Methods.*[4]

If you are an agile seller, you must be sure to clearly state the need for the customer's involvement throughout the project as well as the consequences should the customer fail to uphold this requirement. Many companies have included clauses that allow both parties to make continue-or-cancel decisions at the end of each iteration—the customer may cancel if the agile seller is failing to make deliveries as agreed, and the agile seller may cancel if they do not receive the input needed from the customer.

Usually a set of standard forms are utilized by the project management office when creating the documents needed to support the Request Seller Responses and Select Sellers processes. When an additional document is needed, the team can assist; sometimes, legal involvement is necessary.

Table 12-2 presents a summary comparison of the traditional and agile approaches to planning contracting.

Table 12-2
Plan Contracting

Traditional	Agile
Create procurement documents.	Meet with the team to determine the best language to put into the request for proposal.
Create evaluation criteria to help select the best seller.	The team may establish and review potential vendor candidates' evaluation criteria.

Request Seller Responses

"The Request Seller Responses process obtains responses, such as bids and proposals, from prospective sellers on how project requirements can be met."[5] This part of the process monitors the responses and timelines for those responses from suppliers.

A good measure—whether traditional or agile—is to communicate with the sellers who are making a bid for your business. The seller response takes time, and substantial cost is incurred to do so. Making sure that they understand your needs is critical to receiving quality responses from your sellers; in fact, they will probably need an explanation of Agile at the very least, and it is in both party's best interest to have a face-to-face meeting to set expectations. If a face-to-face meeting does not work for both parties, then a conference call, augmented with a web presentation should suffice. Again, these are activities that you are probably already engaging in as part of your seller response process, and we underscore the need for it for agile projects.

Part of receiving effective responses is setting expectations for the contract: in other words, letting the seller know that you are interested in expedited shipment of hardware, for example, or that the contractor must attend daily stand-up meetings. These details could certainly impact the seller response.

All of this also holds true if you are the agile seller team. Education about agile practices and the benefits of iterative and incremental delivery of working software are usually required, as is the need for continued customer involvement.

Seller responses can be solicited in many forums: newspaper, online, agencies, and via general networking. Often, organizations have a list of "qualified sellers"—that is, sellers who have already undergone a qualification process with the procuring organization. Sometimes, firms may give preference to qualified sellers over nonqualified sellers.

Table 12-3 provides a summary comparison of the traditional and agile approaches to requesting seller responses.

Table 12-3
Request Seller Responses

Traditional	Agile
Conduct bidder conferences.	Conduct bidder conferences and be sure to emphasize the expectations you have about adhering to agile practices—be prepared to educate the bidders.
Create qualified sellers list.	Revisit the qualified sellers list and remove those you know lack the ability to meet your agile needs.
Create the procurement document package for qualified sellers.	Create the procurement document package for qualified sellers and ask for the team members' help in reviewing it for their agile needs.
Receive proposals from sellers.	Receive proposals from sellers and review with those on the team who are interested.

Select Sellers

Selecting good vendors is critical to our projects. Not only must we know and understand the solutions they plan to provide but also how they plan to work with us in delivery. If our agile teams are accustomed to delivering working features every two weeks, and the vendor team is used to working in a waterfall fashion, then we could be setting ourselves up for disappointment and risk in our project. Likewise, if the provider of services is agile and the RFP came from a waterfall organization, there is an educational component that is critical to ensuring a satisfactory relationship.

The *PMBOK® Guide* recommends creating a weighting system for sellers; that is, rating sellers along a set of weighted criteria so that the most appealing rise to the top. The weights then create a "negotiating sequence" that determines the selection order of sellers. Cost is certainly a criterion, but there are also other things to consider: Will the vendor staff the job with dedicated resources? Are they skilled and reliable? Have we done business with them before? Were the results satisfactory to us? Do they understand agile values and principles? Are they willing to work with us in this fashion?

Contract negotiation is the art of ensuring that both buyer and seller are satisfied with the terms of the contract in order to agree to doing business. If the project manager is not the lead

Agile Only

I was working with a company for a period of months that really "got" agile—Scrum in particular. This company provided development solutions and services to its clients, many of whom where not accustomed to working in an agile fashion. After a couple of months, this company finally decided to draw a line in the dirt when it came to taking on new work. The CEO stated that "We will not provide services or technical solutions to a customer who cannot work with us in an agile fashion. That is, they must be committed to the project right there alongside of us, utilize the inspect and adapt checkpoints, and work with us to refine requirements to their specifications." Ever since, this perspective has been reflected in the company's contracts and in the way it does business.

negotiator on the contract, it is vital that she be included in the discussions leading up to contract finalization. Think of the project manager as the product owner in this instance, defining requirements in order of importance to the lead negotiator and being available to provide further clarity, answer questions, and grant final acceptance of the contract and its terms.

Once the seller and buyer agree to the contract and its terms, there must also be a plan in place to manage the contract. You may want to consider the following questions: What are the terms for payment of the contract? How will we manage the progress made by the service provider? Are we prepared for frequent releases? Do we need to establish a staging environment for the iteration deliverables? Does the buyer expect to have a formal UAT phase, or will this be a part of every iteration? What are our quality measurements for the deliverables provided by the seller? What eventual outcomes are we expecting? The answers to these questions (and others) will determine the overall contract management approach.

Additionally, the agile project manager must determine how status will be reported in accordance with the contract. Will there be a status report once a week? Once a month? Daily as part of the daily stand-up meeting? The contract could be written such that the buyer gets the status through a combination of informal documentation (burndown charts, iteration summaries, task board webcam) and an open-door invitation to observe the daily stand-ups. In any case, it is the agile project manager's responsibility to coordinate and facilitate the status reporting activities such that they satisfy the signers of the contract and yet still protect the team from unnecessary ceremonial meetings that pull team members away from the work waiting to be done.

As we've discussed elsewhere in the book, the best form of project status is a demo of working product. However, some buyers do not work in an agile fashion and do not want to consume deliverables as such (see the sidebar). Sometimes, the agile project manager will get creative in the way the team and the customer collaborate; regardless of how this is handled, the project manager must help set expectations for both parties when it comes to the status of the project.

Table 12-4 presents a summary comparison of the traditional and agile approaches to selecting sellers.

Balancing Customer and Project Needs

One client I worked with had a very demanding customer, and it made sense to respond very quickly because this customer contributed about 20% to the overall bottom line. It just so happened that this customer did not want to hear the word "agile" or "sprint" or "demo" from my client; in fact, the client specifically asked for waterfall-style milestone updates. This was very demanding for my client's product owner, Jim, who was constantly managing a high-level schedule—or agile release plan—in tandem with the customer's milestones. Jim worked with the project manager to allow time for things such as a four-week user acceptance testing period, while keeping the team busy on new work. It was a constant juggle, which meant that successfully managing and delivering the requirements from this demanding customer hinged on team, project manager, and product owner partnership.

Table 12-4
Select Sellers

Traditional	Agile
Use tools such as weighting and screening to determine qualified sellers.	Use tools such as weighting and screening to determine qualified sellers, and include items that quantify your agile needs and expectations.
Select sellers and negotiate a contract.	Make negotiation as collaborative as possible, allowing time for agile education and including text regarding agile expectations around involvement and delivery.
Establish a contract management plan.	Identify end-of-iteration contract management activities.

Contract Administration

Contracts are administered in order to make sure both parties meet their contractual obligations. Simply put, a seller administers a contract to make sure that the buyer is paying, and the buyer administers the contract to make sure that the seller is performing to expectation. Although legally the relationship's expectations are managed by a contract, there is also the day-to-day relationship management that happens as a result of working in an agile fashion. I like to use the marriage analogy: There is a contract that outlines the legal relationship of two people, and those people also have the day-to-day relationship that they "manage." The marriage contract is "high level" to allow for interpretation and negotiation along the way; it doesn't tell us how to relate to each other on a day-to-day basis—how to make the coffee, how to pick up the spouse's dirty sneakers without complaining, deciding who's going to pick up the kids. How we interact beneath the legalese of our contracts is critical to building and sustaining a real partnership with our clients; Agile provides natural mechanisms for this to occur.

The *PMBOK® Guide* lists a number of project management processes in its section 12.5 that apply to contract administration; of course, actions are not limited to these:

- **Direct and Manage Project Execution to authorize the contractor's work at the appropriate time.** In an agile project, we can leverage the release roadmap and agile release plan to have an early look at when a contractor might be needed, and then manage the contracts to these releases. For example, if I met with my project team yesterday to plan a release, and the team members determined that they are going to need a data architect for the fourth iteration because the architecture will be extended in such a way that prescribes this, I will start looking for a DA now. I will write the contract so that the DA will be a part of the team for that iteration or perhaps a little before and after that iteration to allow for proper ramp-up and knowledge transfer. I will also write the contract such that the DA works onsite in an agile fashion with the rest of the team, attending iteration planning, stand-ups, and review meetings, among other things.

- **Performance Reporting to monitor contractor cost, schedule, and technical performance.** The agile project manager will have a contract amount and expectations for performance before the contractor comes on board; this is written into the contract and discussed at length as part of the contractor interviewing process. Deliverables can be managed through the daily stand-up and review meetings—however it is determined best by the contractor and the project manager/team. When a contractor is part of an in-house agile team, technical performance will be known immediately due to the visibility and transparency of the work.

- **Perform Quality Control to inspect and verify the adequacy of the contractor's product.** Here, quality and the definition of "done" are determined by the team as a factor of customer expectations. Agile teams do keep metrics about quality, and the same rules should exist for the contractor on the team. For example, some metrics that we hear include the following: Every developer should have written unit tests and have a McCabe less than ten;[6] test cases have been written and fully cover the deliverable of the iteration and have been executed; and only severity four or lower are acceptable for the end of the iteration. From the contractor's point of view, this information should be written into the contract at a high level, as in "contractor shall create functionality in accordance with the definition of done set forth by the team," and managed at a day-to-day level by the team. This "control" is thus part of the exit criteria for each iteration's deliverables. If the team is meeting its goals, and the contractor is part of the team, then in an agile project that means the contractor is contributing appropriately (because the team commits to and delivers the work). This implies a significant amount of trust.

- **Integrated Change Control to ensure that changes are properly approved and that all those with a need to know are aware of such changes.** Agile teams want flexibility to allow for the changes that need to occur, so while they have a plan to follow, there is also room to respond to the changes that will occur. It is important that the contractor participate in iteration planning with the team so that she has the same expectations as the team for what is to be delivered. Likewise, if any mid-iteration changes are necessary, the contractor is just as responsible as the team to voice this information to the team and the project manager.

Contracts must be managed from a financial perspective as well, determining how the contractor's performance links to contractual expectations, as well as managing how the payment process occurs. It is for this reason that a buyer will often have a person capable of contract administration on the staff. As the *PMBOK® Guide* states, "The legal nature of the contractual relationship makes it imperative that the project management team is acutely aware of the legal implications of actions taken when administering any contract."[7] If a contract administrator is handling the contract, it is critical that he is in contact with the team and project manager to understand how the contract will be executed. The contract administrator should understand the expectations by the team (what the definition of "done" is, for example) and any other assumptions that the team has made.

Communication Eases Contract Administration

My very first independent contract was with a team in South Florida. I was charged with a software tool implementation to help manage internal workflow. My duties ran the gamut from interviews with "actors" in the system to understanding the workflow, configuring the tool to support the workflow, and training all users on the system. I decided that even though the contract was written on a month-to-month basis, I could leverage the iteration review mechanism of agile and schedule weekly review meetings with the director and the internal team that brought me on board. This worked extremely well! Not only was I able to show the "value" of my work on a weekly basis, but by working with the internal team so closely, we were also able to easily gauge when changes needed to be made and incorporate those into the next week's work. I eventually formed an implementation backlog in order to plan for and prioritize work with the customer. Bottom line: Frequent communication led to both a happy contractor and happy client. There were no surprises when the contract had to be extended because of new work that had been discovered. By the same token, I had worked to develop in-house staff capabilities such that when the time came for me to move on to another contract, key employees could take over with minimal transition and disruption. Because I worked with this team of key employees as a bona fide team member, the transition was easy.

Table 12-5 provides a summary comparison of traditional and agile approaches to contract administration.

Table 12-5
Contract Administration

Traditional	Agile
Determine how best to administer the contract (performance reviews, audits, payments, changes, etc.).	Engage the team in defining the expectations in the contract, familiarizing the contractor with the agile release plan and associated duties, and helping to monitor schedule, cost, and technical performance by the contractor via the use of daily stand-up and review meetings.

Contract Closure

Contracts may be closed (that is, verified that all work and deliverables were completed and accepted) on a per-project basis or as part of the exit phase of the project in which a contractor was involved. Let's go back to our data architect contractor: If the contractor was only hired for one iteration, the contract will be closed after that iteration, even though the project itself is not over. However, if the DA had been hired for the entire length of the project, then contract closure would be part of the overall project closure process.

In an agile project, organizations will also hold a retrospective with the contractor as a part of contract closure. The project manager and team will meet with the contractor to discuss what worked well during the contractual period, and what could be improved for the future in case another contract is sought. The "exit retrospective" results become a part of the contractor's file.

Contract closure in the general sense means that contracts are formally closed out at the end of the project from an administration point of view. This means that payments are processed, files are updated to reflect actual progress against the contract (if necessary), and the contractor's file would be updated to reflect whether his work was satisfactory. Some organizations will add a contractor to a "preferred" list, meaning that this person will be considered first in any future project requiring the same skills. Each organization's closure process is different.

Table 12-6 provides a summary comparison of the traditional and agile approaches to contract closure.

Table 12-6
Contract Closure

Traditional	Agile
Close the contract and update records on the seller.	Close the contract by confirming customer acceptance of the deliverables; update records on the seller to include results of the project or iteration retrospective of which they were part.

Summary

Your takeaway from this chapter should be the following:

- The act of planning, writing, and administering contracts really doesn't change that much in agile projects, with the exception of the need to educate parties as to what it means to work in an agile fashion.
- The project teams may take a more active role with the project manager in evaluating and selecting sellers and noting sellers' performance.
- Contract documents are preferably written and negotiated in face-to-face meetings. The contract may specify the expectations of the seller

working with an agile buyer or the expectations of an agile seller working with a buyer. If you're lucky, you'll both be agile and the contract will then be easy to write and administer.

- Contract administration can be done such that contractor deliverables match iteration deliverables.
- Project retrospectives, in addition to iteration retrospectives, are useful for understanding what went well and what could use improvement in the overall contract delivery process.

Table 12-7 compares the procurement management activities of a traditional project manager to those of an agile project manager.

Table 12-7
Agile Project Manager's Change List for Procurement Management

I used to do this:	Now I do this:
Evaluate sellers.	Engage the team in helping me evaluate sellers.
Negotiate contracts.	Negotiate contracts with an eye toward the seller's ability to enact the contract in an agile fashion.
Judge the quality of the contractor's deliverables.	Engage the team to plan and evaluate the contractor's deliverables on an iterative basis.
Prepare a lessons learned document.	Ask the contractor or contractor's agency to engage with me and/or the team in order to understand areas of excellence or improvement as the contract is underway through the use of retrospectives.
Close the contract.	Close the contract and include the results of a project retrospective.

Endnotes

1. *PMBOK® Guide*, 274.

2. Mary Poppendieck. "Lean Contracts." http://www.poppendieck.com/contracts.htm.

3. *PMBOK® Guide*, 282.

4. Karen McCabe. "IEEE Revises Software Project Management Standard, Starts Agile Software Standard." IEEE, http://standards.ieee.org/announcements/pr_1490p1648.html.

5. *PMBOK® Guide*, 284.

6. The McCabe metric measures the number of linearly independent paths through a program. Minimizing the number of independent paths reduces code complexity.

7. *PMBOK® Guide*, 290.

Part III

Crossing the Bridge to Agile

IN THIS PART

Chapter 13

How Will My Responsibilities Change?

New knowledge always begins with the individual.

—*Ikujiro Nonaka*

Twenty years from now, the typical large business will have half the levels of management and one-third the managers of its counterpart today.

—*Peter F. Drucker, 1988*

Although for some becoming an agile project manager is second nature, we've found that many managers struggle with their new responsibilities. If you happen to be in the change-resistant camp, or just curious about our perspective on how the agile project manager role should be expressed, please read on.

Whatever our reasons for resisting change, the first step is to realize that we are indeed resisting it. Resisting change can manifest itself in a myriad of ways. Those who resist it can become territorial, "check out," or become fiercely involved in a project in order to appear important, as if their current status were good enough to shield them from any change at all. Some managers have expressed to us that they believe the traditional project management role validates "my power, my accomplishments, my reward." Agile teams require their leaders' focus and assistance; this turning of the focus to others—this externalization of effort—is difficult and doesn't feel rewarding to people who derive power from managing. Many managers complain of feeling like a "gofer" and feel a loss of control and a deep sense of, well, personal loss.

So, the question remains, how do we make the transition? As Virginia Satir points out in her widely accepted change model, a transforming idea[1] is necessary to bring a group or a person to a new status quo; in other words, a person needs to identify with an idea that can help him see the benefit of the change and thus move on to establish a new norm. For me (Stacia), who was very uncomfortable with agile in the beginning, my transforming idea was along two dimensions: First, I realized that there had been a drastic increase in morale of the team after only a couple of iterations. Second, I found a new way to add value by focusing on reporting agile projects to senior management, thereby making progress visible so that timely decisions could be made. I realized what a service I was providing by helping organizational stakeholders "see" progress in terms to which they were not accustomed, and more importantly, I realized that a profound change had taken place in my team members. Their spirits were lifted. They had time for their families. They were empowered—and agile was *working*. I grew to realize, slowly over time, that I shouldn't be afraid of change, that the benefits outweigh the pain by tons.

Looking back, I believe that I grew to support the change because my life became easier after a few months; I had successfully transitioned project decisions about time and scope to the product owners and the team, where those decisions belonged. It wasn't as simple as you might think, that I was sitting in my office, legs propped up on the desk, drinking a latte, exclaiming, "Oh, I have nothing more to do these days, so whoopee! My life is so much easier! I can surf the 'net!" Rather, my life was simpler because I wasn't forcing teams to uphold commitments that they didn't make; I had always struggled with this as a traditional project manager as it violated my values, but I didn't know another way until agile came along. In this new agile setting, I realized that I could bring the right people together to make the right commitments. This was empowering to everyone—even me, ironically, as I often pondered how the loss of control could at the same time empower. I grew to realize that the once-mystical realm of leadership was actually possible for me to learn as I observed myself becoming more competent and confident, iteration by iteration.

As a result of reflecting on these discoveries, I started to embrace and look forward to change. The ability to introspect (and retrospect) became life transforming, but the first step was realizing how I could provide value under the new circumstances. Once I could seize this attitude and adopt new daily actions, only then could I drop the old ways in which I had perceived to add value.

Let's look at how an agile project manager's role is different from that of a traditional project manager. Although we know that the argument will be made that "a good project manager does this stuff anyway," we respond, "Yes, AND in agile, these are the core characteristics that an agile project manager must possess; second to this comes reporting, charts, and so on. Reports and charts are easy. The human fundamentals are most difficult because they are most important."

Management styles in the knowledge worker organization are changing rapidly. We see evidence of this everywhere. What characteristics, then, does the agile project manager possess in order to support teams of knowledge workers in this postmodern "agile" approach? The following characteristics are explored in this chapter: allows teams to self-manage and adapt their process empirically; assumes different leadership styles for different stages of team formation; leads by serving; possesses self-awareness; partners with managers for the good of the team; relinquishes the inner taskmaster; facilitates collaboration; and removes impediments.

Allows Teams to Self-Manage and Adapt Their Process Empirically

Peter Drucker told us decades ago that knowledge workers are more intelligent than their managers when it comes to their work tasks. Workers know best the intricacies, the complexities, the ins-and-outs of the work and the heaps of red tape within which they must wield their scissors; they are simply closer to the work than their managerial counterparts. We cannot, then, expect to manage them in the traditional sense of the word. Time-and-motion studies don't quite cut it in a world of collaborative product development. Ralph Stacey, a well-known professor who has authored several books on complexity in business, reminds us that in a complex environment of instability and uncertainty, traditional methods of planning are insufficient; conversely, these direct and controlling methods do work well when there is stability and certainty.[2] In an article titled, "A Leader's Framework for Decision Making," David J. Snowden and Mary E. Boone extend Stacey's complexity matrix to discuss appropriate management and leadership techniques; in fact, they discuss how leaders should "create environments and experiments that allow patterns to emerge" whenever faced with complex situations, as well as create boundaries.[3] We see agile boundaries as iterations, within which team members self-organize and self-manage; iterative learning occurs in an ad hoc fashion during the iteration, and formally, at the conclusion of the iteration, in the retrospective. Through this cadence of iterations, patterns for work emerge as discovered by the teams doing the work. This is completely different from a traditional organization in which managers solve the problems by deriving solutions themselves and then directing their workers one step at a time; managers in an agile context must learn to wait for the best patterns for work to emerge, which can feel dangerous, uncertain, and risky. It is always good to feel as though we can predict the future, to know what will happen next. Agile managers, over time, accept that the future cannot be foretold, that we can plan to the best of our abilities, but surprises in fact will always occur. Agile managers learn to trust their teams and listen for new discoveries that increase the team's effectiveness, instead of trying to plan this themselves, and they become comfortable with the fact that iterations are, in fact, experiments.

Resisting the urge to leverage command-and-control techniques in complex situations is a management behavior that Snowden and Boone also identify in their article. We see this in everyday practice with agile teams: at release time, the team goes into crunch mode, so the manager assumes that because one daily stand-up is good, then two must be better! It's fine if this is a process that the team creates and supports, but it's different if these two-a-days are created by the manager out of fear. This "reverting to form" is a concept known in psychology as regression. Identified by Anna Freud, regression is when people who are confronted by stressful events abandon coping strategies and revert to patterns of behavior used earlier in development.[4] It is important to be aware that when you are faced with stressful situations, your natural tendency might be to go back to the old way of doing things. Resist this pressure! I can remember the exact moment I became aware of nearly regressing during a high-pressure project in 2003. I had three teams all working together on various parts of an integrated product.

One of the teams had caused defects in another team's part of the code. Everyone came running to me to solve the problem. I remember thinking to myself, "Okay, I need to call a project status meeting with everyone, and call the VP of development and senior architect so that they can figure out the best solutions." I immediately jumped into problem-solving mode. Then, as I was about to retreat to my office to begin writing emails, it hit me: The best people to solve this problem were not the project stakeholders and the vice president of development. Rather, the teams themselves could solve these problems by iterating solutions together. I left my office, stopped by the teams' war rooms, and asked whoever was involved in the situation to gather in the main conference room. Seven people showed up and solved the issue in fifteen minutes. My lesson: getting the right brains in the room together can solve any problem. Managing the solution or trying to solve it alone is not the right approach. Watching those seven people that day identify the problem and tether a solution opened my eyes to the power of self-managed teams. I simply created the space and focus for solutions to happen.

Learning happens (or should happen) continuously in an agile environment; the retrospective is the time to stand still and thoroughly assess the current situation in order to make changes moving forward. Agile project managers, then, must be receptive to continuous feedback and embody the notion of continuously improving, as sometimes the proposed changes from the team may directly relate to the changes the project manager himself must make. A project manager who is afraid of change will impede the team that is attempting to apply the collective knowledge gleaned from prior experiences.

Assumes Different Leadership Styles for Different Stages of Team Formation

Managers of any type, and that includes you, dear reader, cannot say to a team, "Go forth and be self-managed." If it were only that easy! Rather, teams need hand-holding at certain points in time. Bruce Tuckman created a model for the stages of team formation: forming, storming, norming, performing, and adjourning. These stages are recognizable by certain behaviors exhibited by the team, behaviors that clue in the observant manager as to which management or leadership style he or she must embrace appropriate to each stage.

During times of forming, which is the stage when a new team is formed, managers need to be directive and paint a clear tactical picture for a team to meet its goals, as well as keep teams focused on the big picture. Mike Cohn says that "providing leadership is about every interaction with a team: what we tell them, what we don't tell them, how we tell them, how we listen."[5] In addition to giving a team permission to be self-managing, we must also show them how to become self-managing by providing clarity and details.

Here's an example: With new agile teams that we coach, we help them break down their features to very small tasks in the iteration planning meeting, as well as have them assign owners and estimates in hours to each task. Because they are new at agile, and new to each other, we suspect that they're still thinking in terms of hand-offs and their own individual roles on the team. We want to allay fears of "What about me and my role?" by helping each team member realize that he or she plays an important part on the team. Advanced teams, on the other hand, can plan at a more mature level, only breaking down tasks for the feature at hand, with the next available team member taking the next task in the queue. This more advanced approach would find most new forming teams running for the hills out of concern for their jobs and security.

Teams that can make it past forming will move to the storming phase. Storming is characterized by conflict and open, sometimes harsh dialogue. Although storming can feel uncomfortable, these tumultuous behaviors should be welcomed and appreciated by the manager as a sign that real communication is occurring; team members no longer feel like they must veil their discussions and comments. Rather, saying how they really think and feel is important because that is how true collaboration occurs. Managers must listen intently to the conflicts that are surfacing and help the team members resolve this conflict without damaging relationships in the process. By resolving conflict in a healthy manner, team members learn to trust each other. With trust comes the ability for teams to move into the more advanced stages of team formation—norming and performing—where collaboration is unrestrained.

I once had a team that had a very vocal tester. This tester would yell, "That's not agile!" any time a situation smelled of waterfall or hand-off. Although I knew that her comments were correct in many situations, I could also see that several members of the team were growing resentful of her criticism. After some thought and reflection, I realized that this was because she was acting as Agile Police, but not offering up any new ideas for behavior that would be more agile-like. Team members were frustrated because they couldn't see a way around the problems without reverting to the old way of doing things. I did some research and the next time the tester yelled, "That's not agile," I jumped in and gave some examples to the team to get them thinking about her comment (as they rolled their eyes). I asked them to read a case study of a team that went agile, and we talked about it at our next team meeting. Once the other team members had an idea of what it meant to act in an agile fashion, they started yelling "That's not agile!" also! Their new collective wisdom helped them get past the criticism and start thinking in new ways to fix old problems. My lesson: Managers can help team members picture where they are trying to go. When team members see this picture, they can figure out a way to get there. Agile is a big shift for all the team members, and they don't know what they don't know. Making time for education and self-study within each iteration is time well spent.

It may seem that when a team matures into a norming phase, the agile project manager then goes on cruise control and doesn't have to pay so much attention to the team. Not so: Norming simply means that the team has found a way to create rules to help govern itself. It will still need help with conflict resolution, as well as reminders to enforce the rules—or norms—that it has created. Although the detailed, day-to-day involvement of the project manager is not as necessary as when the team was forming, the norming team still needs high-level goals to strive for. Challenge norming teams with high-level goals such as the following: Everyone owns testing, always leave the code in better shape than you found it (and make it demonstrable), and work on crafting messages to the business about things such as velocity, iteration goals, and areas of progress resulting from the retrospective.

Because of traditional organizational structure, teams are seldom left alone long enough to evolve into the "high-performing" class. Agile methods seek to change this so that every team can reach this ultimate work existence—the culmination of trust, collaboration, and hard work. The ultimate nirvana for a project manager, high-performing teams are self-managing, self-policing, empowered, and brazen. They usually can be heard before being seen by the laughter and banter that emanates from the group. They are comrades, friends, and partners. They usually don't need much from a manager, except which direction to take off in. They can interface with a customer and act as consultants. They will be quick to let you know when you're cramping their style and when they don't need you. As a project manager, you must be accepting of their mob mentality, especially so that you don't take it personally when they say that they don't need you for something. You must challenge them with new ideas, goals that seem improbable, as well as help them become mentors to other teams. You may be asking right now why a performing team is desirable? Many studies—too numerous to cite—have proven that individuals who can self-manage, make decisions for themselves about the work, and have management support (versus control) are many times more effective and productive than the alternative. Additionally, they innovate.

A similar model to Tuckman's is Paul Hersey's situational leadership,[6] which combines the ideas of self-awareness of the project manager and the need for varying levels of direction in creating a self-managed team. From helping an unconfident team win small victories by leading them day by day, to delegating decisions to a mature team, situational leadership involves the project manager's awareness of the team's willingness and ability, adapting his behavior accordingly. One of the ways in which we've observed agile project managers display situational leadership is to ask the team, "Help me to see it." This question enables the team members to go into detail and think a tough situation through; often they realize the solution in the middle of the details. Another tactic is to ask, "What ideas do *you* have to overcome the issue?" This puts the team member into problem-solving mode, moving them away from the tendency to look to the project manager for solutions. When should a project manager try these questions? She should try them whenever she can feel that people are on the verge of speaking up, when the confidence in the room is rising. This is a subjective assessment; a manager who can listen and stay tuned in to these subtle behaviors will know when to apply different situational leadership styles. Recognizing these subtleties takes immense focus by the manager on team members' language choices, inflection, and speaking tones, body language, and other nonverbal cues. Study and learn about leadership as well as the dynamics of individuals and groups; take a course, or meet once or twice a month in a study group with your peers to discuss the issues that you are encountering, as well as new techniques you have learned to help teams (and yourselves!) conquer challenges. The best step to take is to get to know your team, understand what motivates each team member, and support an environment of creativity and learning.

Leads by Serving

Robert Greenleaf coined the "servant leader" phrase some thirty years ago, describing said leader as someone who ensures that "other people's highest priority needs are being served."[7] The agile project manager also embodies this ideal, that whatever the team needs to be productive, the team gets. We often use the mantra "Everything for the team, for the customer" as a way for project managers to think about serving. Sometimes serving can feel administrative—the gofer who gets snacks for meetings, writes purpose and agendas, and processes meeting results. And, yes, sometimes these tasks can become mundane and seem trivial. Yet serving in this manner provides untold value to a team (or teams) in that it is free from these tasks and can focus on what knowledge workers do best: create expressions of knowledge in the form of products.

Let's consider the ceremony around eating. The seemingly small task of gathering, preparing, and serving food has deep meaning to humans from a ritual and ceremonial perspective. Think about your own religion, for example, or your own family customs. How does food play a part in how you celebrate? Why, then, would ordering the "iteration planning pizza" or taking the team out for an afternoon latte be any different? It is through the act of eating as a group that we share a sense of community and tribalism. The next time you think of that pizza order as merely "gofer-ish," think about the thousands of years of tribal instinct you are evoking, subconsciously, for your team. Eating together is an important team activity.

And there are myriad other quite challenging responsibilities that a servant to the team must address. Protecting the team from outside distractions, educating others who interact with the team or affect the team's performance, and removing impediments to the team's progress all require a high level of political tact, professional and personal communication, and intelligence to perform. You must also serve each individual, meeting with the team members on a regular basis, to help them resolve personality clashes, improve their skill base, and map a career path—as well as gaining feedback into how they think you are doing!

When teams feel that you are doing your very best to serve them, that you are putting their needs before anything else, they will in return do their best work for the good of the project. It's easy to write this, yet a very difficult existence to create, and it boils down to one word: trust. When the team feels as if it can trust its leader, understands the importance of the goal, and is left alone to craft a solution, it will usually perform. The first step you need to take with your team is to earn its trust. A servant leader can do this by rolling up her sleeves, getting involved in the work from a support perspective, and making visible the actions that she takes to remove greater impediments.

So while you're doing all these very important things, don't forget that we are all equal in our humanity—and don't feel that it's beneath you to order a pizza and clean up the breakroom.

Possesses Self-Awareness

Although certainly an inherent trait in some people, self-awareness is a skill that can be honed by opening yourself up to understanding how others react to you. This takes a tremendous amount of courage and objectivity, but receiving feedback—both positive and critical in nature—helps us improve. This is a form of a self-retrospective—or introspection.

The hardest part about self-awareness for some people is processing the negative feedback. People naturally have an emotional response to negative feedback, often because they desire to do well and do not wish to disappoint. Negative feedback can be perceived as rejection. If you fall into this camp, consider the following advice. When you receive less-than-stellar

The Benefits of Being Self-Aware

I realized about a decade ago that when engaging in deep discussion, I would assume a scowling expression—that is, a furrowed brow that has somehow managed to remain permanently etched into my face. (Mother was right—our faces can get stuck!) This expression, which is my usual "deep thinking face," came across as anger or frustration to others. I could sometimes sense apprehension or reluctance in those talking with me, and didn't always know why. It wasn't until a good friend of mine pointed out the scowl that I realized what was happening. Of course, I could have gone into denial, blaming it on my audience's poor perception of me, but I took ownership of this issue. Becoming aware of this small outward expression of deep inner thought and reflection caused me to become conscious of "the face." I am aware of when it happens and can focus intently on relaxing in order to project a confident, objective exterior, regardless of what's going on beneath the surface.

—Stacia

I will often feel I am passionately discussing a topic, when I notice my colleague's body language change into more of a protective stance. I have to be careful to always state that I am passionate about the subject, but equally excited to hear a differing viewpoint—then I shut up and smile. That seems to help!

—Michele

feedback about yourself and you're feeling red in the face, the first thing to do is think about it before responding. A simple "Thank you for your feedback" will suffice while you take the time to process it. In your journal or diary, or discussion with yourself in the mirror, ask, "How did I earn this feedback?" Think about the scenario. What did you do? What did others do? Was it a misunderstanding of the information, or did you unintentionally cut off someone in a meeting? Why are you having an emotional response? Take some time to look at the situation objectively while the emotional response subsides. Sometimes it may take you a day, weeks, or months to fully understand the situation. In the meantime, display good leadership by supporting the relationship until you've figured out a new behavior or a new way to proceed. Once you have identified it, have a discussion with the team member to let them know that you have a solution. Ask for future feedback about the changes you have decided to implement and keep the dialogue open.

Whether it's the scowling face, the loud voice, or the tendency to cut off people mid-sentence, we must be aware of our actions and how they cause reactions in others. Our effectiveness as leaders depends on a deep understanding of how we impact our teams. Michele once coached a team whose ScrumMaster, as told by one team member, "wears her feelings on her sleeve. When she has a bad day, we *all* have a bad day." This represents a person who may be aware of her mood but chose to let it impact her team anyway. Her team then "walked on eggshells" to escape the wrath of her mood. Although it's important to be self-aware, it's only effective if we act responsibly on that knowledge.

Partners with Managers for the Good of the Team

Many project managers who become leaders, servants, and facilitators for their teams often ask how their role coincides or conflicts with the traditional development or QA manager's roles. My advice is to partner with the skill managers to create the most effective teams possible. Gain an understanding of each team member's desires. For example, if the DBA has a personal goal to learn Java, it's important that his manager know this; likewise, it is important that his team knows this as well. Pairing opportunities can be found within an iteration to provide learning situations to help this person reach his goal.

Additionally, the agile project manager can be quite helpful in reinforcing the definition of "done" with the team, and helping the team discover obstacles to reaching this very strenuous product goal. The agile project manager can partner with the skill manager to get the team the resources it needs in order to upgrade the development environment, for example, or implement automated testing tools. The agile project manager, by nature of being the guardian and impediment remover for the team, has first-hand knowledge about what the team feels it can improve. Acting as a voice and a partner to the skill manager is imperative to helping the team meet its goals.

This is easiest when the teams are organized with focus on the project's outcome. In matrixed organizations where teams are organized to report to their skill manager and simultaneously are "on loan" to projects, loyalty is usually felt toward the skill manager, not the project's outcome. If you are in this scenario, have discussions with the skill manager to gain his or her support for the project as well as the commitment to reinforce this message to his or her subordinates. Work with the skill manager to help remove obstacles for the team.

Relinquishes the Inner Taskmaster

Because agile project managers can effectively let go of the day-to-day task management of the team, they can move on to find more valuable expressions of their roles. You can think of agile project management on two levels: There's the micro level, which is composed of the tasks that fit within the timebox. The team manages itself within the boundaries of this timebox. Then there's the macro level of agile project management. This level consists of contract procurement, contract administration, working with product owners to formulate and communicate roadmaps and stage the product backlog, and partnering with skill managers to help keep teams effective and productive—basically, everything that is involved with keeping the team ready to go for the next iteration. Additionally, project managers can help standardize reports and educate stakeholders about how to gain visibility into agile projects. You can read more about this in Chapter 15, "How Can a Project Management Office Support Agile?"

Facilitates Collaboration

An agile project manager realizes the criticality of facilitation skills. Because the agile project manager acts simultaneously as a liaison and a buffer between the business and the delivery team, this person must hone her ability to facilitate discussions and negotiations. From knowing how to set up, facilitate, and process a meeting, to helping resolve conflicts, to knowing the right teambuilding activity to engage in at the right time, the agile project manager should have at her fingertips a plethora of facilitation tools.

We've learned how to facilitate by practicing with hundreds of teams. Each new team presents a learning opportunity for the facilitator, and facilitation is a skill that can be honed and refined, just like any other. At the very least, an agile project manager should be able to craft a purpose and an agenda for every meeting. Sure, after a week of daily stand-ups a purpose and agenda may be slightly overkill, but you'd be surprised at the amount of teams who do not realize that the purpose of the daily stand-up is to inspect and adapt their work on a daily basis! Likewise, agendas keep the team focused on how they are going to meet the purpose of each meeting.

Other facilitation skills include deep listening, intense focus, conflict resolution, as well as the observation of verbal and nonverbal cues so that the team benefits from each individual's contributions. Because agile project iterations are book-ended by meetings that plan and close each iteration, it is imperative that these meetings are facilitated effectively. Teams can become more successful when they meet their meeting objectives. A well-facilitated planning meeting, for example, allows a team to plan its selected features in detail; a granular level of decomposition means that tasks get better estimates, which reduces the possibility that the team will over- or under-commit and miss its commitments. Check out Appendix B, "Typical Agile Artifacts," for sample meeting agendas. We also highly recommend *Collaboration Explained,* by Jean Tabaka, for a deeper pass at facilitating agile teams.

Removes Impediments

The agile project manager also recognizes that her primary role within the iteration is to remove impediments that affect the team's progress. Obstacles can come in all shapes and sizes. Some are obvious: "Bob broke the build." Some are not so obvious and require sharp listening and the Socratic approach: "I am stuck on my task *again.*" The agile project manager has the difficult task of working with the team to determine which obstacles belong to the team, and which belong to the manager to resolve. In the case of Bob breaking the build, I asked the team to figure out how to resolve the broken build, and more importantly, what it would do to prevent this from happening again in the future. The team responded with a process for determining at any point in time if the build was broken, and a new rule that the person who broke the build would have to wear the "build monkey" until he or she fixed the problem (the build monkey was a plush toy with long arms and Velcro hands). The agile project manager must walk the tightrope; lean too far one way and you fall headfirst into old patterns of directing work, lean too far the other way and take a tumble into the cesspool of inaction.

Removing impediments means that the agile project manager must listen as if life depends on it. It means that we must slow down to hear all of the words, as well as what lies beneath the words.[8] So much of what our co-workers say is infused with culture, religion, gender, and life's overall experiences. Rarely will we hear a statement that is only a statement; rather, there are undercurrents of life always running throughout words.

Summary

In conclusion, an agile project manager—or any manager for that matter—should possess all of the characteristics outlined in this chapter, as well as demonstrate fluency in job-specific responsibilities. However, the agile project manager should continuously self-assess and adapt to grow in these areas. What were once considered soft skills and secondary to book smarts are now taking a front seat in the knowledge management realm. In an environment of self-managed and empowered teams, today's agile project manager must practice continuous improvement in order to best support her team.

Endnotes

1. Virginia Satir. *The Satir Model: Family Therapy and Beyond.* (Palo Alto: Science and Behavior Books, 1991).

2. Ralph D. Stacey. *Complexity and Creativity in Organizations.* (San Francisco: Berrett-Koehler Publishers, 1996).

3. David J. Snowden and Mary E. Boone. "A Leader's Framework for Decision Making." *Harvard Business Review*, November 2007, 73.

4. Kendra Van Wagner. "Defense Mechanisms." About.com, http://psychology.about.com/od/theoriesofpersonality/ss/defensemech_7.htm.

5. Mike Cohn. "Situational Leadership for Agile Software Development." *Cutter IT Journal* (June 2004), 1.

6. Ibid.

7. Robert Greenleaf. *Servant as Leader.* (Indianapolis: Robert K. Greenleaf Center, June 1982), 1.

8. Peter Senge. *The Fifth Discipline Fieldbook.* (New York: Doubleday Currency, 1994), 376–379.

Chapter 14

How Will I Work with Other Teams Who Aren't Agile?

"A new doctrine goes through three stages. It is attacked and declared absurd; then it is admitted as true and obvious but insignificant. Finally, its true importance is recognized and its adversaries claim the honor of having discovered it."

—William James

"Lord, give us the wisdom to utter words that are gentle and tender, for tomorrow we may have to eat them."

—Sen. Morris Udall

Agile methodologies were designed with small co-located, cross-functional teams in mind. Due to the expectation and economic requirement to respond rapidly to market pressures, companies with large and geographically dispersed personnel are compelled to still forge ahead as they adopt agile approaches to software development. The implementation of these new methodologies begins in their historically waterfall organizations. The challenge is that because it's simply not practical to just "flip a switch" and have a 1,000-person department start doing agile all at once, these organizations must wade through a thick transition period where agile and waterfall are forced to coexist.[1]

And it may not be only for the transitional period. Agile and waterfall teams may also be forced to coexist for the long-term, because not all companies will choose to move every single software development project to an agile framework. The trick is in *how* they can coexist peacefully and not detract from operational stability and continued project success. Every transitional environment, agile or otherwise, has to deal with duality until the transition is complete. Doing this with the least amount of pain and disruption means tightly embracing one of the key agile tenets: inspect and adapt. Reviews of the process and the progress the teams have made at the end of every iteration guide decisions on how to best proceed in the next iteration. This enables teams to tweak some of the agile practices so that they work best in the current environment, knowing that these agile practices will change and become more "pure" as the environment and culture slowly change over time.

Some agile purists will say that by stretching the process it's no longer "agile"—and in many cases they may be right. But semantics aside, it's still about improving the overall software delivery system. What label we apply to the process itself is secondary. However, teams must be careful not to stretch the practices so much that they revert to their more comfortable waterfall-like habits. When agile is viewed as an ala carte menu of practices that can be adopted as the consumers see fit, it's critical to adhere to a lean diet of key principles when ordering from that menu: continuous improvement through timeboxed iterative deliveries and reviews, implementing the most important items first, and constant collaborative communications. When teams keep these principles in mind, they are able to find ways of integrating the traditional and the agile approaches as they begin the transition.

In this chapter we discuss working as an agile team in a waterfall enterprise, working on multiteam projects where some teams follow an agile approach and some do not, and getting around other obstacles to adopting agile practices in a waterfall enterprise.

Working as an Agile Team in a Waterfall Enterprise

Large companies usually have clear and valid reasons for requiring more traditional activities on an otherwise agile project. Project approval processes that are designed to weigh benefits, costs, and strategic alignment with corporate objectives are one example of a reasonable standard upfront process requirement. Independent Validation and Verification (IV&V) is a typical at-end process requirement for those companies in the government or healthcare industry who must comply with federal regulations. And teams saddled with an organization whose leadership hasn't grasped the intent behind adopting agile are unreasonably forced to address traditional process requirements in tandem with agile approaches throughout their project.

None of these requirements will cease to exist simply because the teams are employing agile practices. Instead, the teams must learn to factor these corporate needs into their existing agile procedures, and management must begin the investigative work of determining how to streamline these requirements and activities, eliminating wasteful process, so that they don't hamper the project.

Integrating Traditional Process Requirements Upfront

Project approval processes are the most popular waterfall upfront activities. There are two ways that projects can be initiated: One is after the paperwork has been submitted and approved, and the other is as a provisional project that receives limited funding and resources prior to official long-term approval. You can see an example of both approaches integrated with the agile framework in Figure 14-1. Sometimes this first iteration that addresses these types of tasks is called the "initiation iteration," or "iteration 0."

If the documentation must all be submitted prior to obtaining project approval, use Alistair Cockburn's "barely sufficient" philosophy in order to prevent doing more than is absolutely necessary.[2] Using the "barely sufficient" guideline, the team members should ask, "Is this something that we really must do?" If it is, then they should ask, "What is the simplest thing we can do to satisfy this requirement?" Being an agile team, you would not want to prepare a detailed spec outlining all the functional requirements of the system just to gain approval. Instead, the agile project manager must work with those who do the approving in order to find out what the minimum criteria is for acceptance. (See Chapter 4, "Integration Management," for a story about how one team handled this upfront process requirement.)

If the team has provisional approval, then the process requirements simply become part of the product backlog. Even though the items are not directly related to the creation of a potentially shippable increment of software, they are indirectly related because they are required for the project to exist at all—and thus are prioritized accordingly. To prevent the team from reverting back to a waterfall-like approach where it spends the entire first iteration doing nothing but analysis, it is important to deliver at least one feature in parallel with the required project approval documentation. Not only does this serve to get the team "into the groove" so to speak, but it also can serve as proof to the approval board that your team is already off and running. Whether the feature is something as simple as being able to log on via a secure environment or as complicated as developing a proof of concept for a feature that was deemed "high risk," everyone benefits from the work.

Figure 14-1
Integrating traditional process requirements upfront

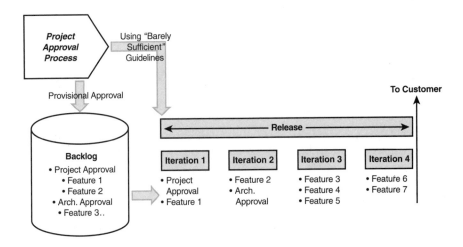

Integrating Traditional Process Requirements At-End

Having to deal with traditional process requirements at-end, such as the transfer to production, audit, or IV&V agencies, generally means allocating an iteration at the end of the release to prepare those deliverables. Passing through the required phase-gate of a typical production department means that documentation, meetings, end-to-end system testing, system compatibility testing, and sign-offs all must be planned as part of the release. Figure 14-2 shows how this accommodation would look in an agile team's release plan.

Again, use the backlog in conjunction with the team's definition of "done" to ensure that this work is recognized and planned for. It is not uncommon to devote the entirety of the last iteration, often referred to as the "hardening iteration," to production-readiness. Team members do not implement any new features during this iteration; instead, they produce documentation for production, customer support, the architecture review committee, auditors, the IV&V agencies, and sales and marketing. Meetings are held to facilitate the hand-off, and any sign-offs or audits may be attended to as well. If the team members have any spare time left in this iteration, they spend it refactoring code, installing development and test system upgrades, investigating new technologies, training staff, performing a project retrospective—and celebrating!

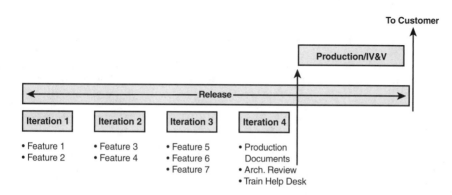

Figure 14-2
Integrating traditional process requirements at-end

Even if your agile team does not have to pass along the product for outside approval, you can use this iteration to capture final screenshots for marketing and training materials, finalize the release notes, do performance and load testing, and carry out other activities that make sense in your organization and industry. Just be sure that your team isn't using this last iteration solely as a bug-fixing opportunity—that's a signal that the team is committing to more features in each iteration than it has time to test.

Integrating Traditional Process Requirements in Tandem

Having to address traditional process requirements at either the beginning or end of an agile project is preferable over having to deal with process distractions throughout the project. When the traditional process requirements are no more than a set of bookends, as in Figures 14-1 and 14-2, then the agile team has the opportunity to spend the majority of its time focusing on the iterative and incremental delivery of working software. Requests for compliance with a waterfall methodology throughout the project, however, can severely limit the team's ability to focus on speedy delivery. Teams finding themselves in this situation tend to be either those that have adopted a "stealth" mode of doing agile (that is, using an agile framework but not telling anyone that they are doing so) or teams working in an organization that is only paying lip service to an agile transformation as it continues to expect compliance with its current process.

In either situation, the team must continue to adhere to the key principles of continuous improvement through timeboxed iterative deliveries and reviews, implementing the most important items first, and constant collaborative communications. Teams should continue to keep to their iteration timeboxes, using the backlog as a way to prioritize both product-specific and traditional process requirements. Improving their lot will be the result of negotiations with those who are forcing the old practices on them, showing them how the removal of unnecessary process speeds up the delivery of working software. Although teams may at first be limited in the amount of success they can achieve, they should be able to slowly integrate more and more agile practices into the mainstream of the organization, as each new change generates improved productivity as noted in the team's iteration review and retrospective.

Working as Part of a Multiteam Project where Your Team Is Agile and Others Aren't

Sometimes the system under development is so large and complex that multiple component teams, often working on different platforms, must work together to prepare a release. Ideally, all teams would be following the same methodology, but this is not always the case. As with any project, communication and coordination are important for the project team to be able to deliver as a whole.

First, talk with the waterfall stakeholders about how you would like to work together. Answer their questions about agile, and ask for their help in making the relationship as pain-free as possible. The executive sponsor should be part of the initial discussion to share her commitment to the process, her dedication to removing roadblocks, and the importance of each team's involvement. Don't try to force the waterfall teams to convert to agile! No one likes having something shoved down their throat. Instead, let your agile team's increased performance and success speak for itself and generate a desire on the part of others to learn more. Be clear that you want to work with them toward your common goal of a successful delivery.

Teams need to coordinate regularly, and the agile planning meetings provide the perfect forum for this synchronization (see Figure 14-3). Especially important are the release planning meetings, where milestones/deliverables are determined by both agile teams and waterfall team managers. Include the waterfall stakeholders in the agile planning meetings so that everyone can understand what qualifies as barely sufficient deliverables, what assumptions the teams are making, and what dependencies exist across teams. If the waterfall team managers balk at attending all the planning meetings, then at a minimum the release planning meeting should be the one meeting they must attend.

Continued follow-up and subsequent course adjustments are covered in iteration planning meetings and daily stand-ups. Again, the waterfall team managers should be invited to attend, and the agile team manager should be sure to meet with them afterward to answer any questions they may have. It is common to find that the waterfall team managers simply do not have enough time to attend all the agile team's planning meetings. In this case, see if there are proxies who might wish to attend. Perhaps the lead programmer or architect could attend in the place of the waterfall team manager, share information and input from his team, and take the information learned back to his team. You will have to experiment with what works best for all.

For those waterfall team managers/proxies who do make an effort to participate, and for those multiple agile teams, a second tier of daily stand-ups should be added for team coordination. This is the Ken Schwaber "Scrum-of-Scrums" model from the Scrum process framework, where the daily stand-ups are referred to as "daily scrums."[3] Having a fifteen-minute stand-up meeting at the team level enables the team to plan its day and brings to light the obstacles that the team manager must focus on removing.

Scaling this to meet the needs of multiple teams means that all team managers hold their own daily stand-up following the team stand-up. This Scrum-of-Scrums enables the team managers (or the appropriate representatives from the team) to coordinate daily and tackle issues that prevent their teams from meeting their goals.

Figure 14-3
Integrating agile and waterfall teams in a project

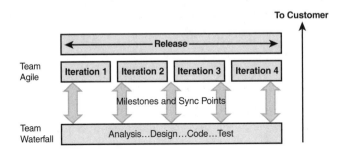

Scale the iteration review and retrospective in the same fashion. Each agile team should hold a review and retrospective at the end of each iteration; following this an iteration review and retrospective should be held for the team managers. This will give the leads an opportunity to analyze the benefits and challenges you've just experienced from your efforts to coordinate and work together and make recommendations on how to improve the experience in the next iteration. (Again, this may be difficult to schedule with the waterfall managers—aim for a review and retrospective at the end of each release at a minimum.)

Finally, have a project retrospective at the end of the project, and invite all stakeholders to participate. These meetings are crucial at helping to identify and implement broader transition changes that affect the entire enterprise. Executive and middle management should have their own prioritized backlog of transition issues they need to focus on, many of which are raised in retrospectives such as this. Transitioning to agile involves making corporate process and organizational changes iteratively and incrementally, in much the same manner as the agile process involves developing software iteratively and incrementally. Project retrospectives enable the reviews of those changes and recommendations for improvement.

Don't be surprised to find your agile teams moving ahead of waterfall teams who aren't inclined to cooperate or who are unable to deliver. Agile teams usually figure out a way to keep making progress even without the expected deliverables they had been relying on. The agile team will stub out that subsystem and provide workarounds, or more often than not, the team members will simply build the module themselves.

Clearing the Hurdles in a Waterfall Enterprise

We've looked at ways an agile team can incorporate some traditional practices at the beginning, end, and throughout a project. But there are non-project-specific instances as well, where agile project managers will have to focus their energies on communication and coordination in order to clear the hurdles that a waterfall enterprise can throw in their path. Here are a few of the most common hurdles and what you can do to clear them.

Resistance

Agile project managers will run into resistance from management, from the business, and from the team. In fact, resistance—or healthy skepticism—is such a common hurdle that we've included an entire chapter just to address it (Chapter 16, "Selling the Benefits of Agile"). In the meantime, here is a high-level look at some things you can do to clear the bars to change.

One way to hurdle management resistance is to just avoid it entirely. As long as you are delivering (in a legal and ethical manner that doesn't expose the company to liability) then the management will be happy. So do your agile in "stealth mode," and begin your adoption of agile as a grassroots effort. Just be prepared to share your approach with management when your productivity begins to really catch their eye!

Also consider advocating agile using their language, and not the jargon of the agile movement. Instead of using terms such as "agile," "extreme," "velocity," and "iteration," use phrases that will resonate with them and give them a baseline for understanding. Talk about improving technical practices in order to increase the speed in which you deliver and improve the quality of the product. Talk about increasing ROI by changing the way you interact with the business. Focus on terms such as "cooperative endeavor," "speed to market," "increased customer satisfaction," and "increased revenue" to get your agile points across.

To reduce resistance from the business, be sure you engage them early and often. They won't be happy to learn that the technical division has been planning an agile rollout that will directly affect the business and how it functions, without even including them in the planning effort. And while you're working on hurdling the business resistance, have your teams focus on improving their technical practices, so that the only roadblock you'll have to high performance is the cooperation of the business representative.

The team may have issues as well, primarily with some of the tactical approaches that agile presents. Help the team solve these problems and concerns by providing the education and training the members need and the opportunities to learn and apply those lessons in an iterative fashion. Empower them, but give them an agile guide to help their crossing of the bridge go more smoothly.

Culture

The culture that a company or an organization has can help to elevate the agile approach or help to kill it. Identify the corporate values in your company, and pay attention to whether the values noted on paper are the same that are exhibited by its employees in everyday interactions and decision-making (see Chapter 9, "Human Resources Management," for more detail). Are these values in keeping with the agile values your team has embraced?

Some difficult conversations might be required to address any value mismatches you may find. This is also the agile project manager's opportunity to dispel any misconceptions that linger about what agile software development is and what it is not. Sometimes an agility assessment by an unbiased outside advisor can help in identifying cultural (and other) issues that need to be addressed before the adoption of agile can be truly successful.

It is common for many organizations to see high turnover in their CIOs, having a new one every few years, who brings new ideas on how to approach software development. If agile is viewed as yet another temporary "methodology-du-jour" by your staff, then your resistance hurdle will be high indeed.

At the end of the day, an agile approach will surface all impediments that stand in the way of agility. If the organization is not prepared—or vehemently opposed—to working through these issues, then your implementation of agile will fail. So be prepared to not do agile. If the culture won't support your efforts and won't bend to the changes required, your teams won't be successful in the long run.

Resource Management

Resource managers will still want to know when you need certain skilled personnel, and for how long. Procurement managers will still want to know when you need certain equipment, materials, services, and facilities. As we noted in Chapter 9 and Chapter 12, "Procurement Management," you can use the release plan to indicate to resource management where in the project these needs must be addressed. Remember to advise your resource managers that agile release plans change as the team makes progress and incorporates its learning and that you will provide them with regular updates to the plan and your team's resource needs.

Vendors and Contracting

When it comes to vendors, the first thing you'll want to do is determine whether or not it is worth your time to explain agile to them. Will the vendors be around a long time? Then you may want to educate them. Are they contractors? Then you'll want them to attend the daily stand-ups. Are they onsite long-term contractors? Then you'll want them involved in everything. Are they short-term with a clear delivery? Then set expectations of what you want and when, as well as how you want to communicate updates and status—don't bother to explain agile. Use common sense, but always be sure to communicate, and communicate again, to your vendors.

If you are a provider of software developed in an agile environment, you may need to have a careful discussion with your non-agile customer. In addition to the information we provided in Chapter 12, here are some questions you can ask during the conversation to steer your customer toward a more agile contract:

- Do you often find that your requirements change mid-stream, even after everything has been captured and analyzed?
- Would you like to be able to change your mind every two weeks about the features you've requested?
- Would you be willing to spend some time with us to help us better understand what your vision is for the implementation of these new features?
- How often have you seen working software in the past, and how often would you like to see working software on this project? Would you like us to show you what we've accomplished by demonstrating the product to you every two weeks?
- How should we mitigate against time constraints? Or against potentially building the wrong thing? Do you have a prioritized list of work that could help us with this?
- People typically roll on and off projects, which can cause delays as information needs to be transferred and absorbed (and can sometimes be lost). How would you like us to handle this?
- Would you like the right to close or cancel the project at any time with only thirty days' notice?

Although a time and materials contract (or "pay-as-you-go") is better suited to an agile project, it is not always possible to negotiate. If, after all the preceding questions, your customer balks at a T&M contract, consider responding with, "Let's spend $5K and build a backlog of work that we can estimate, and confirm if we can do it based on a fixed price." Then be sure to gather not only the user stories, but also the conditions of satisfaction, or acceptance criteria, for each. As trust between your customer and the delivery team grows, these types of contracts will become easier to procure. You'll find a bit more on this topic in Chapter 16, "Selling the Benefits of Agile."

Also note that an IEEE standard is currently being drafted (P1648) that will help to guide both customers and vendors. Its working title is "Recommended Practice for Establishing and Managing Software Development Efforts Using Agile Methods." Although the standard is not close to release at the time of this writing, you can check on its status via the IEEE website (http://standards.ieee.org/db/status/index.shtml).

Facilities and Tooling

Agile teams don't do their best work when relegated to their separate cubicles. Having a common work area, often known as a "war room" or "bullpen," enables the team to work together and share information. Commandeer a conference room for starters, to provide your team with all the wall space, whiteboards, and communal work space the team members will need. In the meantime, work with your facilities staff to create a larger communal space for the team. (We've observed some teams who, even though co-located, are not collaborative—they sit inside their war room and type away in quiet isolation. Even though you may have the best facilities at hand, it does not remove your responsibility of helping the team learn how to work as a cohesive unit. Isolation and introversion can be one of the team's biggest obstacles.)

When teams are distributed, proper tooling to create virtual shared space is critical. Luckily, many open-source tools are available to help your agile teams get started, so budget woes won't have to stop you. Wikis allow teams to share information. Instant messaging keeps everyone connected, as do Skype and web cameras. Use planningpoker.com to help you estimate stories, cardmeeting.com and XPlanner to help you plan, CVS to handle configuration management, and Fitnesse to help you test.

Cost Accounting and Reporting

The two most prominent hurdles are those of determining capitalization versus expense, and reporting project status. Both can be cleared by having discussions with those who need the information.

First talk with your finance manager to determine the minimum required information you'll need to provide to resolve the capitalization question. If necessary, work those documentation requirements into your backlog, as outlined in the section "Integrating Traditional Process Requirements Upfront" earlier in this chapter.

Then have a conversation with your PMO and management staff to determine what metrics would be helpful to track and how to best report them without derailing the team's efforts at software delivery. You'll soon reach an amicable compromise that shows how your team is progressing, as you begin to introduce management to the new types of information radiators that agile uses (burndown charts, task boards). You'll find more information on this in Chapter 16.

Auditors and Assessors

Again, conversations with these individuals to determine the bare minimum (or "barely sufficient" deliverables) is a must. Do what you can to keep documentation to a minimum, but do so with the understanding that some forms of auditing (Sarbanes-Oxley, FDA) will require documentation that cannot be negotiated. Work these into your iterations by placing them into the backlog and asking your product owner to rank them accordingly.

Communications

Communication is a constant in all of these hurdles, and in all of agile, but we give it its own category nevertheless, due to its criticality. In particular, these areas are extremely important but often overlooked:

- Include a communications plan in your transition/rollout plan. This communication plan should account for ways to keep staff updated regularly—even when you feel there is little to report. Reporting that "We didn't really accomplish anything this month because of the server issues, but we still really want to go agile and hope to get back on track with some pilot teams next month" is better than hearing nothing at all. Practice high visibility into the status of your rollout, just as you will ask your teams for high visibility into the status of their software development projects.
- Provide full support for the sharing of experiences and knowledge. Do this by offering brown-bag lunches, speakers, cocktail hours, pizza socials, regularly scheduled meetings for your agile project leaders, and so on. Set up the venue, give the team members time to go, do it regularly, and make clear this is a supported activity.
- Define escalation and issue resolution. Make sure there is an escalation process for teams who can't get satisfaction. Is this the transition

committee? The PMO? How about an issue resolution process for the customer? Is there a customer advisory board?

- Be prepared to provide constant education to customers and vendors, to new employees, and across the business. Turnover, the hiring of new staff, and reorganization efforts will make this an ongoing necessity.

It's never easy making changes, especially of this magnitude. But we've been told over and over again by most teams that the hardest part was just getting started. Once teams begin adopting some of the practices, they find the rewards surprising and well worth the continued effort. Organizations find that being able to better respond to the marketplace isn't the only reason to switch to agile—the cooperative and collaborative nature of the approach provides a more supportive, meaningful, and exciting work environment for the members of the team. Agile is a commonsense approach to software development, and applying that common sense to a waterfall/agile enterprise means success lies in creating a transition plan to excellence through the cycle of inspection, adaptation, and execution. Just as building software systems is an emergent process, so is the way in which agile is adopted by an organization's teams.

Summary

The takeaways from this chapter include the following:

- Traditional process requirements and working with waterfall teams are two areas that agile teams in a waterfall enterprise must address.
- When agile and waterfall must coexist, keep in mind these key principles to ensure a cooperative relationship: continuous improvement through timeboxed iterative deliveries and reviews, implementing the most important items first, and constant collaborative communications.
- Traditional process requirements can be like bookends, occurring at the beginning or end of an agile project, and therefore can be placed into the agile team's product backlog to be prioritized and worked as appropriate.

- Being asked to fulfill traditional process requirements throughout the agile project lifecycle indicates that those who are asking have either not bought into agile philosophy or do not understand agile principles.
- Agile and waterfall teams on the same project must coordinate regularly, and the agile planning meetings provide the framework for doing so.
- Retrospectives provide both the agile and waterfall teams with the means to continually improve the way they work together.
- There will still be hurdles to clear: resistance, culture, resource management, vendors and contracting, facilities and tooling, cost accounting and reporting, auditors and assessors, and communication. Apply common sense in overcoming these obstacles, and have the conversations necessary to negotiate solutions and embrace change.

Endnotes

1. Portions of this chapter were originally published in *Better Software* magazine. Michele Sliger. "Bridging the Gap: Agile Projects in the Waterfall Enterprise." *Better Software*, July/August 2006, 26–31.

2. Alistair Cockburn. "Balancing Lightness with Sufficiency." http://alistair. cockburn.us/index.php/Balancing_lightness_with_sufficiency.

3. Ken Schwaber. *Agile Project Management with Scrum.* (Redmond, WA: Microsoft Press, 2004), 121.

Chapter 15

How Can a Project Management Office Support Agile?

The real problem is what to do with problem solvers after the problem is solved.

—Gay Talese

Do not repeat the tactics which have gained you one victory, but let your methods be regulated by the infinite variety of circumstances.

—Sun Tzu

Imagine logging in to check your online bank account. You expect to see a balance of $5,000, minus a few ancillary purchases you made over the weekend. To your astonishment, you see a balance of a million dollars! Your heart starts to pound a little, and your palms get a little sweaty. Upon closer inspection, you notice that the purchases you made over the weekend total ten thousand—but that cannot be! All you remember buying was gas for the car, some groceries, and a bottle of wine for your neighbor's house warming party. You now become really nervous. What if someone has stolen your identity? How else can you explain the large transactions and balances? You call the bank and are asked to wait 20 minutes to speak to an agent (phone lines are jammed due to unexpected volume). Finally, the exhausted agent tells you that there is a glitch in the system, that all of the online transactions and balances for the past 48 hours were somehow recorded in Hungarian Forint (HUF). She reassures you that many people have called in, nervous and scared because they don't know how to tell the balances of their accounts, but there is nothing to worry about: All accounts will be converted to their expected currencies by the next business day.

Think of a PMO (project management office)[1] like a bank, and imagine a similar scenario; an executive stakeholder arrives at work Monday morning and over coffee decides to review the portfolio dashboard. He expects to see earned value analysis in terms of dollars and performance indices, yet instead sees release burndown charts and estimates expressed as "story points." Imagine how frustrated, frightened, and confused he would be!

As a financial institution provides multiple services to its clients, from mortgage services, to investments, to loans and bank accounts, the PMO, similarly, provides stakeholders of an organization insight into the value that projects have delivered, and thus the ability to make informed, educated decisions about investments. An agile PMO can help the organization stick to a currency that everyone can understand, and can change this currency when it's not working.

Instead of a PMO that first dictates policy and then measures projects according to those rules, we envision an agile PMO that makes visible the most effective team practices by amplifying retrospective results and sharing that knowledge across the organization. The PMO, the organization traditionally charged with managing a collection of projects to meet broader business goals, must then be considered as part of the agile transition, or at least identified as an organization that will soon be impacted by projects whose project managers decide to employ agile methodologies.

Some will argue that the existence of a PMO flies in the face of agile values, that self-organizing teams determine their respective processes empirically, led by a servant leader who clears obstacles. We would agree that the traditional role of a PMO—govern, control, and direct—is opposite of what agile culture attempts to instill in the organization; we also have had experience with vast organizations (tens of thousands of employees) that need guidance and information from the PMO in an agile organization. Think of contracts in an agile project; a little entity called the Judicial System forces us into mitigating risk by putting it on paper. Likewise, the PMO acts as the guardian of consistency and adherence to outside forces such as Sarbanes-Oxley,[2] accounting, legal, and so on, yet engages the team to help create a process that considers all perspectives!

We would like to propose an agile PMO—an enabler and uber-facilitator of agile projects and communication to the organization. If the agile project manager is the obstacle remover of the team, then the PMO is the obstacle remover of the program and the magnifying glass of reality. Also, we think of the PMO as agile ambassadors, working to educate others within and outside of the organization. Like the Brinks money truck, the PMO delivers the right amount of education to the right people, just in time to keep the entire operation running. Creating a project management office that can be as nimble and flexible as its project teams is no small feat, yet this is imperative for retaining a high level of agility in the organization.

When do we engage this agile PMO? Obviously, keeping a minimal level of overhead is in line with Lean Product Development. PMOs typically exist in the midst of a large organization, when there is need for overall analysis and synthesis of hundreds—even thousands—of organizational initiatives. Aside from tearing down and rebuilding your existing PMO to be agile, consider the following ideas about how a PMO can adapt the following in order to support agile initiatives:

- Product management
- Project initiation
- Compliance
- Resourcing
- Control
- Metrics
- Education and coaching
- Retrospective
- Role

An Extension of Product Management

Just as the agile PMO is the magnifying glass to project team progress, it also functions as an extension of product management. The agile PMO keeps the product management team informed of all programs' statuses (remember the bank?), enabling the product managers to have the ability to change investment strategy or make changes to the emerging products. The agile PMO synthesizes the information coming out of multiple teams' iteration and release backlogs, helps the product management team update the individual product backlogs, and helps in the preparation and updating of product roadmaps. Figure 15-1 illustrates how information flows from teams to the agile PMO (which is made up of the teams' project managers); from there, the agile PMO orchestrates and helps information flow between resource managers and the product management team.

Figure 15-1
The agile PMO functions as a knowledge amplifier and conductor of information between resource managers, teams, and product management.

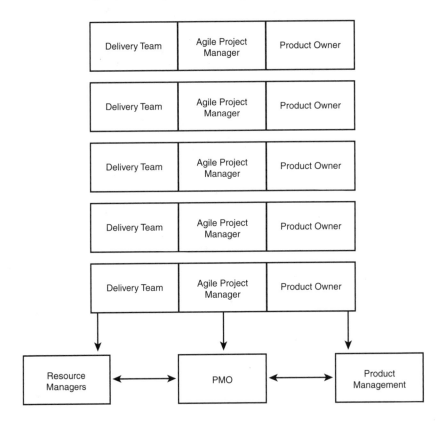

One area in particular where an agile PMO can be helpful to product management is by reporting on the product roadmaps within the organization. A product roadmap is an effective way of looking at the product's evolution over time. The typical timeframe for a product roadmap is quarterly; that is, product development milestones are set on a quarterly basis and the plan is updated based on actual delivery and current and future needs. Considerations that affect a product roadmap are things such as product launch windows; for example, we wouldn't dare consider upgrading our entire retail database in the middle of the holiday season. Other examples include fiscal year, shareholder announcements, and large customer needs. The agile PMO can report a project's status relative to its roadmap in order to enable product management to make decisions about the products relative to what is emerging in the marketplace. An example of a roadmap/release report appears later in the chapter in Figure 15-3.

Project Initiation

Traditionally, a PMO would need a full set of requirements with estimates from which to determine costs that would then help the organization determine whether or not the initiative is advisable. This "project initiation phase," as it is commonly referred to, is important because the PMO is trying to help the organization determine if the project is worthwhile. Many PMOs have discovered that they can leverage the rapid start nature of agile, invest in a release plan with the team, and allow the team to work for an iteration, after which iteration the business can make a go/no-go decision about the project. Figure 15-2 represents this idea. The flow at the top of the graphic represents the traditional waterfall approach; while the initiation phase begins up front, many organizations will only authorize the project after the detailed functional and technical design is complete and when all tasks are estimated. This bottom-up approach to planning provides the budgeting group with an expected cost based on this very detailed analysis, from which point it can make a funding decision. The flow at the bottom is an agile approach to the initiation process; that is, the organization provisionally funds for a team to engage in release planning as well as conduct one iteration. The first iteration's deliverables include, among other things, the team and the customer fleshing out the product backlog, as well as the team delivering at least one feature. Once the first iteration is reviewed, along with the updated release plan, the budgeting group can make an informed decision to proceed or not. Many organizations have found this approach to be much less costly than the investment in upfront requirements analysis and design; plus, the organization benefits from a demo of early thought work and can make collaborative decisions based on real results.

As Figure 15-2 depicts, project funding can then be reevaluated at the end of each iteration.

A Traditional Project Initiation Approach

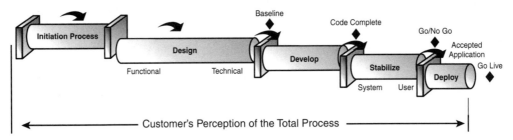

An Agile Project Initiation Approach

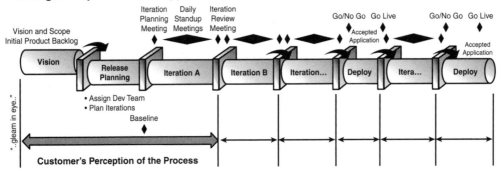

Figure 15-2
A traditional and agile approach to project initiation

Are We Compliant?

The agile PMO is the informer of compliance information and the amplifier of teams' and external departments' needs regarding these compliance situations. Instead of acting as a dictator and enforcer, the agile PMO seeks to inform teams of the external compliance challenge, negotiate a reasonable process to satisfy both team and business, and most importantly, listen to the teams to understand what works and what does not work. Instead of the PMO as a sole determinant of process and ensuring compliance, the PMO listens to what is working for teams and helps to amplify knowledge of other teams and programs. Sometimes the PMO staff is referred to as "the process police," and often this is not a term of endearment. But remember, many police cars have the words "to serve and protect" painted on them. Even though police have many responsibilities to ensure that civilians are obeying the law, their foremost duty is to serve. The PMO can be thought of in much the same way; serving the organization by helping it define a process that is effective and valuable.

Working to Get to Compliance

We worked with a client who was scaling 12 product teams in an effort to rewrite a 15-year old "cash cow" legacy system. In addition to all of the technical complexity, this public company also suffered from the complexity of compliance to Sarbanes-Oxley standards. And it was taking on all of this while implementing an agile process. Talk about challenging!

Its traditional process dictated that a thorough design document be written before any work could begin. This clearly flew in the face of agile methods. The teams were challenged with answering the question, "How do we get started when external compliance won't allow us to?" The director in charge of the PMO met with several teams to understand the issue, and then met with auditors to determine how the teams could use agile methods, yet still meet compliance standards. After many meetings and discussions, the teams were allowed to begin work with an overview document that described basic architecture. Additionally, they had as an acceptance criterion for each feature to document the decisions that were made during each iteration. Documentation, then, became a living representation of the system. Even though the teams felt as though this extra step was not necessary, it was very necessary from an organizational compliance perspective.

It was the work of the PMO in listening to the problem from both sides and then helping drive a suitable resolution that enabled the teams to move quickly and nimbly.

Resourcing

Although agile teams (and arguably agile organizations) should be self-organizing, we have seen tremendous value in a PMO that can work with product management and resource managers to satisfy a project's needs for people.

Although most agile projects can be staffed by dedicated, cross-functional teams, every now and then there is the person who needs to be dedicated to more than one team. The most common roles that fall prey to multitasking are the roles of the DBA (database administrator) and technical writer. Additionally, many projects have non–human resource needs as well, such as servers and routers.

Figure 15-3 is a representation of a roadmap and release plan report. This report was given to product management after a round of strategic planning in the fourth quarter of the preceding year. As you can see, iterations for the first quarter have been planned at the user story level in release planning, and all of the other quarters are defined by themes at this point in time. In this report, the PMO designates hardware and other resource constraints based on the information the team provided in release planning; these items will impact the projects' budgets. Also, product management can see that the teams in Project B are currently not scheduled for work in Quarter 4, 2008. As a result, the product management team may begin thinking of a new initiative for this team once detailed planning for the fourth quarter is on the horizon. Right now, however, product management can begin to count on extra headcount in the fourth quarter; this availability will be observed and revised, if needed, based on the actual progress of the teams against the roadmap and release plans.

The roadmap and release planning meetings help teams identify additional resource needs early, so that by the time their first iteration arrives they are ready to create slices of functionality. Additionally, the agile PMO can work with teams to understand their resource bottlenecks and institute measures to help relieve the constraints. These efforts include working with the training organization to help cross-train roles within teams and aligning these efforts with resource managers who have identified new training needs as a result of helping their staff with career development. The PMO can also see the split in user stories across multiple teams as designated by the asterisks.

The agile PMO can also assist in streamlining the processes in resource acquisition. For example, one client we worked with had a 90-day window for ordering and acquiring new hardware. When we investigated the steps in the process, we realized that the hardware procurement team allocated ten days for the request ticket to get into the system! By helping the procurement team understand the ideas behind prioritization and backlogs, we were able to reduce the time for ticket entry to one day, saving about 10% of the overall time for hardware purchase, which translated to valuable time savings in the project.

	Quarter 1 2008			Quarter 2 2008	Quarter 3 2008	Quarter 4 2008
Project A	Iteration 1	Iteration 2	Iteration 3			
Team 1	User Story A User Story B User Story C	User Story D* User Story E User Story F User Story G	User Story I User Story K	Theme A Theme B Theme C	Theme D Theme E	Theme F
Team 2	User Story H	User Story H	User Story J			
Team 3	User Story A User Story B	User Story D* User Story E User Story F	User Story J			
Project B	Iteration 1	Iteration 2	Iteration 3			
Team 1	User Story A User Story B*	User Story C	User Story D User Story E*	Theme A Theme B Theme C	Theme D	
Team 2	User Story B*	User Story C	User Story E*			

Project A—Teams 1 and 3 have hardware dependencies for Iteration 2.
Project B—Teams 1 and 2 have a need for a data architect in Iterations 1 and 3.

Figure 15-3
A quarterly roadmap and release planning report from the agile PMO to product management depicting resource needs

Finally, the agile PMO can guide product owners on figuring out how many teams are needed to "keep the lights on" for a product—that is, how many teams are necessary for the support and maintenance. Additionally, the PMO can help make visible the investment across several initiatives from a resource perspective—from new product development, support of existing versions, and finally, sun-setting product versions.

Backlog Control Versus Change Control

Although agile teams have the product backlog to leverage for communication about scope, the agile PMO can help the product management team look across multiple backlogs in the effort to coordinate cross-program initiatives across multiple projects. An agile PMO, for example, may want to report on amount per project spent and amount of budget remaining in each product backlog at a summary level. Depending on where the focus shifts in the overall corporate strategic plan, product owners can choose to open or close the budget valve on projects and programs based on overall spent and what's left to spend.

In Figure 15-4, because the Platform Rewrite project has encountered unforeseen architectural expenditures, product owners may agree to go ahead with the team's recommendation of dropping the last 20 points of work on the new dashboard and invest the $40,000 "surplus" in the Platform Rewrite project. The agile PMO can help synthesize all teams' project information in order to help product management make effective investment decisions about projects.

Project	Initiated	Total Points in Release	Total Points Remaining in Release	Cumulative Team Velocity per Iteration	Comments	Budget Spent to Date	Remaining Budget
Version 11.0 Sunset	5/9/2006	240	100	40		$127,328	$50,000
Platform Rewrite	1/9/2007	750	250	75	This project incurred 20 new PBIs this iteration; due to unforseen architecture refactoring, remaining budget increased from $156K to $254K; needs discussion	$750,000	$254,786
New Dashboard	6/2007	150	20	20	Team and product owner feel that functionality meets user needs; consider dropping last 20 points of backlog due to stagnation	$200,000	$40,000

Figure 15-4
Trade-off matrix. The PMO can roll up project reporting in an effort to aid product management's ability to make timely decisions about where to spend money.

Project Metrics

The agile PMO can help teams standardize on meaningful metrics that enable timely and effective decision-making, and review these metrics and resulting team optimizations regularly for areas of improvement. Whereas some measurements should be standard regardless of methodology (customer satisfaction, profit and loss, return on investment, business case realization), other metrics, such as release burndowns, customer support, and cycle times (from concept to first release, from feature request to deployment, and so on), should be investigated as new ways to measure agile team productivity.

One agile PMO we worked with was solely focusing on the number of points completed per iteration. Additionally, it was giving out a cash award to the team that exemplified the most thorough completion of points. Not surprisingly, teams were optimizing around this metric by "completing" as many points as possible, in some cases inflating the point estimates to appear as if they had taken on and completed more work. Also, not surprisingly, the resulting quality of each iteration's work was poor and there were no standards for automated builds and integration. Each team was working its own way, which was causing a nightmare, especially for the products that required multiple teams' work.

Figure 15-5 shows how multiple teams' iteration burndown charts can be aggregated to make visible the burndown of the release. This is critical from an overall product perspective, enabling product managers to decide if they should extend the number of iterations, add another team, or negotiate scope for the project. The agile PMO can leverage the natural break points—at the end of one iteration and the beginning of another—to consolidate and make available this summary information.

Additionally, the PMO can leverage the teams to come up with metrics. A metric is more valuable (and valid) when those who create the data believe in its worth. Because the PMO has the duty to make many teams' project information visible, it can coordinate metrics used among all the teams in all projects. Another area of value is to communicate variances and meaning behind metrics to senior management; for example, a story point estimate of 8 in one team will not map perfectly to another team's estimate of 8. Finally, the PMO can ask questions to understand which metrics management finds most useful and communicate that back down to the teams.

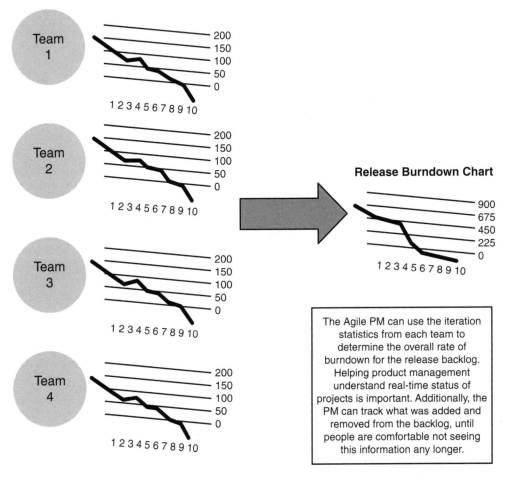

Release Burndown Chart

The Agile PM can use the iteration statistics from each team to determine the overall rate of burndown for the release backlog. Helping product management understand real-time status of projects is important. Additionally, the PM can track what was added and removed from the backlog, until people are comfortable not seeing this information any longer.

Figure 15-5
A release burndown chart

Many lean teams employ Six Sigma or Lean Six Sigma techniques, which compose a set of concepts intended to systematically improve processes by eliminating defects. In an agile setting, we've seen PMOs well-versed in agile utilize the concepts of Critical to Quality and Defect, as well as Process Capability to derive metrics in order to help teams get better in these three areas. Two common Six Sigma techniques are Pareto diagrams and root cause analysis. Pareto diagrams help us focus on the problems that have the greatest potential for improvement, and root cause analysis helps determine the underlying reasons for nonconformance with a process. An agile retrospective is another way of thinking about root cause analysis (what are we currently doing that is impeding us?).

The PMO as Educator and Coach

We see immense value in the PMO partnering with the training services division of the organization to plan and deliver educational sessions about agile. These sessions can run the gamut from Agile101, to retrospectives, to test-driven development. The PMO should coordinate the creation and delivery of courses in response to the organization's current level of agility and stage in the adoption cycle. Some agile project managers learn to teach courses themselves, realizing what a powerful tool this is in helping others achieve agility!

Additionally, the PMO can act as coach to the entire group of agile project managers. We've recognized that project managers thrust into the role of a "servant leader" have a challenging time reconceiving self-worth and esteem, because the focus shifts to the team. Creating leadership courses, scheduling group meetings and retrospectives, as well as providing forums for agile project managers to share experiences (either internal or external, such as conferences) are all exceptionally helpful in aiding the personal transformation.

Keepers of the Retrospective

Because we've worked with so many organizations that struggle with agile simply because they fail to retrospect, we feel that the agile PMO can play an integral part in reinforcing the purpose and value of this meeting, as well as assisting agile project managers in removing the resulting obstacles from their impediment backlogs.

Agile PMOs should ensure that qualified facilitators are on hand to help lead these meetings, or invest in training if these qualified individuals do not exist.

Who Is the Agile PMO?

Because the minutia of acting as "taskmaster" to the team is removed when going agile, this frees the project manager to provide more value. The agile PMO is a perfect fit for this project manager; this person acts as the liaison between the need for visibility into teams' work, and how teams' work fits into the strategic vision. What we've found is that this role duality exists in many organizations already; in fact, we're hearing the title "program manager" used with almost equal frequency as "project manager."

A PMO can be just another layer of management complexity if not leveraged properly.

PMO members need to be educated in the values and practices of agile processes, including ideas such as dedicated teams, points-based estimations, and burndown charts. They need to manage themselves in an agile fashion as well, creating their own backlog of issues to resolve, timeboxes to iterate in, demonstrating their progress, and then retrospecting on how well they are serving the organization and what they can do to improve.

Indeed, PMOs should leverage the power of retrospectives to consistently ask (and answer) how they can continue to provide visibility into projects, help teams and agile project managers get better at employing agile techniques, and enable teams and the business to come together to make effective product decisions.

Do You Really Need an Agile PMO?

By now, you should be thinking about whether your company really needs an agile PMO. Remember, many agile approaches follow one of the basic tenets of Lean: "eliminate waste." If your product owners are directly driving projects, even in multiteam scenarios, if your HR department is involved with and supports team training and knowledge-sharing, if teams are making results visible, and/or if you are leading projects in a very small company, then a PMO might be redundant. Sometimes, not all of the parts fit together when the organization transitions to a new way.

Summary

The takeaways from this chapter include the following:

- The agile PMO makes all project and program results visible so that the business can make timely decisions.
- The agile PMO engages in agile education and socialization activities throughout the greater organization, including, but not limited to, teaching executives and managers about agile project metrics and partnering with the training organization (if applicable) to educate teams and managers about agile practices.
- The agile PMO will revisit processes such as project initiation to understand if they still make sense for agile projects. Additionally, the agile PMO can work with outside groups such as auditors and accountants to most effectively coordinate the reporting for agile projects.
- If appropriate, the agile PMO can work with line managers to help them understand the benefits of cross-functional, multidisciplinary teams, as well as help them see when key resources will be necessary for teams by utilizing release and iteration planning outcomes.
- The agile PMO can be effective in amplifying learning as a result of teams' retrospectives to the rest of the organization. The agile PMO can leverage these findings to streamline project coordination and execution.

Endnotes

1. Some enterprises refer to a PMO as a *program* management office.

2. Sarbanes-Oxley (SOX) is a controversial United States law passed in 2002 in response to various corporate scandals. The most contentious aspect of SOX is Section 404, which requires management and the external auditor to report on the adequacy of the company's internal control over financial reporting. (Source: www.wikipedia.com)

Chapter 16

Selling the Benefits of Agile

Are we selling or building trust?

—*Hubert Smits*

I really don't 'sell' anything, and don't even think that I can do so very well. What I can do, on my best days, is to listen to what someone wants, what they are having trouble with, and suggest a specific thing to do to make that part of their life better.

—*Ron Jeffries*

We've provided you with the foundational and historical information regarding agile, its evolution into modern software management, and ways you can move from your existing traditional practices to agile practices. However, we also recognize that as an agile project manager, you will ultimately be asked by a group of people (whether a team, another manager, or an executive or customer), "What's in it for me?" Congratulations! Part of your role as an agile project manager is to help others understand how the team is working and the role that others play in the process.

We're sure that this is not unlike what you have done in the past as a traditional project manager; however, this chapter is intended to provide some helpful hints when thrown into the situation of selling, persuading, or convincing others about agile. What we call "selling" is really the act of finding what interests people and seeing if an agile approach can help meet their needs. You might be involved in an organizational change to agile methods, and understanding how to relate information to certain groups of people will greatly help in the transition.

This chapter looks at selling agile in several ways: selling in general, selling it to the team, selling it to management, selling it to the customer or product owner, and selling it to other departments in your organization. We finish with a look at *not* selling (that is, finding other ways to share and promote agile).

Some General Ideas about Selling

Ask any salesman and he'll be sure to tell you that it helps if you believe in the product yourself before you try to sell it to somebody else. The same is true for agile. How can you convince someone of the benefits of something if you do not receive or have not observed these benefits yourself? It can be a little difficult to do.

In addition to believing in an idea, there's another aspect of selling: know what is motivating the buyer. Some refer to this as "pain points," which is a level of difficulty sufficient to motivate someone to seek a solution or an alternative. In other words, knowing enough about agile to position it against various pain points of the organization will surely help the sell. Our standard response to most protests is, "How do you handle that now?" This followed by, "And how is that working out for you?" After a momentary stammer and some nervous laughs from those witnessing this exchange, the protester usually admits that his current method isn't working out very well. An admittance that a new way is needed is the best way to start the discussion.

Although it's nice to present a perfect picture of an idea you're wild about, it's also important to acknowledge the weaknesses. Nothing is bulletproof; there is never a one-size-fits-all solution that will fix everyone's pain and make lives perfect. The same is true with agile; although it does improve the management of complex projects, it does not fix everything. Difficult situations and tradeoffs will still exist, no matter the approach.

In fact, part of your message should be that the problems that exist in the organization today will be exacerbated and magnified with agile. Because of the two-tier inspect-and-adapt cycle (daily and iteration), issues and problems are uncovered and made highly visible on a regular basis. If these issues are not addressed, the organization could be worse off than it started.

Part of selling is learning when not to sell. Sometimes you have to plant the seed of an idea within people's minds and then let some calendar time pass. Learn when to push and when to back off—and educate throughout the process.

Now let's discuss some of the groups you may wish to sell agile to as it takes hold in your organization. We've compiled a list of the most popular questions and have provided some food for thought for each. Note that this is not an exhaustive list, and the ideas are not prescriptive. We just want to expose you to many of the questions that we are often asked and ways these questions can be addressed.

Selling to the Team

The team can be your hardest sell, especially in the situation where agile has been brought in from top management. Developers, quality assurance staff, technical writers, and other professionals do what they do because they are smart. They will challenge you, and they have every right to. Arming yourself with information about principles and values is vital to helping a team understand why the discipline in agile approaches is necessary and how that discipline can ultimately benefit them.

There Are Too Many Meetings

After we dispel the notion that agile teams don't plan much, there is a general horror expressed by many of our clients at the number of meetings agile requires. We've found that this negative view of the meetings is usually based on their own experience with their current ongoing meetings. Usually starting late and lasting too long, with no agenda, and too much politicking and finger-pointing, these nightmare meetings set the tone for what they expect agile meetings to be like.

When we encounter the pushback regarding the number of meetings involved in agile—iteration planning, iteration demos, reviews, retrospectives, daily stand-ups, not to mention release planning—it is time to be clear about the differences in how these meetings are run, and how all the "overhead" as they see it is actually quite productive.

The first question to ask is, "In the process you're using now, how do you know what to work on?" The answer generally centers on documentation: "I'm given a spec and I code to what I interpret the spec to mean." The second question to ask is, "Yes, and how is that working out for the customer? Are they getting software they can use?" What we've heard from hundreds of teams is that this process generally doesn't work out well. With this acknowledgement comes the uncertainty of how to lighten up the heavy documents. Well-timed meetings help us accomplish this.

First, agile meetings are in keeping with one of the basic agile tenets, that face-to-face communication is the most efficient and effective way to communicate. Combine this with another agile tenet, that of "the art of maximizing the amount of work not done,"[1] and the meetings become the most efficient way to communicate information, plan the work, make improvements to both the product and the process, and eliminate quality errors caused by misunderstandings. These meetings require team involvement and focus on the next best thing to do. They are efficient in that there is an agenda, the planning is limited to the timebox at hand, and information does not need to be repeated or heavily documented, because everyone who is affected is there and participating in the decision-making.

Sometimes it helps to do the math. Five daily stand-ups equal 75 minutes at most, not much more than a weekly status meeting, so that's a wash. Four hours in an iteration planning meeting multiplied by six two-week iterations equals 24 hours, which is less time than you would normally spend planning a quarterly release. And don't forget, you're not supposed to be attending agile meetings *and* other non-agile project meetings! Asking the team to follow two different processes isn't efficient at all—the agile meetings should replace existing ones.

Probably the most contested meeting in an agile setting is the daily stand-up. Teams often complain that they feel as if this is a mechanism only in place so that managers can micro-manage. Remind the team that this meeting is *their* meeting, designed for them to inspect and adapt their work tasks in response to how the iteration is unfolding.

One technique we've used in the past to push the team to run its own meeting is to walk away and let the team continue the meeting solo. This sends the message that "I trust you as professionals to run this meeting on your own." Afterward, stop by and talk to a team member or two to see if any obstacles were brought forth in the meeting and take these down. Of course, we wouldn't do this with a brand-new team. We would do it with one that has the hang of how to run this meeting (which doesn't take too long). Mike Cohn tells a story of how he had to attend daily stand-up meetings with a magazine and pretend to read during the meeting. Deprived of his eye contact, the team started speaking to each other, which is the whole point of these stand-ups.

Often, the "roll up your sleeves" approach is very beneficial. Give the status of the impediments in your own backlog as the agile project manager. How are things going with getting Support's presence at the product review meeting? How did the discussion go with the vice president regarding publishing agile reports to the dashboard? Visibility into this information will build trust with the team. The members will come to understand that you have work that you are doing for the good of the team, and you are open to sharing it in the daily stand-up meeting. When the team members feel like you are supporting and serving them, they will begin to trust you.

It's just fifteen minutes. Remind the team members that their engagement in this meeting is meant to keep them out of other meetings, hopefully saving them some time. Also, remind them that the daily stand-up is also a mechanism to promote visibility into work and that anybody is invited. This meeting, while primarily to serve the team, also serves the greater organization by promoting transparency.

Eventually the team begins to realize that even though these meetings are called "meetings," they really are collaborative working sessions to build the right product increment. They are necessary discussions for the team and customer to plan, negotiate and create. If these three basic actions are not happening in the team's agile meetings, redefine it as a "work session" and reset or reemphasize its purpose. An example of this is a team who feels like the purpose of iteration planning is to create tasks with estimates; while

Selling Themselves on the Stand-Up

I once had a team who fought me tooth and nail on the daily stand-up meeting. The members didn't get the idea, they very much disliked it, and regardless of the amount of time I spent "selling" it, they refused to embrace it. After one heated retrospective, the team convinced me to let them try an iteration without the daily stand-up. I agreed, in the spirit of self-managing teams. To my surprise, within five days they resumed the daily stand-up, on their own, because they found that communication and task dependency management were floundering because of the lack of the meeting. I never said, "I told you so." Instead, I just let them gain momentum from the self-discovery.

this is an *outcome* of the meeting, the true purpose is for the team to design the solution, plan its approach, and commit to a plan.

We Don't See the Point in Gross-Level Estimating

Teams will resist high-level (gross) estimates of feature complexity, mainly because they've felt pressured to give "perfect estimates" in a plan-driven environment. Gross-level estimates, usually given in something called "story points" (for more information on story points, see Chapter 6, "Time Management") feel like "fuzzy logic" to engineers.[2] They've on occasion received punishment for "bad" estimates by having to work late to make up the time. Sometimes, they don't want to give estimates at all because sales and management make promises based on these numbers or replace the team members' estimates with a "better estimate" anyway.

Remind the team that gross-level estimating was devised as a way to abstract time from the estimates in order to focus on the complexities surrounding implementation of the feature; additionally, this level of estimating provides for a look into longer-term, or strategic, planning. Our experience is that over time, teams become very effective at estimating using this technique. It is important to remind the team that the time to implement a feature is important, but we must not confuse expected duration with estimates of the level of effort. In agile, the durations are always the length of the iteration. Instead, explain to the team that the time a feature takes to implement is impacted by many things: skill, technology, culture, distributed teams, code complexity, and so on. The gross-level complexity estimates provide a way of factoring in these elements as part of the overall complexity of the feature, and understanding that complexity helps us to better determine a range of time and resources that will need to be expended in implementing that feature. History has shown us that trying to predict time rarely leads to accurate estimates; predicting complexity, however, does give us a better view into what to expect.

This gross-level complexity estimating is also important to the customer or product owner who manages the product backlog. Knowing the level of complexity involved helps this individual make decisions based on the return on investment the company would receive from the implementation of the feature. If a feature receives a high complexity estimate from the team, the customer may decide to prioritize it lower than another high-value feature with a lower complexity estimate. It's about getting the most return for the investment, and providing team-generated gross-level complexity estimates is the fastest and simplest way to indicate potential risk, effort, and size.

If We Don't Do Any Technical Planning, Our Architecture Will Fail

We would tend to agree! Although the Agile Manifesto states that "the best architectures, requirements, and designs emerge from self-organizing teams,"[3] that's not to say that emergent design simply pops into existence from thin air. The design begins with a high-level plan, appropriate to the time horizon and in keeping with the overall product vision.

In the same way the product owner is planning the vision around the product and how it will serve the customer, the architect (or members of the agile team) should plan for how the system can support that vision and provide enough flexibility to meet the inevitable changes in requirements. In his book *Scaling Software Agility,* Dean Leffingwell refers to this agile architectural planning as the "architectural runway."[4] Architectural planning is still emergent, but the idea of having a "runway" in place for the team means that the architecture, like the high-priority items in the product backlog, is being designed and detailed in the existing iteration for the next iteration or next few iterations. The idea is that an architectural foundation, or runway, will be in place and ready for the team to use as it takes off on its next iteration. Portions of the runway continue to be built out as the project progresses and the "plane," or product, gets larger and heavier with features.

While considering the architectural runway, it is important to remind the team of the statistics: 60% of software features are rarely or never used![5] Many have attributed this to the fact that in traditionally managed projects, every conceivable feature is planned for and expected to be implemented. This is frequently a symptom of fixed-price, fixed-scope projects with little-to-no room for change. Because these types of products historically were created in horizontal layers, one layer at a time, by hand-off from one group to the next, the architecture would be built to support any and all features outlined in the analysis phase. Unfortunately, many companies realized that after anticipating and building for all of these possibilities, by the time the system was complete, the customers' business had changed, making some (or all) of the features and underlying architecture obsolete. In agile, we build product increments as we go, and this also means the supporting architecture; however, we keep an eye on the horizon, making sound architectural decisions based on what we know today. It's like swimming across the English Channel: We know where we need to go and start making strokes to get there, but every so often we have to come up for air and make sure we're heading in the right direction. Agile teams don't want to waste time building something that will never be used, as well as add to future waste of time maintaining that functionality for the life of the product. Refactoring existing features and architecture to appropriately integrate new features is a regular discipline of agile teams. Support this practice on your teams.

We Aren't Co-Located, So We Can't Be Agile

When you have a geographically dispersed team, communications simply take longer. Teams have to figure out ways to work together so that they communicate verbally as often as possible. Technology exists to support this: telephones, Skype, video conferencing. Throw in a few face-to-face meetings to build understanding and team cohesion, and even nonverbal instant messaging can then work well.

You can help build a sense of team and collaboration by helping team members learn about each other. Create trivia quizzes that allow team members to guess little-known facts about each other. Post photos on the wiki, along with favorite programming languages or hobbies. Invite remote team members to key planning meetings to kick off the project with everyone on board. With a little effort and the right tools, virtual teams can be just as effective as co-located teams.

Some Unspoken Reasons

We've talked about some of the more obvious pushbacks from teams who don't wish to adopt agile (and by no means have we covered all of them). However, there are also many *unspoken* thoughts that contribute to a person's reticence. They are all centered on fear and discomfort, and although we have no pat answers as to how to address these concerns, it is good to at least be aware of them. You'll find that despite what team members (and project managers) are saying, they are often really thinking:

- I'm afraid of change.
- I'm afraid I will have nothing to do.
- I'm afraid I will lose my job.
- I'm afraid people will see how little I actually do.
- I'm afraid I won't be able to keep up.
- I'm afraid I won't be able to learn the new software.
- I'm afraid this will mean hard work.
- I'm afraid I'll be fired if the decisions we make don't work out.
- I'm afraid I won't get raises or promotions anymore.
- I'm afraid of conflict and trying to reach consensus.
- Nuts! There go my three-hour lunches.
- Nuts! That means I can't mosey in at 10:30 anymore.
- Nuts! That means I'll have to really think now.
- Nuts! That means I'll actually have to talk to people now.
- It's just so much easier and safer when someone else tells me exactly what to do.
- It's just so much easier and safer when I can tell them exactly what I want them to do.

The best thing you can do to help people through these issues is to create and maintain an environment where failure is viewed as an opportunity for learning and growth. Although you can make promises and clearly communicate that this is your intent, it has been our experience that people don't begin to really relax until they see the truth of it in action. Additionally, provide hands-on coaching and leadership for team members to help them envision their new roles and how to add value in new ways. For example, working with the developers to write unit tests can help them see how they are contributing to overall product quality. Helping testers get the time of the product owner can help testers understand the acceptance criteria for the next iteration's backlog items. Helping technical writers learn incremental writing and editing techniques can help them scale to multiple teams. Assisting customers with product backlog preparation and inviting them to iteration demos can show them the influence they really do have over development.

Selling to Management

Management sometimes has the same concerns as the team, but often managers' issues center around perceived lack of control and loss of identity. Many managers feel personally tied to the current state of development because they helped create this current state. Asking them to change to an agile approach is sometimes perceived as a criticism.

Agile Doesn't Allow for Long-Term Planning. How Are We Supposed to Do Our Budgets?

This is a misunderstanding born from the initial focus on doing iterative and incremental delivery. Because this is such a new way of thinking, it takes a while before newcomers learn about more strategic and long-term levels of planning, such as release planning and defining a product roadmap. You can read more about these different levels of planning in Chapter 5, "Scope Management."

It Has Worked So Far, Why Do We Need to Change?

Well, if this is really true, and your customers are satisfied, then you probably don't need to change. However, it has been our experience that this type of general resistance to change hides a different issue.

Traditionally, managers create metrics, reports, budgets, and career paths. They have goals and they try to meet those goals, not only for themselves but for their departments, and they are rewarded on how well their departments perform.

The focus in agile development shifts to that of cross-functional teams of people, not a group of individuals with similar skills, otherwise known as "skill silos." The focus is also on creating self-managed, empowered teams. This notion troubles many managers because they feel like they will lose power or control. Because they must redefine their existence within agile, they will often resist the very notion of it. Sometimes, the personal change is just too great.

You can help managers by showing them how they can support a team. You can partner with them to help remove the biggest impediments. You can have discussions with them to find out what they are being asked to measure, and offer to talk with their bosses about how measurement is conducted on an agile project. You can also discuss ideas for career paths in an agile setting.

At the end of the day, you want to create a partnership with the managers. Help them see the results of the team, and engage them to help you help the team get past difficult times. Help them reconceive the value they provide by learning about agile engineering and testing practices, creating centers of technical excellence, coordinating releases, and so on, so that product development "flows." In an organization that's agile, the work of continuous improvement never ends.

> ## Working on the A-Team!
>
> Agile team structure can change the career path approach. One development organization had a team called the "A-Team." This team was responsible for critical customer support issues, spanning all areas of the system. At first, senior programmers would rotate in and out of this A-Team, so that everyone had a chance to lend his or her expertise. This team slowly evolved into a career path; new hires would "do their time" on the A-Team because it was an extremely good way to learn about all of the system. Senior team members would be on hand to help with problems. Once a newbie put in his three months, he would then be "promoted" to a new product development team. This approach increased overall system domain knowledge and provided a new career path within the development organization.

Our Situation Is Just Too Complicated for Agile

We hear this all the time: "Our situation is so special, so unique, so complex that we can't *possibly* change!" This is a mindset that is difficult to get past, and it is often only by demonstrating results that people can begin to think differently.

Help managers by referring to case studies of companies in similar situations. Remind them that change does not happen overnight. Ask what things they think they *could* change, or help them envision the desired state and what must change in order to get there, no matter how wild or wacky. Encourage them to create an impediment backlog and work through these issues in order of priority, in iterations. Echo discoveries of the teams, and get teams and managers in a room to help solve issues or change the current way of doing things. Offer to help.

We Need to Matrix Resources to Get Maximum Efficiency

The industrial and maximum efficiency mindsets of the 1920s and 1990s, respectively, insist that software can be created and managed by matrixing people across multiple endeavors so that nobody is ever idle. Although software *can* be created this way, it is not the most effective approach. What thousands of teams across the world are learning is that the multidisciplinary, dedicated team approach is the best possible scenario for focused work and innovation.

You can arm yourself with data here. Plenty of reports show the productivity hits when people are time-sliced across multiple initiatives—up to 40%![6] This statistic does not include the immense overhead of the management necessary to orchestrate the dependencies between matrixed staff. Moving to an environment of dedicated teams means a big leap in organizational structure to support this setup. Not everyone will see the benefits immediately, and experts will suddenly become constraints to building functionality every iteration. Investment must be made in cross-training and knowledge-sharing from senior to junior resources and across skill sets. The working environment must be safe for people to jump into another role when the team must meet its commitments. Management will need some convincing, however, that the learning and ramp-up hits to productivity in these early days will be worthwhile in the long run.

Our People Can't Be Trusted to Self-Organize

Agile won't solve this problem, but it will certainly highlight it on a daily basis. The problem is usually with management at this point, and not with the team. When there is no trust or respect from managers to workers, agile implementations will fail in that teams won't be self-managed. You will have to decide whether or not you want to stay and work to build a trusting environment, or flee.

How Can We Make Strategic Decisions without Gantt Charts?

Executives need timely and accurate information in order to make sound strategic decisions about the future of the business. They really don't care how product is created, as long as it meets the functional and quality needs of the customer, there is reliable delivery, and it is done in such a way as to meet legal and ethical obligations. But they do care about getting information about the effects of product development: the ROI, the market share, the customer satisfaction rates, and so on. When they log in to the project dashboard or look at their weekly reports and see burndown charts instead of schedule and cost performance indexes, it can be incredibly annoying and frustrating for the executive. They feel that they don't have the information they need to steer the business. Educating them about agile is critical so that they can make the transition to new ways of analyzing project data.

Let them know they'll still have access to all the information they've come to expect from projects, except that it will exist in a different format, most notably as working software. If you can get them to agree to support an agile pilot team, then the best way to do this is to have the teams create information radiators and then invite the executives to the team room and help them understand what's being built and how the progress of the team can be tracked. Ask what information they get the most value out of, which information is confusing, and work to improve the value and visibility of this information. Also, several tools on the market are specifically designed for agile project management, and these should be investigated as possible solutions to the reporting problem.

Another effective approach is to invite the executives to the pilot team's product review meetings. Often they are very impressed to see working code so early. This transparency helps create trust by the executives in that the process is working and that delivery is reliable and consistent. Build on this trust by interviewing executives to understand what information is useful for them to run the business, and work with the teams to help make this visible.

Over time, education and making results visible will greatly increase the level of trust with the executives, enabling them to make timely decisions about products relative to the organization's strategy.

Selling to Customers/Product Owners

Customers want value. They want results. They are paying for a product and want to be able to use it as they've envisioned. We've included a few statements that you'll hear from some customers when they find out the team is using an agile approach.

You Just Want Us to Contract with You on a Time and Expenses Basis So You Can Bill Us for Eternity

This is probably the number-one reason why customers will be reluctant to engage with the team in an agile fashion. In order to understand this, one must examine it from a contract perspective. It is important to understand the nature of contracts; they protect somebody from risk. Sometimes they are written as mutually binding agreements, but usually they favor one party over another. Fixed-time/fixed-scope contracts are written to place most of the risk on the vendor; a penalty is applied if the vendor does not deliver to the specified scope by the specified time.

This type of arrangement puts pressure on the customer to specify all of the scope up front, and calls for a change control meeting to allow for any change. The vendor doesn't want to change the scope because there are uncertainties of the related impacts in doing so. The customer wants the change, but has to fight for it, and the vendor retaliates, feeling as though the customer should have thought about it in the first place. It is usually an uncomfortable situation for both parties.

Changing contracts from fixed-scope/fixed-price to a pay-as-you-go time and expense means that customers are now more responsible for the success of the product. They directly control the cost of the contract because they authorize its existence on a recurring basis, every iteration. As Ron Jeffries so succinctly states in a posting on the XP Yahoo! discussion board on July 1, 2004:

> Right now, this appears to be a 200-point project. Based on our performance on other projects (or a random guess), with N programmers on it, and your intimate involvement in the project, a project of this size will take between four and six months. However, we will

be shipping software to you every two weeks, and we'll be ticking off these feature stories to your satisfaction. The good news is that if you're not satisfied, you can stop. The better news is that if you become satisfied before all the features are done, you can stop. The bad news is that you need to work with us to make it clear just what your satisfaction means. The best news is that whenever there are enough features working to make the program useful, you can ask us to prepare it for deployment, and we'll do that. As we go forward, we'll all see how fast we're progressing, and our estimate of the time needed will improve. In every case, you'll see what is going on, you'll see concrete evidence of useful software running the tests that you specify, and you'll know everything as soon as I know it.

With agile projects, the customer drives the priority of the requirements, so one benefit to your customer is that the priority can change at any given moment (except for the iteration at hand). No more uncomfortable change control meetings. We can trade a new requirement for an unstarted requirement of equal value.

Also, the customer has the ability to stop production at any time he feels that the product meets his needs, and he will see new functionality at the end of each iteration, which provides for a natural decision point. This does not mean that there is no overall plan going into the relationship—it would be very difficult for vendors to do their resource planning if they had no targeted end date! Release plans are defined at a high level and revisited throughout the engagement.

You may still run a fixed-time/fixed-scope project using agile, and you may still ask for prioritization of the requirements, even though they are fixed up front. You may still ask if the customer is interested in an early review of functionality (they usually are). For more information on ways to contract with your customer, refer to "Clearing the Hurdles in a Waterfall Enterprise" in Chapter 14, "How Will I Work With Other Teams Who Aren't Agile."

There's Not Enough Time to Work with the Team Every Iteration

We hear from product owners, especially, that they are too busy working with the end users to have the time necessary to dedicate to the delivery team. Granted, agile puts a new set of job requirements on the product owner; whereas before agile they didn't really have to interact with the team much, except for in the beginning when scope was being identified and solidified.

The collaborative nature of agile—that is, the product owner working with the team—can be a stressful situation for the product owner, merely from a time management perspective. Try to understand that the product owner is going through the agile change just like everyone else on the team, and try to partner with him or her in order to keep the backlog staged for the team's next iteration. Advise the product owner that scheduling "office hours" through the week, like college professors do, is a good short-term solution.

I Can't Wait an Entire Iteration for That Feature!

The idea of the iteration is deliberate in its attempt to control the anarchy associated with forever fluctuating requirements. This chaotic environment, one that does not allow the team to focus, often means that many things get started, but none are completed. The idea of the timebox—the iteration—was created as a way to control the chaos in a complex project, as well as a way to force the business to keep its work in a backlog, staged and ready to be worked on by the team. Using both of these concepts together allows the right product to be created iteration to iteration.

Product owners, customers, and other stakeholders can get antsy when forced to wait an entire iteration for work on the new requirement to begin. You may want to discuss with them the possibility of shortening the iteration length to better accommodate their needs. Usually, once the stakeholders see that delivery is reliable and consistent, this pressure subsides.

Selling to Other Departments in the Organization

When teams "get agile" (that is, they are responsive, creating working software reliably and consistently, and have established a "flow" of product creation), they inevitably start to affect other departments in the organization.

Although we cannot cover every scenario in this chapter, we urge you to work with the other departments to discover their needs and talk with the team to see how to best meet those needs. Additionally, the team may want to invite certain representatives from these organizations to a retrospective or working meeting in order to identify and work out the issues together.

The ultimate goal is to provide reliable delivery to customers and to respond accordingly to their needs. The other departments in the organization are part of that value stream—all of the steps required to bring a product or service from a raw state through to the customer—and it is important to work together to understand how to make that stream flow as efficiently as possible.

Other Ways to Sell Agile

Information must be communicated repeatedly in different forms before it takes hold and is ingrained in the minds of the message recipients. We often hear educators say that their mantra around education is "seven times, seven ways." Sometimes, even the most basic message—a product vision, for example—must be communicated repeatedly until the team and other stakeholders can really internalize it.

We wanted to outline some ideas for you to think about in communication of agile or the artifacts of the teams. Always err on the side of overcommunication. The alternative just isn't sufficient.

- **Socialize, don't evangelize.** Nobody likes to have change forced upon them. Sometimes it's better to simply share your ideas about agile processes without using the word "agile" and without demanding change. Just make some suggestions for ways things might be done in a more effective manner, using terminology others readily understand, and see what happens. One way to do this is to simply make some changes in your own team—when the team starts delivering product faster than expected, people will notice and will come to you to find out how you did it. That's the time to share.
- **Promote brown-bag sessions.** These lunch sessions are intended to gather anyone who may be interested in a particular topic. It is a wonderful way to promote education about agile (or any other topic) in a comfortable, informal session.

- **Entice colleagues to join you at local chapter meetings.** If you're lucky enough to live in a city with a local agile chapter (see www.agilealliance.org or www.apln.org) you'll find the chapter usually has monthly meetings and often provides free sodas and pizza.
- **Get an outside consultant to bring in the news.** Sometimes, hearing the message from an objective third party is more effective than hearing the message from within. An experienced coach can help the team identify areas of improvement and can communicate difficult messages to others in the organization.
- **Don't bother trying to sell anything.** As Jim Highsmith once said in response to a question asked of him at a conference, "Don't bother trying to sell agile to management. Just do it. They don't care what you're doing anyway." Management usually doesn't care, as long as you deliver working software when you say you will. So go stealth. Do as much as you can and see what happens.

Part of selling, persuading, and convincing is knowing enough about your audience to do this effectively. We recommend that you study team-building, team dynamics, motivation theory, Myers-Briggs, and so on, in order to prepare yourself for the situations you may encounter in building teams and working with the rest of the organization. After all, agile is about people, and the more you know about people, the better off you and the team will be. Sometimes it's as simple as listening and creating a safe environment for change, and not trying to sell anything at all.

Summary

The takeaways from this chapter include the following:

- "Selling" agile is usually best done by not selling per se, but instead by listening, offering alternative solutions, and by being (or providing) a great example of what agile teams can accomplish.
- When presenting agile to the team, the members will usually object to the number of meetings, having to do gross-level estimating, the perceived lack of architectural planning, and the issue of needing a co-located team. Although all of these issues can be addressed, don't

forget to look for the hidden objections—such as fear of change—that may be driving the resistance.

- Management resistance is frequently centered around the perceived loss of control and personal identity. Although objections such as the concern for lack of long-term planning, missing Gantt charts, and matrix organizational issues can all be addressed, other issues may be deal-breakers: insistence on the success of the current method, lack of trust, or refusal to change for personal/political reasons.
- Issues of resistance from the business or customer that can be addressed include a reluctance to contract on a T&M basis, a lack of time or willingness to spend it with the team, and a need to make changes at the drop of a hat rather than on an iterative basis.
- Other methods of selling agile include socialization, brown-bag sessions, attendance at local chapter meetings, outside consultation, and simply not bothering to sell at all (going agile in "stealth" mode).

Endnotes

1. From the "Principles Behind the Agile Manifesto," the full quote is "Simplicity—the art of maximizing the amount of work not done—is essential." In other words, by keeping things simple, you don't end up wasting time doing work that did not need to be done. You can read all of the principles here: http://www.agilemanifesto.org/principles.html.

2. Fuzzy logic is an approach to computing based on "degrees of truth" rather than the usual "true or false" (1 or 0) Boolean logic on which the modern computer is based.

3. Kent Beck et al. "Principles Behind the Agile Manifesto." http://www.agilemanifesto.org/principles.html.

4. Dean Leffingwell. *Scaling Software Agility*. (Boston: Addison-Wesley, 2007), 204.

5. The Standish Group International. *The Standish Group's CHAOS Report 2004.* (West Yarmouth, MA: The Standish Group, 2005).

6. Mike Cohn. "The Dark Side of Multi-Tasking." *Better Software*, July/August 2005, 10.

Chapter 17

Common Mistakes

If you don't make mistakes, you can't make decisions.
—*Warren Buffett*

The road to hell is paved with good intentions.
—*H. G. Bohn, Hand-Book of Proverbs 514*

One rarely ever sets out or intends to make a mistake. A mistake is made by misunderstanding a situation or perhaps by not understanding it completely. At other times, there simply is no knowledge platform from which to spring forward. Consequences of mistakes vary from a loaf of bread that doesn't rise, to world wars. People generally do the best work that their capabilities enable, yet sometimes these good efforts result in failure.

The title of this chapter is meant to catch your eye so that you give pause to the common mistakes we've seen in the field. Sometimes, mistakes are in the eye of the beholder, and we've attempted to remain as objective as possible. However you view it, try to remember the values of the Agile Manifesto, and remember that your translation of those values will most likely be different from that of your neighboring companies. Remember that variety in translation is the purpose behind agile, so that it doesn't become an out-of-the-box methodology. As you are reading about these pitfalls, it is most important to understand *why* these are considered pitfalls. If you find your organization suffering from one of these pitfalls, check out the tips strewn along in this chapter to help you rectify those situations.

The mistakes covered in this chapter have to do with documentation, implementation, the rest of the organization, championing, leadership, crunching/death marching, adhering to the schedule, self-organizing, participation of the business, retrospectives, and values.

Thinking That Agile Means "No Documentation" and "Cowboy Coding"

Education is critical in helping the organization understand what agile really means. It is a set of project management and engineering practices for developing software. This iterative and incremental approach adheres to the Agile Manifesto and follows the manifesto's guiding principles. Although we place a greater emphasis on working code over comprehensive documentation (the former the customer will buy, the latter the customer usually is not as interested in), this doesn't mean that documentation goes away. It is simply reassessed according to the value it provides.

As we have discussed throughout the book, it is worth reiterating how important it is to discuss the types of documents that the customer needs and wants to pay for, as well as the types of documents that add value to the product development process and support the product after it has been deployed (though the customer probably wouldn't pay for these documents even if the customer knew they existed). On the other hand, if your environment is one of heavy contracts and big analysis/design up front to substantiate those contracts, you may have a difficult time convincing your customers that a ton of documents is not what they really need.

You can easily facilitate this conversation. First, set up a time and space to have the conversation with the product team (and customer if appropriate). Then, divide the types of documents into three categories: documentation deliverables (such as help manuals, release notes, and so on), internal project documents (project plans, PERT charts), and internal product documents (technical specs, product requirements documents, and so on). We suspect that customers would be disappointed to not receive help manuals, for example, so we leave that category intact. In each of the "internal" categories, prioritize the list of documents by the value they bring the customer; if the customers are part of this conversation, they can help by telling the team what's valuable to them. Then, for each high value document, ask what is the criticality of each of these documents to the team during the product creation process. Do these documents clarify or corrupt knowledge? Or, do we write and maintain these documents because we've always done so? Can we write a little detailed documentation at the end of each iteration in order to document our decisions instead of writing everything up front? Leading a conversation this way will help you whittle away at the most important pieces of documentation to write and maintain. Additionally, it will provide the team a new perspective on streamlining work so that only valuable documents are written.

Furthermore, agile is not an invitation for the team members to code whatever they find interesting, or fun, for as long as they'd like to work on it. There is a strict discipline to the iterations and iteration commitments, and the business or the customer decides which increments of the product will be created by the team each iteration. Remember that product backlog items are of insufficient detail. They should be discussed by the team and the customer before every iteration in order to determine the assumptions, acceptance criteria, and decisions moving forward. This is the built-in scope "control" mechanism in agile. Also, it is important to remind the team members that they should never compromise internal quality for the sake of completing a product backlog item. Code should not be hacked; rather, it should be clean, simple, adhere to coding standards, and it should work.

Regardless of your chosen process, it is a waste to write documents that don't add value, as well as a waste of time to fix deliberate hacks and/or maintain code that a customer does not want. Agile, by connecting silos of people, forces us to fix these issues that are otherwise symptomatic and often tolerated in an industrial process where groups of people do not talk to each other. If you're doing agile, you'll have these conversations with your team and customer in the spirit of eliminating waste from your processes; otherwise, these issues will force themselves to front and center as obstacles to creating quality software each iteration. For both documentation and coding, the final arbiter is the value each brings to the customer.

Thinking That You Can Piecemeal Agile Practices and Gain All the Benefits

You can implement individual practices here and there, but they will not give you the same return as if you implemented all the pieces that make agile what it is. All of the pieces and parts of agile work together to make one big working system. For example, your team can remain a waterfall team, and only implement the practice of a daily stand-up meeting, and certainly derive the benefits of improved communication—or so you think. But now this team feels micro-managed even more than it did before this daily meeting. And because the real meaning behind the daily stand-up meeting (empowered team members inspecting and adapting their work on a daily basis) is lost, the meeting starts to drag on past 15 minutes. Now you have a daily project status meeting and everyone on the team is complaining about too many meetings again. Additionally, only implementing the daily stand-up without working in iterations, the team won't be able to quickly move its work into production. Without working closely with the product owner, the team won't be able to make adjustments based on the feedback. Without a regular retrospection, the team won't be able to analyze how well the current process is working and make changes to improve. Without a prioritized backlog of work, the team may find itself working on the wrong things. Without a new set of engineering practices to help shorten the feedback cycle from idea to inspection, the team will flounder and find it very difficult to complete work in small timeboxes.

Put the agile framework in place and follow it—all of it—in order to be able to realize the multiple benefits that together increase productivity.

Expecting a process—any process—to solve all your business and technical problems is unrealistic. Even if you put all of the pieces of the agile framework in place, agile is not magic. What agile does is provide a way to develop an innovative product quickly, using feedback, inspection, reflection, and refinement in order to deliver in an iterative and incremental fashion. And in this process, the roadblocks to delivery become highly visible, enabling the team and the organization to remove them. But it does not magically make the roadblocks disappear. It requires hard work and discipline from everyone involved.

Thinking That Agile Stops at the Engineering Teams and Won't Affect the Rest of the Organization

Although agile often starts as a grassroots effort, it eventually starts poking at the organizational walls around it. The ways that the company determines project capitalization, how it plans and forecasts, how it manages its portfolios, how it is organized and manages resources, what the career paths are and how individuals and teams are recognized and rewarded—all of these things begin to change when agile teams become mature. Companies eventually all reach a tipping point: Either they make the organizational changes necessary to move forward in support of their agile teams, or they choose not to and begin to lose their agile team members, sliding back into the waterfall.

If you find your grassroots agile engineering team bumping its head on the glass ceiling of the organizational greenhouse, it's time to get those other departments involved. One team we worked with put Support representatives on each team so that their involvement could help catch early misassumptions about the product; previously, Support was always a bottleneck to releasing the product. If your team doesn't have a tester or QA representative, try to get a promise for just one headcount to start. Nurture this team and its relationships as it finds new ways of working, and then scale the learning to other teams and the rest of the organization. Remember, agile is organizational change, and connecting silos of people to support the product for the customer is a huge shift from the traditional suboptimization approach of just measuring the silos.

Not Having a Champion

Without a real champion who fully supports the agile efforts of the teams, political and financial pressures can derail even the most earnest agile endeavor. Someone needs to be the voice of change for the organization and unite both the business interests and the engineering interests in a joint effort at improving their ability to deliver. Because there is always a slowdown with any first foray into something new due to the learning curve, the champion has to protect the teams as they begin this process of learning and incremental improvement. And because the team will need tools to aid its collaborative efforts, the champion needs to be ready with the checkbook. Note, however, that many open-source collaborative tools are now readily available, and the hit to the budget can be minimized. Because organizational evolution will also need to be addressed, the champion has to prepare executive and mid-level managers for these coming changes—not just changes in process and approach but changes to the fundamental value system and culture of the organization.

If you can't find a champion at the highest level, then start with mid-level managers in engineering. Although an engineering champion can jumpstart the initiative, you'll find that by producing working software every iteration, the team will soon have a business champion as well, helping to promote agile throughout the rest of the organization. Having this champion can help the engineering teams break through the greenhouse ceiling to streamline deliverables of product each iteration.

Having the Wrong People Lead the Effort and/or the Teams

Because agile is a collaborative approach to problem solving that relies on the power of self-managing teams, motivation is derailed when a command-and-control manager sucks all the creativity out of a room with his dictatorial style. Fearful leaders who are more interested in numbers rather than results can completely squash an agile effort. Managers who do not understand their new agile role as a servant-leader will turn the team into their own fiefdom, with serfs who merely do as they're told. Then when the effort fails, agile is blamed. Although this can be an honest mistake due to the misunderstanding on the part of the agile leader, we are sorry to say that we have also seen this done intentionally as a form of sabotage. When an individual values his own personal comfort more than his ethical obligation to deliver value to customers, then the *implementation* of agile will indeed fail. Agile is all about individuals and interactions; management must support empowered, self-managed teams.

Hanging On to the Death March as a Solution

Organizations that frequently push a team to "crunch mode" or a death march as the project nears its deadline will also try this same push-hard approach in every single iteration—because now the deadlines are more frequent, and the sense of urgency is no longer limited to the last few months of the project. This is a fine way to burn a team to a cinder, increase the instability of the product, delay the release, and lose your finest engineering staff. We recommend working at a sustainable pace in every iteration in order to avoid this.

Managers can help a team create a sustainable pace by listening to the types of issues the team encounters, asking the team to make its progress visible throughout the iteration, and helping facilitate effective retrospectives so that the root causes of frantic pace are identified and eradicated for the next iteration. Remember, it takes a few iterations to get it right; be patient with the team.

Allowing the Team to Say, "You'll Get It when You Get It. We're Agile Now and Only Plan One Iteration at a Time."

Again, this is a misconception that proper education can allay. The business needs to be able to plan for the future, and the teams need to recognize this fact and respect it. Teams should conduct release/quarterly planning, guided by the vision and product roadmap created by the business. The business must understand that time estimates—guesses that turn into commitments—are not the best way to plan at a strategic level because they take too much time up front and degrade over time. Help the business or the customer understand gross-level complexity estimates for high-level planning, and help the team utilize hours and burndown charts for tactical-level planning during the iteration.

ALLOWING THE TEAM TO SAY, "YOU'LL GET IT WHEN YOU GET IT.
WE'RE AGILE NOW AND ONLY PLAN ONE ITERATION AT A TIME."

• 291 •

Allowing the Agile Team Leader to Say, "You're Self-Organizing—You Figure It Out."

Frustrated or fearful agile leaders often want to wash their hands of the team during conflict, and flinging this phrase at the group does nothing to help the team members. Your job as an agile leader is to guide these individuals in learning how to achieve consensus by working through conflict. Although no doubt the team members will figure it out on their own, it is better for everyone if you make the process one that the team feels comfortable with. Make sure the environment is safe, allow differing opinions to be expressed, allow time for analysis and insights, and after considering the alternatives and hearing arguments for and against each, facilitate the convergence on a decision made collaboratively by the team.

Lack of Participation by the Business

Because agile values customer collaboration over contract negotiation, the lack of participation by a business representative will prevent the team from realizing its full potential regarding its ability to deliver what the customer wants and needs. When introducing agile concepts and practices to the team, be sure that the product owner is part of that team and is educated alongside the team members. Waiting until after the engineering team has been trained leaves an "us vs. them" attitude in place. Working in an agile team is a joint effort between team members and the customer, and therefore it should start out that way.

Continued lack of participation by the business may mean that although a team is able to perfect the technical skills of a high-performing team, you will never know if what the team is working on is the right thing to be working on. This situation presents a significant business risk that you can escalate.

Not Bothering with the Retrospective

Inspecting and adapting every iteration is key to the continued success of the agile team. When this reflection stops happening, teams can stagnate or, even worse, begin to go back to older more comfortable habits. This ceremony reminds the team that it has the power and the responsibility to self-organize and gives the team the time and setting in which to do so.

A Values Mismatch

When an agile team focuses on delivering value to the customer and adhering to a set of values in working together in order to make that delivery, attitudes and culture can change. This is where the agile teams begin poking at the rest of the organization, inviting them to change, too. If the rest of the organization is rewarded based on metrics that are not aligned with customer satisfaction, then their definition of value will not be the same as those participating in the agile process. A culture that does not support learning and innovation will not be able to support agile in the long term. A values mismatch requires one side or the other to change. Which will it be in your organization?

Although the instances of agile implementations vary greatly from organization to organization, the basic values hold true: Deliver quality product early and often to customers by working with them to understand their needs, and eliminate the waste in doing so. Changing from a traditional to an agile organization means that certain traditions must be challenged. As an agile project manager who is tasked to remove obstacles, you will win some battles, take lots of time to win others, and lose some. Resting on your laurels is the only true mistake.

Summary

The takeaways from this chapter include the following:

- Agile development does not mean that teams hack code or cease writing any documentation at all. For both documentation and coding, the final arbiter is the value each brings to the customer or the necessity for the organization.
- The framework in agile is tightly coupled; dropping one or many pieces means that the selected pieces will fail or become meaningless.
- The grassroots engineering team will eventually run into obstacles as it tries to work with other parts of the organization; a champion can support the agile team to find new ways of working with other departments in support of the product and in support of the customer.
- Managers who cannot adopt a true leadership style will hinder their teams' ability to become empowered and self-managing. A team that always looks to its manager for direction will suffer the inefficiencies of a command-and-control management style.
- Teams and managers will revert to death marches when pressured; habits run deep. Keep an eye out for this, and use strategic planning techniques to anticipate key project milestones so that the pace remains sustainable.
- Employ the retrospective as a way to identify and improve any failure points.
- Traditions must be challenged—doing nothing is a mistake.

of three phases: pre-project, project lifecycle, and post-project phase. The project lifecycle phase is broken down into five parts: feasibility, foundations, exploration, engineering, and deployment. A bit more prescriptive than some other agile frameworks in defining project artifacts and specific roles and responsibilities, DSDM remains responsive to changing requirements. Its nine principles are closely aligned with those in the Agile Manifesto. DSDM V4.2 now advocates the use of XP in conjunction with its process.

Available only to DSDM Consortium members until 2007, its V5 release, Atern, is now available to the public.

Download free publications at www.dsdm.org.

Crystal Methods

Crystal methods are a collection of agile methods that can be tailored based on project complexity and team size. The focus is on people rather than process, and the priorities of all the crystal methods are safety (with respect to project outcome, efficiency, and habitability), frequent delivery, reflective improvement, and close communication.[2] Like individual facets on a crystal, the dimensions of projects—technique, roles, tools, and standards—sit atop a core of principles and values. A color scheme helps teams to determine the minimum set of standards to employ: Maroon is for very heavy projects in terms of the number of people involved, the criticality, and the project-level priorities. Then in descending order there is Red, Orange, Yellow, and finally Clear, for the lightest approach. The intent is to be "barely sufficient" in the amount of process imposed on the team. Crystal enables teams to use the color grid to define the basic process or starting point and customize the process as they go. If a process helps people work together, then the team should keep it—and if it isn't helping, they should discard it.

Crystal Clear, by Alistair Cockburn

Lean Software Development

Lean Software Development was adapted from Lean Manufacturing, the Toyota Production System, and Bob Charette's Lean Development. It focuses on seven principles: eliminating waste, amplifying learning, deciding as late as possible, delivering as fast as possible, empowering the team, building integrity in, and seeing the whole. A set of tools—set-based design, value stream mapping, and queuing theory are some examples—are provided to help teams adhere to the principles and achieve their goals.

Lean is a management approach for streamlining the process of providing value to the customer. It goes beyond the tactical software development team, yet complements its existing practices. Lean principles and tools are well-suited for strategic execution at the enterprise level.

The Machine That Changed the World, by James P. Womack et al

Lean Software Development: An Agile Toolkit, by Mary and Tom Poppendieck

Implementing Lean Software Development: From Concept to Cash, by Mary and Tom Poppendieck

Feature-Driven Development

Feature-Driven Development, or FDD, is a marriage between Jeff De Luca's lightweight development approach and Peter Coad's feature-oriented object modeling. FDD's focus is the domain model, the creation of which is the foundational step in the FDD process. The five activities to be followed in FDD are: develop an overall model, build a list of features, plan by feature, design by feature, and build by feature. Sets of features are worked through to completion in two-week iterations. The features to be built are small aspects of client-valued functionality that can be expressed in the form <action> <result> <object>. For example, "Calculate the total in the shopping cart" and "Show the list of hotels to the user" would both be good examples of features. Like in DSDM, there are multiple specific roles and responsibilities in a project, all clearly defined.

Unlike XP, FDD prefers individual code ownership and seeks to avoid refactoring by focusing on domain modeling. FDD is also scalable and works with multiple teams or large teams.

A Practical Guide to Feature-Driven Development, by Stephen R. Palmer and John M. Felsing

Adaptive Systems Management

Developed by Jim Highsmith and Sam Bayer, Adaptive Software Development (ASD) is adapted from Rapid Application Development (RAD) practices and Complex Adaptive Systems theory. The focus of ASD is continuous adaptation to change as a result of learning. The typical static plan-design-build lifecycle is replaced by ASD's dynamic Speculate-Collaborate-Learn approach, which is intentionally "messy, nonlinear, and overlapping."[3] ASD is mission focused, feature based, iterative, timeboxed, risk driven, and change tolerant.

Adaptive Software Development: A Collaborative Approach to Managing Complex Systems, by James A. Highsmith III

Agile Unified Process

This is a simpler and more agile adaptation of the artifact-heavy Rational Unified Process. It is summarized by Scott Ambler as being "serial in the large, iterative in the small, and delivering incremental releases over time."[4] There are four major phases divided into one or more iterations: inception, elaboration, construction, and transition. Techniques such as test-driven development and agile model-driven development are part of the AUP process. AUP is risk driven, and contains many optional artifacts that teams may or may not choose to use.

http://www.ambysoft.com/unifiedprocess/agileUP.html

Endnotes

1. Ken Schwaber. "What is Scrum?" www.controlchaos.com.
2. Martin Fowler. "The New Methodology." http://www.martinfowler.com/articles/newMethodology.html#ShouldYouGoAgile.

3. Jim Highsmith. "Messy, Exciting, and Anxiety-Ridden: Adaptive Software Development." *American Programmer*, Volume X, No. 1; January 1997, http://www.adaptivesd.com/articles/messy.htm.

4. Scott Amber. "The Agile Unified Process." Ambysoft, http://www.ambysoft.com/unifiedprocess/agileUP.html#Overview.

Agile Artifacts

This appendix will guide you through a simple agile project, providing you with sample project artifacts along the way. Keep in mind that it is impossible to provide you with a prescription to follow, because the documents you may need in your own project scenarios will vary greatly from organization to organization and are often based on personal preference. We felt it important to include this appendix to give you some ideas about what you should track, what the teams should track, as well as what to consider communicating to stakeholders.

Project Initiation

All projects go through an initiation phase, whether it's a simple meeting to discuss the high-level needs, or a more formal phase with approvers, analysis and design, and details before the proverbial check is signed. In many cases, receipt of funding means having a signed contract from the client in hand.

The traditional input to the initiation process is the PRD (product requirements document); some also refer to this as the MRD (marketing requirements document). If you are in a contract world, this is known as the proposal. We like to refer to this lightweight summary as the product overview document, which is similar to a project charter, also common in agile projects. (If you'd like more information on developing agile project charters, refer to Jim Highsmith's *Agile Project Management* book.) The product overview document is a starting point for the customer that outlines a high-level description of the product, followed by bullet points that describe the capabilities or features to be delivered in the product. As the team begins to learn more about the product to be built, the team will augment the product overview document with information about the architecture, technical trade-offs, and so on (again, at high level). You can think of this product overview document like an abstract you would read about a book—it tells all the pertinent information in a summary form. Subsequent project details can be gleaned from the product roadmap and product backlog.

In a traditional project setting, the team responds to a PRD by creating functional and technical specifications. In agile projects, documents like these may exist, but we tend to see them as an *output* to the iteration, and only when deemed necessary by the team or the business. Again, this is an important conversation in which you will need to engage both your customer and team in order to find the right amount of documentation at the right time for the project's specific needs.

Figure B-1 illustrates the different artifacts in the traditional and agile processes. Usually, both the PRD/MRD and the functional and technical specifications must be fleshed out for a budget to be allocated in a traditional project setting. In agile, because teams work from a prioritized list of features, the initiation of a project can happen earlier in the project lifecycle; as long as the team has enough to get started for the first iteration, the product owner or customer can continue elaborating features for future iterations in parallel.

Figure B-1
Artifacts in traditional and agile processes

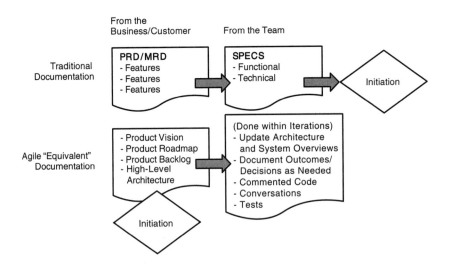

One team we worked with wanted to make notes of the decisions it made during the iteration and track these in a project wiki; this was efficient because any team member had the ability to update the project information on a real-time basis. The team was willing to maintain the documentation in this form, and it met the business needs.

Product Overview Document

Following is a sample product overview document, something you might see hanging on the team room wall or living in a project wiki. This document is the responsibility of the customer or product owner and contains high-level information such as product vision, product roadmap, and product backlog.

Product Overview Document: AgilePM Space

Product Name: AgilePM Space

Product Vision Statement: For agile project managers who want to collaborate with each other, AgilePM Space is a website that provides a place to build community; unlike other sites such as YouTube and MySpace, AgilePM Space is specifically for agile project managers and allows for any type of media to be exchanged.

Dedicated Team: The Click Team: Bob Bradshaw, Amy Allegheny, Mary Mason, Stacey Ralph, Tom Thompson, and George Jefferson. Billy Edwards is on loan for DBA work.

Project Manager: Stacia Broderick

Customer/Product Owner: Michele Sliger

System Overview: This is a brand-new product. Even though several products on the market currently provide some of this functionality, we are leveraging the acquisition from last year to build this from the ground up. Eventually, this Space idea will grow to accommodate other specific professions, but that is out of scope for this project.

Architecture: To be determined by team.

Features Backlog:

- Registration
- Profile
- Create page
- Photos
- Ads
- Video
- Video Player
- Chat
- Search
- Project Simulator
- Job Board

Product Roadmap:
Four quarterly releases for this year, as follows:

1st Quarter Theme: Establish a Presence	2nd Quarter Theme: Enhance Media Capabilities	3rd Quarter Theme: Bells and Whistles	4th Quarter Theme: TBD
• Registration • Simple Profile • Create Page • Upload Photos • Ads	• Upload Video • Video Player • Simple Chat • Search	• Project Simulator • Expanded Chat • Advanced Search • Jobs	• TBD by Market

Risks/Rewards: Significant risk if our competitor beats us.

Success Criteria: High quality, fast TTM (time to market). Time to market is critical, but we want to build a product that's extendable to other industries in the future. Keep this in mind.

Flexibility Matrix:

	Most Flexible	Moderately Flexible	Least Flexible
Time			X
Resources		X	
Project Objectives			X

We have the ability to add a team should we need to. Let's see how the first release goes before we increase funding.

The Release Planning Meeting

Once the product overview document has been created by the customer, the delivery team should meet with the customer to understand, decompose, and estimate the features. Additionally, a release plan should be created by the team at this time. If your contracting situation is such that your customer requires a release plan before the contract is signed, you perhaps will be doing this much earlier in the cycle.

Creating a release plan relies on a well-facilitated release planning meeting. The customer or product owner, delivery team members, and the agile project manager must be there; sometimes other stakeholders or interested parties will show up to observe. Here is an agenda that we frequently use when facilitating these meetings:

- Introductions, ground rules, review of purpose, and agenda (Project manager)
- Do we need to review our current situation and/or existing product roadmap? (Project manager, architect, customer/product owner)
- Do we remember the product vision? Has it changed? (Customer/ product owner)
- What is the release date? How many iterations make up this release? (Project manager)
- What is the theme for this release? (Customer/product owner)
- What are the features we need for this release? (Customer/product owner)
- What assumptions are we making? What constraints are we dealing with? (Team)
- What are the milestones/deliverables expected? Do we have any LRM (Last Responsible Moment) decision points? (Team)
- What is the capacity of the team (iteration velocity)? (Team)
- Can we move the features into the iterations? Do we need to break them into smaller features so that they can be completed in a single iteration? (Team)
- What issues/concerns do we have? (Team)
- Can we commit to this release as a team, given what we know today? (Team)
- Close: empty parking lot, action items, next steps (Project manager)

While the team and the product owner/customer are discussing the features, the agile project manager should be facilitating and writing down assumptions, concerns/risks, dependencies, decisions, and actions as they come up in conversation. The walls of the meeting room should be prepared with flip charts on which to record each of these items of discussion. This keeps the ideas fresh in all of the participants' minds, as well as makes transcribing easier after the meeting.

The Release Plan

Creating the release plan is similar to creating a project schedule, except that specific tasks, owners, and hourly estimates are not identified at this point in time. The release plan is a high-level overview of the upcoming iterations, along with which features will fit into those iterations; most importantly, the release plan is created out of a conversation between the customer/product owner and the team. First, we have an example of an informal release plan done by a co-located team using flipcharts and sticky notes; we then show what this might look like if placed into a more formal document.

The flipcharts for the informal release plan from the release planning meeting would look like that shown in Figure B-2.

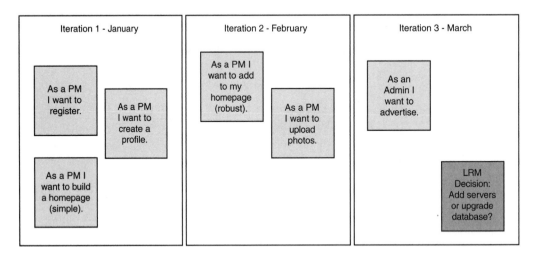

Figure B-2
The informal release plan

AGILE ARTIFACTS

The formal document used to communicate the release plan (created by project manager for stakeholders) follows:

1st Quarter Release Plan: AgilePM Space

Release Date: March 31, 2009

Today's Date: December 20, 2008

Here is the original information from the product roadmap:

1st Quarter
• Registration • Simple Profile • Create Page • Upload Photos • Ads

Theme: Establish a Presence

Iteration 1: January 1–January 31

Iteration 2: February 1–February 28

Iteration 3: March 1–March 31

Project Wiki: http://www.clickprojectwiki.com/index

Team Room: Safari conference room

	Size	Planned Iteration
The team and the customer have created the following user stories out of the high-level features listed in the product overview document. The team estimated the user stories and Michele ranked them in priority order. Additionally, based on an estimated velocity of 10 points per iteration, the team placed the user stories into iterations (see right-hand column called "Planned Iteration").		
1. As a project manager, I want to register for AgilePM Space because I want to access the features of the website.	5	1
2. As a project manager, I want to create a simple profile so that others may be able to search for me in the future and build communities.	3	1

3. As a project manager, I want to create my own homepage so that I can list the projects I am working on, the technologies I am interested in, and success with using agile approaches.	8	1, 2
4. As a project manager, I would like to upload photos so that I can share ideas about task boards, teambuilding, burndown charts, etc.	3	2
5. As a website administrator, I would like to allow for advertisements from other companies so that our company can generate more revenue.	5	3

Estimated Release Burndown:

As of today, the team has estimated a total of 24 points for all of the features requested in Release 1. Based on an estimated velocity of 10, the team feels it can complete the features within three iterations' time.

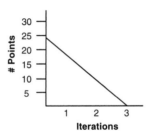

Assumptions: Ralph won't be taking family leave until Iteration 4.

Concerns/risks:

Decisions: We're going to use Java and adhere to Bob's "Shared Codebase Rules."

Dependencies: LRM decision on adding servers or maybe changing the database—will affect how we handle video in the next release.

Actions:

The Iteration Planning Meeting

Once the team has planned the release, the team should start its first iteration. The team should meet on the first day of the iteration in order to plan the iteration. Here is an agenda that we use in facilitating iteration planning meetings for teams:

- Introductions, ground rules, review of purpose and agenda (Project manager)
- Do we know our iteration start and end dates? (Project manager)
- Do we know the team's velocity? (Team)
- Do we know what "done" means? (Team)
- What are the features we need for this iteration? What are the acceptance criteria for each feature? (Customer/product owner)
- Do we have enough information about the features so that we can task them out? (Team)
- Can we estimate those tasks? (Team)
- What assumptions are we making? What constraints are we dealing with? Are there dependencies that affect our prioritization? (Team)
- Are we within our velocity limits? (Team)
- What issues/concerns do we have? (Team)
- Can we commit to this iteration as a team, given what we know today? (Team)
- Close: empty parking lot, action items, next steps (Project manager)

Just as in the release planning meeting, while the team and the product owner/customer are discussing the features, the agile project manager should be facilitating and writing down assumptions, concerns/risks, dependencies, decisions, and actions as they come up in conversation. The walls of the meeting room should be prepared with flip charts on which to record each of these items of discussion. This will keep the ideas fresh in all of the participants' minds, as well as make transcribing easier after the meeting.

The Iteration Plan

The outcome of the iteration planning meeting is called the "iteration backlog," which is composed of the team's iteration goals and list of tasks that must be completed for the iteration. So next let's look at a sample iteration backlog based on the team's iteration planning meeting, one done on flipcharts and the other as a compilation.

The informal iteration backlog from iteration planning done as flipcharts would look like what is shown in Figure B-3.

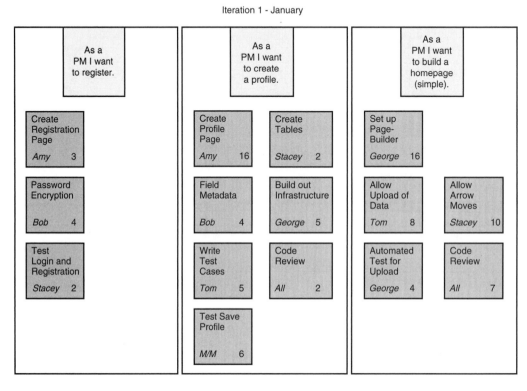

Iteration 1 - January

Figure B-3
The informal iteration backlog

The formal capture of the iteration backlog in a spreadsheet would look like this:

Iteration 1 Click Team		
Goals: Enable an agile PM to log in, create a profile, and upload project data to a homepage.		
1. As a project manager, I want to register for AgilePM Space because I want to access the features of the website.	**Owner**	**Hours**
Task: Create registration page.	Amy	3
Task: Encryption for passwords.	Bob	4
Task: Test registration and login.	Stacey	2
2. As a project manager, I want to create a simple profile so that others may be able to search for me in the future and build communities.		
Task: Create profile page.	Amy	16
Task: Create metadata for fields on profile page (for future search).	Bob	4
Task: Create tables in database.	Stacey	2
Task: Infrastructure work.	George	5
Task: Write test cases.	Tom	5
Task: Code review.	All	2
Task: Test "save profile."	Mary, Michele	6
3. As a project manager, I want to create my own homepage so that I can list the projects I am working on (technologies and agile success stories deferred to iteration 2).	Split; this story is now 2 points	
Task: Enable PM to create homepage using PageBuilder technology.	George	16
Task: Enable PM to list projects via simple upload of static data.	Tom	8
Task: Enable PM to rearrange project list by arrows.	Stacey	10
Task: Code review.	All	7
Task: Create automated test for uploading static data.	George	4

Figure B-4
Iteration backlog in spreadsheet form

You will notice very detailed tasks in this iteration backlog. Traditionally, this is the level of task breakdown detailed in the Work Breakdown Structure of a waterfall project plan. In agile, we still break down tasks to this level, but only at the time of the iteration in which the tasks will occur. And the other big difference is that instead of the project manager of a number of leads breaking down the tasks, the team does this work itself, in addition to estimating and assigning owners.

Just as with release planning, iteration planning needs an agenda to help the team and the customer stick to the goals of the meeting. Remember, this meeting can take up to eight hours for a 30-day iteration (four hours for a two-week iteration).

Working in the Iteration

As the team is working on its features during the iteration, it will produce artifacts such as the updated iteration backlog and an iteration burndown chart.

Iteration Backlog

Here is the Click Team's iteration backlog as of the fifth day of the iteration. You can see that the original hourly estimates are recorded under the column labeled "1." This represents the first day of the iteration, or "Day 1." You will then notice that each team member updated his or her own task on a daily basis to recalculate the number of hours remaining on each task. These numbers are recorded under the column headings "2, 3, 4, 5," or "Day 2, Day 3, Day 4, Day 5." For illustration purposes, we've only gone five days into a 30-day iteration; in the real project, your team's iteration backlog would go up to Day 30 (or so, depending on the month or the structure of your iterations).

Iteration 1 Click Team						

Goals: Allow an agile PM to log in, create a profile, an upload project data to a homepage.

1. As a project manager, I want to register for AgilePM Space because I want to access the features of the website.	**Task Owner**	**Day 1**	**Day 2**	**Day 3**	**Day 4**	**Day 5**
Task: Create registration page.	Amy	3	0	0	0	0
Task: Encryption for passwords.	Bob	4	4	2	0	0
Task: Test registration and login.	Stacey	2	2	2	2	0
Task: Write test cases for registration and login.	Mary		4	4	5	0
2. As a project manager, I want to create a simple profile so that others may be able to search for me in the future and build communities.						
Task: Create profile page.	Amy	16	16	20	10	8
Task: Create metadata for fields on profile page (for future search).	Bob	4	4	4	0	0
Task: Create tables in database.	Bill	2	2	0	0	0
Task: Infrastructure work.	George	5	5	3	2	0
Task: Write test cases.	Tom	5	5	3	0	0
Task: Code review.	All	2	2	2	2	2
Task: Test "save profile."	Mary, Michele	6	6	6	4	4
3. As a project manager, I want to create my own homepage so that I can list the projects I am working on (technologies and agile success stories deferred to iteration 2).						
Task: Allow PM to create homepage using PageBuilder.	George	16	14	10	10	5
Task: Allow PM to list projects via simple upload of static data.	Tom	8	8	5	3	2
Task: Code review.	G, T	7	5	5	4	4
Task: Create automated test for uploading static data.	George	4	4	0	0	0
Task: Write test for create homepage.	Mary			1	4	4
Total hours:		84	81	67	46	29

Figure B-5
Updated iteration backlog

highlighted for you some of the common updates you'll see in a team's iteration backlog. First, notice for both the first and third features, a new task was added for each (these tasks are underlined). The team member who found the new task simply went into the iteration backlog and added it to the list. Second, notice that Amy's estimate for creating the profile page increased from 16 hours to 20 hours on Day 3. This means that she found more work than was originally planned for in iteration planning. Additionally, take a look at the third feature and notice that a task was removed by a team member; this task was deemed unnecessary by the product owner. The team member didn't have to ask for permission to make these changes in the tracking tool. Adding, removing, and updating tasks are the responsibilities of each agile team member. Finally, notice that the third feature was split into two: "technologies and agile success stories" was deferred and put back on the product backlog.

Iteration Burndown Chart

Although the day-to-day task list is not all that interesting, except to the team, the project manager and other stakeholders are very interested in the iteration burndown chart. This chart reflects the total number of remaining hours each day for the team as a whole and provides a quick, easy-to-read visual about the health of the iteration. In the chart in Figure B-6, we have plotted the remaining hours for each day. You can see that the line does indeed "burn down." By comparing this to the trend line (the dashed line), you can see that the team has clearly undercommitted to the iteration. If you ever notice that the actual burndown line is greater or less than the trend line, the team should meet with the customer or product owner in order to find out which features to add to or drop from the iteration. Also, notice that there are only 21 days in our 30-day sprint. Why? Because this team is only tracking remaining estimates for workdays. Non-workdays such as weekends and holidays (New Year's Day and President's Day, for example) were subtracted from the overall 31 days available in January.

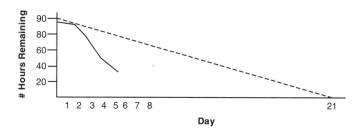

Figure B-6
The burndown chart

In addition to the iteration backlog and burndown chart, many teams also maintain what is known as a "burnup chart." This burnup chart reflects how many points have been earned throughout the iteration. For example, if our team had finished the first feature on Day 6, it would get to burn up the points for it. The estimate for that feature was five points, so the burnup chart would reflect five points as of Day 6. The team would hope to burn up a total of ten points, signifying that all features had been completed by the team in the iteration.

As you can see in the burnup chart shown in Figure B-7, the team is making faster progress than anticipated in the first six days of the iteration. These charts help us see trends or indicators of performance.

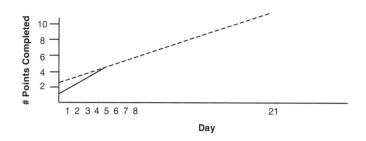

Figure B-7
The burnup chart

The End of the Iteration

There are a few "closure" tasks that the project manager must make sure the team is taking care of at the end of each iteration.

First and foremost, did the team gain acceptance by the product owner of the work it completed in the iteration? If so, the team takes credit for the total number of points for those features that were accepted by the product owner;

this is known as "velocity." Many project managers will keep a velocity log to help the team choose work for future iterations. The average velocity (the average of the last three iterations) can be tracked as well, to be used to estimate the team's iteration capacity for long-term planning purposes.

Velocity Log—Click Team	Estimated	Actual	Average Velocity	Comments
Iteration 1	10	8		Didn't finish upload for homepage.
Iteration 2	7	10		
Iteration 3	12	14	11	
Iteration 4	15	15	13	
Iteration 5	14	10	13	Spring break affected velocity.

Another question to ask is whether there are any carryover tasks. For example, the Click Team didn't finish its third feature, so the unfinished tasks had to be carried over to the Iteration 2 backlog after a discussion with the product owner reflected that these tasks were still very high priority.

Additionally, the *release* burndown chart, in addition to the iteration burndown chart, should be updated and posted on the wall of the team room and/or communicated via wiki or email. Because the team completed eight points instead of ten in the first iteration, the release burndown is updated to reflect this information. As you can see in the updated release burndown chart in Figure B-8, the team had estimated 30 points of work for all three iterations, meaning that it would need to complete ten points of work in each iteration. Because the team completed only eight points in the first iteration, the team and product owner can make the assumption that the team can complete 24 points of work for the release (three iterations of work). Because the original total of the product backlog was only 24 points, there is not a significant risk that a negotiation of scope must occur at this point. As an example, if the team had only completed five points of work in the first iteration, then that would mean, based on a velocity of five, the team would probably only be able to finish 15 points of work in the release, resulting in a discussion and negotiation of the scope of the release early on.

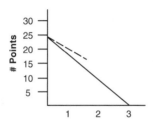

Figure B-8
Updated release burn-
down chart

The product backlog must be updated by the product owner to reflect any changes made as a result of the iteration's work. Here is our original product backlog with points estimates and changes as a result of the Click Team's first iteration. As you can see, user story number three was split into two user stories after the team planned the first iteration; you will also notice the addition of the "Completed Iteration" column, which can be used to designate the iteration in which the user story was actually completed. This is another way of translating the release plan.

User story	Size	Planned Iteration	Completed Iteration
1. As a project manager, I want to register for AgilePM Space because I want to access the features of the website.	5	1	1
2. As a project manager, I want to create a simple profile so that others may be able to search for me in the future and build communities.	3	1	1
3. As a project manager, I want to create my own homepage so that I can list the projects.	2	1	
4. As a project manager, I want to list technologies I am interested in and success with using agile approaches.	5	2	
5. As a project manager, I would like to upload photos so that I can share ideas about task boards, teambuilding, burndown charts, etc.	3	3	
6. As a website administrator, I would like to enable advertisements from other companies so that our company can generate more revenue.	5	3	

It is always a good idea, also, to revisit the product overview document at the end of every iteration to make sure that the delivered functionality is in keeping with the product vision and roadmap.

Last but not least, the agile project manager should facilitate and keep notes from the retrospective. What was traditionally referred to as a "project postmortem" and was associated with the closure of the overall project is known in agile as the "retrospective" and is associated with the end of each iteration.

The agile project manager should facilitate this meeting by, at the very least, scribing each team member's comments onto a whiteboard or flip chart. The bare minimum questions to ask are, What can be improved for next iteration? What did we like about this iteration and wish to continue doing during the next? What obstacles are in our way, and can we (the team) remove them, or does our project manager need to help us with this? In addition to the following sample retrospective, Chapter 8, "Quality Management," has sample outputs of a retrospective meeting.

The project manager should record this information, and with the team's permission, leave the results on display in the team room—both as a reminder and as a starting point for the next retrospective.

Iteration 2 Retrospective Notes		
What we liked	**What we wish to improve**	**Decisions**
Communication was good; we liked daily stand-up meetings.	Make it more of a synchronization style; we relied on the project manager to direct the conversation.	None.
Iteration planning went well, but…	It was a bit rushed from time to time. Help each other stick to the agenda; PM tried to move us along but we couldn't move off of some conversations when necessary.	Use a talking stick.
	A VP was shown our last retrospective results!	The team (only) decides who gets to see the results of our retrospective.
We only committed to 7 points but were able to achieve 10!		None.

Summary

These are the main deliverables you should help the team capture in each project and iterations thereof. As you gain experience with reporting and helping a team to become more self-managing, you will learn what works and what isn't effective. Plan to retrospect on your project documents just as you do any other part of the process. Involve the customers of your documentation to ask what's working for them and what is not.

As you can see, there are still project artifacts to be created and maintained just as in waterfall projects. The main differences in agile projects are the timing and depth of planning and associated documentation, as well as that the team takes a more active role in planning (and owns its tasks).

Glossary

Adaptive Software Development   A software development process created by Jim Highsmith and Sam Bayer. Continuous adaptation of the iteration software delivery process is done using speculate, collaborate, and learn phases.

agile   An iterative and incremental approach to developing software that adheres to the Agile Manifesto and its associated principles. Ideally this is done using small, dedicated, co-located, self-organizing teams who work in close collaboration with a business customer. Agile is value-driven both in the focus on delivering the most important features first and in the ways the teams choose to work together to develop the software.

Agile Manifesto   A statement of principles and values that define agile software development.

backlog   A prioritized list of work to be completed. Backlogs are often divided from largest to smallest: product backlog (items for the entire project/product), release backlog (just the items for a particular release), and iteration backlog (items for the current iteration).

big design up front (BDUF) or big upfront design (BUFD)   The traditional method of trying to define all the possible requirements of a product at the beginning of the project, prior to finalizing a plan and beginning coding.

burndown chart   A chart showing the work remaining over an iteration or release. Time is indicated on the x-axis, work is indicated on the y-axis (hours for iteration burndowns, points for release burndowns).

Crystal   A family of agile methodologies created by Alistair Cockburn that focuses on people rather than process as a way to deliver software more effectively and efficiently.

customer The final user or purchaser of the product, who understands the business problem the product is trying to solve and has the authority to make decisions about the product. The customer is usually regarded as external to the company, whereas the product owner/manager is used as the voice of the customer internally.

daily stand-up Daily meeting of the delivery team to plan for the day and coordinate with one another. It is a 15-minute meeting where all attendees stand for the duration and tell what they did yesterday, what they plan to do today, and what is getting in their way.

done Criteria defined by the team for determining that an item is complete. Typically it means that a feature has been coded, tested, and accepted by the product owner.

DSDM Dynamic Systems Development Method is a software development framework based on rapid application development and iterative and incremental delivery of code. It was developed in the 1990s in the UK by a consortium of vendors and experts in the field of software development.

Evo Evolutionary Software Development, Evolutionary Systems Delivery, Evolutionary Project Management (Gilb), Evolutionary Development (EVO-HP). Evo is an agile project management approach created by Thomas Gilb focused on delivering evolutionary results and high-value-first progress toward the goals, and seeking to obtain and use realistic early feedback.

Extreme Programming (also referred to as eXtreme Programming and abbreviated as XP) A software engineering methodology that focuses on a set of specific engineering practices that lead to a higher quality of software and the ability to be more responsive to the customer's needs.

feature A function that the system should perform. (*See also* "story" and "requirement.")

IID *See* "Iterative and Incremental Development."

information radiator A highly visible display of the current status of a project, available for anyone to view.

iteration A block of time, typically between one and six weeks long, in which a team plans, implements, and delivers a set of functionality.

iteration plan   The breakdown of tasks that the team commits to completing in an iteration. Includes all the results of the iteration planning meeting.

iteration planning meeting   Held at the beginning of each iteration and attended by all members of the team, this meeting determines what items the team will work through to completion in the iteration and their associated tasks and task estimates.

Iterative and Incremental Development   This product development approach was popularized in the mid-1950s with its use in the development of the X-15 hypersonic jet. It is a way of developing a product in a series of "Plan-Do-Check-Act" cycles, delivering a portion of the product (an increment) each iteration (cycle).

knowledge workers   A phrase coined by Peter Drucker, it refers to workers whose chief asset is their ability to think, create, innovate, and problem-solve.

Lean Manufacturing   The production of goods derived from the Toyota Production System with a focus on eliminating waste.

Lean Software Development   A translation of the Lean Manufacturing principles to the software development industry.

planning onion   Coined by Mike Cohn, this refers to the way planning is done in layers in agile, with detail appropriate to the time horizon (the closer the release, the more detail that's provided in planning; the further away the release, the higher the level of detail provided).

product owner/manager   The individual who serves as the voice of the customer, and who has the authority to make decisions about the product. *See also* "customer."

release   A deployable software package that is usually the culmination of several iteration cycles of incremental deliveries, and/or those iterations taken as a group.

release plan   An evolving plan showing what features will be delivered to the business in the upcoming iterations that make up a release. Releases typically occur quarterly; therefore, teams that release software into production more frequently instead call this a "quarterly plan."

retrospective   A meeting with all the members of the agile team where they reflect on the events of the last iteration or project, and make plans to adapt and improve.

requirement   This term is not used in agile because it has connotations of a level of detail that is often too granular for the time horizon. Also, requirements usually begin with the phrase "The system shall…," which tends to place the emphasis solely on the technology. Instead, agile teams focus on functionality from the users' point of view, to ensure that they truly understand the vision and problem to be solved. The use of user stories is common, as is the use of the term "feature" instead of "requirement."

Scrum   Developed by Jeff Sutherland and Ken Schwaber in the early 1990s, this agile approach is an iterative and incremental process for developing any product or managing any work. It produces a potentially shippable set of functionality at the end of every iteration.

sprint   *See* "iteration." Scrum used the term "sprint" to mean "iteration." Sprints are traditionally 30 days long.

story   A system requirement written from the point of view of the user, also known as a user story. A story typically follows the format "As a <user role>, I want to be able to <function>."

story points   A level of complexity assigned to a story using the Fibonacci sequence. It is a gross-level estimate of effort.

task board   A physical board or virtual table showing the status of task items in an iteration. Items move from left to right across the task board from phase to phase (Not Started, In Process, Ready to Be Tested, Testing, Ready for Acceptance, and Done).

Taylorism   The principles that Frederick Taylor laid out in his 1911 book *The Principles of Scientific Management.* Taylor's approach to management held that workers should be trained to do a particular job, directed by management, and offered incentives to perform. Taylor employed assembly-line techniques, time studies, and job differentiation.

timebox   A segment of time with a defined start and end; often refers to an "iteration."

Toyota Production System   The foundation of Lean Manufacturing, the TPS is the process that organizes manufacturing, logistics, and relationships with suppliers and customers at Toyota. Its emphasis is on quality, improving the flow of value through the product delivery process, and the elimination of waste.

TPS *See* "Toyota Production System."

user story *See* "story."

velocity The amount of work a team can complete in an iteration, usually given in story points.

wiki An editable intranet site where details of stories and tracking information may be recorded during development.

working software Software that has been coded and tested and then reviewed by the customer or product owner; software that's ready for implementation.

XP *See* "Extreme Programming."

waterfall A sequential phase-gated method for developing software (analysis, design, code, test, deploy).

Bibliography

Austin, Rob and Lee Devin. *Artful Making: What Managers Need to Know About How Artists Work*. Upper Saddle River, NJ: Pearson Education, Inc., 2003.

Bakke, Dennis W. *Joy at Work*. Seattle: PVG, 2005.

Barton, Brent, Thomas Blackburn, and Tamara Sulaiman. "AgileEVM— Earned Value Management in Scrum Projects." Paper presented at the annual Agile conference, Minneapolis, MN, July 23–28, 2006.

Beck, Kent, Mike Beedle, Arie Van Bennekum, Alistair Cockburn, Ward Cunningham, Martin Fowler, James Grenning, Jim Highsmith, Andrew Hunt, Ron Jeffries, Jon Kern, Brian Marick, Robert C. Martin, Steve Mellor, Ken Schwaber, Jeff Sutherland, and Dave Thomas. "Independent Signatories of the Manifesto for Agile Software Development." http://Agilemanifesto.org/sign/display.cgi.

Beck, Kent, Mike Beedle, Arie Van Bennekum, Alistair Cockburn, Ward Cunningham, Martin Fowler, James Grenning, Jim Highsmith, Andrew Hunt, Ron Jeffries, Jon Kern, Brian Marick, Robert C. Martin, Steve Mellor, Ken Schwaber, Jeff Sutherland, and Dave Thomas. "Principles behind the Agile Manifesto." http://www.agilemanifesto.org/principles.html.

Beck, Kent. *Extreme Programming Explained.* Boston: Addison-Wesley, 2000.

Blanchard, Ken and Don Schula. *The Little Book of Coaching: Motivating People to Be Winners*. New York: HarperCollins Publishers, 2001.

Broderick, Stacia. "A Change in Plan." *Agile Development,* Summer 2006.

Bureau of Labor Statistics. "Charting the U.S. Labor Market in 2005." U.S. Department of Labor. http://www.bls.gov/cps/labor2005/home.htm.

Cohn, Mike. *Agile Estimating and Planning*. Upper Saddle River, NJ: Pearson Education, Inc., 2006.

Cohn, Mike. "The Dark Side of Multi-Tasking." *Better Software*, July/August 2005.

Cohn, Mike. "Situational Leadership for Agile Software Development." *Cutter IT Journal,* June 2004.

Cohn, Mike. *User Stories Applied*. Boston: Addison-Wesley, 2004.

Cockburn, Alistair. "Balancing Lightness with Sufficiency." http://alistair.cockburn.us/index.php/Balancing_lightness_with_sufficiency.

Darwin, Charles R. *On the Origin of Species by Means of Natural Selection, or the Preservation of Favoured Races in the Struggle for Life.* London: John Murray, 1859.

Drucker, Peter F. *Age of Discontinuity: Guidelines to Our Changing Society.* New York: Harper & Row, 1968.

Fishman, Charles. "Engines of Democracy." *Fast Company*, September 1999.

Fowler, Martin. "The New Methodology." http://www.martinfowler.com/articles/newMethodology.html#ShouldYouGoAgile.

Fretty, Peter. "Reconciling Differences." *PM Network,* April 2005.

Greenleaf, Robert. *Servant as Leader.* Indianapolis: Robert K. Greenleaf Center, June 1982.

Heally, Melissa. "We're All Multitasking, But What's The Cost?" *Los Angeles Times*, 19 July 2004.

Highsmith, Jim. *Agile Project Management: Creating Innovative Products.* Boston: Pearson Education, Inc., 2004.

Highsmith, Jim. "Messy, Exciting, and Anxiety-Ridden: Adaptive Software Development." *American Programmer*, Volume X, No. 1; January 1997. http://www.adaptivesd.com/articles/messy.htm.

Hohmann, Luke. *Beyond Software Architecture.* Boston: Addison-Wesley, 2003.

Kane, Tim, Brett D. Schaefer, and Alison Acosta Fraser. "Ten Myths About Jobs and Outsourcing." The Heritage Foundation. http://www.heritage.org/Research/TradeandForeignAid/wm467.cfm.

Katzenbach, Jon R. and Douglas K. Smith. *The Wisdom of Teams: Creating the High-Performance Organization.* Boston: Harvard Business School Press, 1993.

Kohn, Alfie. *Punished by Rewards.* New York: Houghton Mifflin, 1993.

Larman, Craig. *Agile and Iterative Development: A Manager's Guide.* Boston: Addison-Wesley, 2004.

Larman, Craig and Victor R. Basili. "Iterative & Incremental Development: A Brief History." *Computer,* June 2003.

Leffingwell, Dean. *Scaling Software Agility.* Boston: Addison-Wesley, 2007.

McGregor, Douglas. *Leadership and Motivation: Essays of Douglas McGregor.* Boston: M.I.T. Press, 1968.

Moore, Geoffrey. *Crossing the Chasm.* New York: HarperBusiness, 1991.

Ogunnaike, Babatunde A. and W. Harmon Ray. *Process Dynamics, Modeling and Control.* New York: Oxford University Press, 1994.

Ohno, Taiichi. *Toyota Production System: Beyond Large-Scale Production.* New York: Productivity Press, 1988.

Ply, Janet K. "The Impact of Organizational Maturity on Job Attitudes and Intentions Within Software Development Organizations." PhD diss., George Mason University, 2004.

Poppendieck, Mary. "Lean Contracts." http://www.poppendieck.com/contracts.htm.

Poppendieck, Mary and Tom Poppendieck. *Lean Software Development: An Agile Toolkit.* Upper Saddle River, NJ: Addison-Wesley, 2003.

McCabe, Karen. "IEEE Revises Software Project Management Standard, Starts Agile Software Standard." IEEE. http://standards.ieee.org/announcements/pr_1490p1648.html.

Pritchard, Carl. "Where Do You Start in Building a Risk Standard?" *The Cutter Edge,* March 7, 2006. http://www.cutter.com/research/2006/edge060307.html.

Project Management Institute. *A Guide to the Project Management Body of Knowledge: PMBOK® Guide, Third Edition*. Newtown Square, PA: Project Management Institute, Inc., 2004.

Project Management Institute. "The Institute." (From a datasheet included in its media kit.) http://www.pmi.org/Pages/default.aspx (accessed September 2006).

Royce, Winston W. "Managing the Development of Large Software Systems: Concepts and Techniques." Paper presented at the Western Electronic Show and Convention (WesCon), Los Angeles, CA, August 25–28, 1970.

Rubenstein, Joshua S., David E. Meyers, and Jeffrey E. Evans. "Executive Control of Cognitive Processes in Task Switching." *Journal of Experimental Psychology: Human Perception and Performance,* Volume 27, Number 4, 2001. http://www.apa.org/journals/releases/xhp274763.pdf.

Satir, Virginia. *The Satir Model: Family Therapy and Beyond.* Palo Alto: Science and Behavior Books, 1991.

Schwaber, Ken. *Agile Project Management with Scrum*. Redmond, WA: Microsoft Press, 2004.

Schwaber, Ken. "No Applause, Please." Scrum Alliance. http://www.scrumalliance.org/articles/31.

Schwaber, Ken. "What is Scrum?" www.controlchaos.com.

Schwaber, Carey. "Corporate IT Leads the Second Wave of Agile Adoption." *Trends,* a Forrester Research Inc. report, November 30, 2005.

Senge, Peter. *The Fifth Discipline Fieldbook.* New York: Doubleday Currency, 1994.

Sliger, Michele. "Bridging the Gap: Agile Projects in the Waterfall Enterprise." *Better Software*, July/August 2006.

Smith, Preston G. and Roman Pichler. "Agile Risks/Agile Rewards." *Software Development,* April 2005.

Snowden, David J. and Mary E. Boone. "A Leader's Framework for Decision Making." *Harvard Business Review*, November 2007.

Stacey, Ralph D. *Complexity and Creativity in Organizations.* San Francisco: Berrett-Koehler Publishers, 1996.

Stacey, Ralph D. *Strategic Management and Organisational Dynamics, Fifth Edition.* New York: Prentice Hall/Financial Times, 2007.

The Standish Group International. *The Standish Group's CHAOS Report 2004.* West Yarmouth, MA: The Standish Group, 2005.

Surowiecki, James. "Feature Presentation." *The New Yorker Magazine,* May 28, 2007.

Takeuchi, Hirotaka and Ikujiro Nonaka. "The New New Product Development Game." *Harvard Business Review*, January–February 1986.

Tartaglia, Constance M. and Prasad Ramnath. "Using Open Spaces to Resolve Cross Team Issues." Paper presented at the Agile2005 conference, Denver, Colorado, USA, July 24–29, 2005.

Van Wagner, Kendra. "Defense Mechanisms." About.com. http://psychology.about.com/od/theoriesofpersonality/ss/defensemech_7.htm.

Index

agile project managers
 allowing teams to self-manage,
  219-221
 assuming different leadership
  styles, 221-224
 facilitating collaboration, 229-230
 flexibility/adaptability, 225
 leading by serving, 225-226
 overview, 217-219
 partnering with skill
  managers, 228-229
 relinquishing inner taskmaster, 229
 removing impediments, 230-231
 self-awareness, 226-228
agile projects. *See* projects
agile releases, 40-41
*Agile Software Development
 Ecosystems*, 295
Agile Unified Process, 299
AgileEVM (Earned Value
 Management), 123-125
Ambler, Scott, 299
analysis of risk, 188-189
annual performance reviews, 154-155
architectural planning, 271-272
Artful Making, 52
artifacts
 iteration backlogs, 312-314
 iteration burndown charts, 314
 iteration burnup charts, 315
 iteration plans, 309-312
 product backlogs, 317
 product overview
  documents, 303-304
 release burndown charts, 316
 release plans, 306-308
 retrospective notes, 318
 velocity logs, 315-316

ASD (Adaptive Software
 Development), 299
assessors, 246
Atern, 297
auditors, 246
audits, 135-136, 246
Austin, Rob, 52
avoiding risk, 190

B

Back, Kent, 296
backlogs
 backlog control, 258
 iteration backlogs, 312-314
 product backlogs, 41, 317
Bakke, Dennis, 146
barely sufficient philosophy, 53, 235
Bayer, Sam, 299
BDUF (big design up front), 113
Bennis, Warren, 143
Beyond Software Architecture, 71
bibliography, 327-331
Biederman, Patricia Ward, 143
big design up front (BDUF), 113
Bohn, H. G., 285
Boone, Mary E., 220
budgeting
 funding limit reconciliations, 120
 overview, 119
 reserve analysis, 120
 traditional versus agile
  approaches, 120
Buffett, Warren, 285
bullpens, 245

iteration demo and review
meetings, 164-165
iteration planning, 74-76, 309-312
activity definition, 94-97
activity duration
estimating, 97-98
activity resource
estimating, 101-102
activity sequencing, 99-100
overview, 93-94
planning meetings, 52, 309
schedule control, 102-106
iteration retrospective, 44
iteration review, 43
locking down, 122
overview, 42
iterative and incremental
development (IID), 11
IV&V (Independent Validation and
Verification), 235

J

Jackson, Jesse, 83
James, William, 25, 233
Jeffries, Ron, 37, 265
Jenett, Eric, 26
Joy at Work, 146

K

kanban, 168
Kelleher, Herb, 51
Kissinger, Henry, 67
knowledge workers, 85
Kohn, Alfie, 154

L

Last Responsible Moment (LRM)
decision points, 72
"A Leader's Framework for Decision
Making" (article), 220
leadership, 221-224, 290-292
Lean Product Development, 12
Lean Software Development, 297-298
Leffingwell, Dean, 271
lifecycle (project), 28-32, 37
agile iterations
iteration planning, 42-43
iteration retrospective, 44
iteration review, 43
overview, 42
agile projects, 39-40
agile releases, 40-41
agile versus plan-driven
approach, 46
daily work, 44-46
illustration, 38
Lister, Tim, 177-178, 189
locking down iterations, 122
logs, velocity, 315-316
long-term planning, 274
LRM (Last Responsible Moment)
decision points, 72

M

management
integration management
change list for, 65-66
controlling and monitoring
project work, 60-61
handoff iteration, 64

P

performance reporting, 170-172

performance reviews, 154-155

personnel loss, 181-182

phases of project lifecycle, 28-32, 37

    agile iterations

        iteration planning, 42-43

        iteration retrospective, 44

        iteration review, 43

        overview, 42

    agile projects, 39-40

    agile releases, 40-41

    agile versus plan-driven
        approach, 46

    daily work, 44-46

    illustration, 38

Plan-Do-Check-Act cycle, 32

Plan-Do-Study-Act cycle, 32

plan-driven approach, 19, 46

Planck, Max, 25

planning process group, 33

plans

    communications planning, 161

    contracting, 201-202

    human resources planning, 145

    iteration planning, 42-43

        activity definition, 94-97

        activity duration
            estimating, 97-98

        activity resource
            estimating, 101-102

        activity sequencing, 99-100

        overview, 93-94

        schedule control, 102-106

    iteration plans, 309-312

    project management plans, 57-60

Project Scope Management Plans

    change list for scope
        management, 81-82

    overview, 68-69

    scope control, 79-80

    scope definition, 69-76

    scope verification, 79

    WBSs, 77

    purchases and
        acquisitions, 199-201

    quality planning, 130-131

    release planning, 40, 306-308

        overview, 87-88

        meetings, 256-257

        schedule control, 91-93

        schedule development, 88-90

    revising, 18-19

    risk management planning, 183-184

    risk response planning, 189-191

    strategic versus tactical
        planning, 86-87

PM Network®, 27

PMBOK® Guide

    origins of, 26-28

    overview, xvii

    project communications
        management

        change list for communications
            management, 174-175

        communicating basic project
            information, 162-163

        communications planning, 161

        information distribution,
            163-169

        overview, 159-161

        performance reporting, 170-172

        stakeholders, 172-173

Q

storming, 222

strategic planning, 86-87

sustainable pace, maintaining, 291

Sutherland, Jeff, 295

T

Tabaka, Jean, 230

tactical planning, 86-87

Takeuchi, Hirotaka, 295

Talese, Gay, 249

Taylor, Frederick, 12, 149

team working agreements, 59

teams

    acquiring, 146-148

    allowing to self-manage, 219-221

    conformity pressure, 179

    delivery teams, 114, 117

    developing, 148-149

        behaviors, 150-152

        traditional versus agile approaches, 152-153

        values, 149-150

    forming, 221-224

    geographically dispersed teams, 272

    leading by serving, 225-226

    managing, 153-157

    selling agile development to, 267-273

    working agreements, 59

technical debt, 138

technical planning, 271-272

Theory of Evolution, 9

Theory X, 148

Theory Y, 149

time estimates, 291

time management

    change list for time management, 107-108

    iteration planning

        activity definition, 94-97

        activity duration estimating, 97-98

        activity resource estimating, 101-102

        activity sequencing, 99-100

        overview, 93-94

        schedule control, 102-106

    overview, 83-86

    release planning

        overview, 87-88

        schedule control, 91-93

        schedule development, 88-90

    strategic versus tactical planning, 86-87

tooling, 245

top-down cost estimating, 115-116

Toyota

    plan purchases and acquisitions, 200

    TPS (Toyota Production System), 12

transforming ideas, 218

transitioning to agile development, 1-6

Tuckman, Bruce, 221

Tzu, Sun, 249

U-V

Udall, Morris, 233

United States Department of Defense (DoD), 11

W-Z-Y-Z

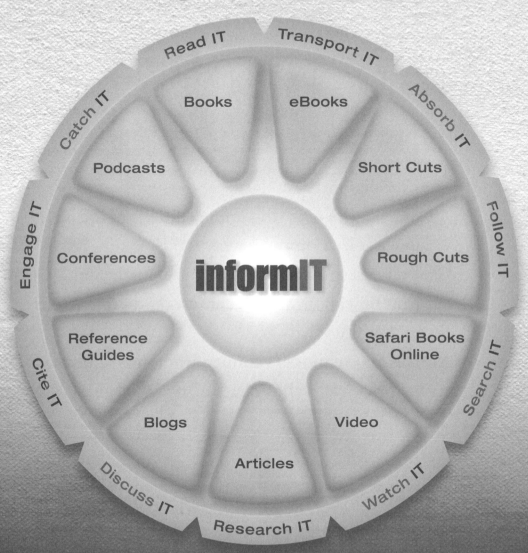

THIS BOOK IS SAFARI ENABLED

INCLUDES FREE 45-DAY ACCESS TO THE ONLINE EDITION

The Safari® Enabled icon on the cover of your favorite technology book means the book is available through Safari Bookshelf. When you buy this book, you get free access to the online edition for 45 days.

Safari Bookshelf is an electronic reference library that lets you easily search thousands of technical books, find code samples, download chapters, and access technical information whenever and wherever you need it.

TO GAIN 45-DAY SAFARI ENABLED ACCESS TO THIS BOOK:

- Go to **informit.com/safarienabled**
- Complete the brief registration form
- Enter the coupon code found in the front of this book on the "Copyright" page

If you have difficulty registering on Safari Bookshelf or accessing the online edition, please e-mail customer-service@safaribooksonline.com.